BUSINESS DEPRESSIONS AND FINANCIAL PANICS

BUSINESS DEPRESSIONS AND FINANCIAL PANICS

Essays in American Business and Economic History

By

SAMUEL REZNECK

Department of History and Political Science
Rensselaer Polytechnic Institute
Troy, New York

With a new preface and introductory
chapter by the author

GREENWOOD PUBLISHING CORPORATION
NEW YORK

Chapter I, "The Sociology of American Depressions in the Nineteenth Century," and the "Epilogue and Bibliographical Note" copyright © 1968 by Samuel Rezneck.

Library of Congress Catalogue Card Number: 68-28644

PRINTED IN THE UNITED STATES OF AMERICA

Greenwood Publishing Corporation
211 East 43rd Street
New York, N.Y. 10017

PREFACE

This collection of essays is the fruit of an idea that germinated many years ago in the midst of the great depression of the 1930's. It has ripened over the years and has matured into the present production. Basically, the idea is that men live in a society that is at once economic, political, social, psychological, and intellectual. These forces and trends act and interact among themselves continuously, in an historical as well as a contemporary setting. Thus, however sophisticated and precise the statistical measures of an economic depression have become, they are never enough by themselves to convey its full scope and impact upon the total community. The history of the United States, and indeed of the world, since 1929 testifies to the complex concatenation of circumstances and consequences, in all levels and segments of society, which has its roots in that earlier depression.

The purpose of the present collection of essays, however incompletely and imperfectly executed, is to demonstrate the validity of this proposition for nineteenth-century America. The modern depression, as indeed the complete business cycle, has its origins in the industrial revolution which spread throughout the western world during that century. As more and more people were drawn into the intricate interdependence of a modern industrial and market economy, its pulsations and swings became universal phenomena, affecting not only the level of business but equally social and political conditions, and particularly the state of mind and spirit of people, whether in a buoyant or depressed direction.

The essays that follow, it is hoped, will speak for themselves, each illustrating obvious differences of time and circumstances, but all contributing to the common concept and pattern of depression as a recurring phenomenon and as a stage of historical and social evolution. The character and composition of this basic concept are developed more fully in the first chapter, entitled "The Sociology of American Depressions."

v

It would be difficult, if not impossible and impractical, to review here all the personal and intellectual influences that have shaped the mind of the author over the many years during which these essays have been in process of germination and production. The sources, primarily intellectual, are embodied in the bibliographical references that accompany the several chapters. Others, undoubtedly, have been omitted, by accident and ignorance rather than by intent. In the personal realm, it is even more risky to name some and neglect others. Especially helpful in their encouragement of this effort have been the late Professor Arthur M. Schlesinger, Sr., of Harvard University, and Professor Earl J. Hamilton of the University of Chicago. The editors of the various journals in which the essays have been previously published deserve acknowledgement, although anonymously, for the improvements that they suggested. My wife, too, has offered constant support and, in particular, the valuable judgment that stems from second and more restraining thought and that serves as a check on precipitate and rash impulse. The errors of omission and commission, it need hardly be added, are the author's alone, for which the responsibility is exclusively his.

—Samuel Rezneck
Troy, New York, 1968

CONTENTS

CHAPTER I

The Sociology of American Depressions in the Nineteenth Century

This essay has never before appeared in print. It was written especially for inclusion in this volume.

THE SOCIOLOGY OF AMERICAN DEPRESSIONS IN THE NINETEENTH CENTURY

This collection of essays, written over many years and concerned with the recurring and intermittent phenomenon of economic depression in nineteenth-century America, is bound together by an underlying theme that may warrant an introductory exposition. The nature of this theme is suggested and delineated in the essay following. Entitled "The Rise and Early Development of Industrial Consciousness in the United States, 1760-1830," it makes, as it were, a double contribution to the purpose of the volume. In the first place, it sketches broadly the beginnings of American industrialism in the critical period of transition from colonial to national status. Obscured by the predominance of westward expansion and the persistence of an agricultural economy, nevertheless there developed in this period an embryonic industrial society, in which a working population of modest size lived, with fluctuating fortunes, in cities and towns. As in England, early industrialism became a major source and factor in the business cycle, particularly in the appearance of recurring, often prolonged depression.

Nineteenth-century depressions were more than commercial crises, which had a long history and involved the decline of prices and profits in the market-place. They also significantly influenced the state of industrial employment and brought hardship and distress to a growing population precariously dependent upon wages for its very survival. The swing of the business cycle in the nineteenth century was thereby intensified, affecting all classes of the population, and the depression phase took on more serious and complex proportions.[1]

Even more, however, the foundations of American industrialism exemplified the role of other than economic factors. As the first essay demonstrates, the pursuit of industrial opportunity was actuated greatly by the political and psychological search for independence and national pride. In this sense, the American people were psychologically and politically prepared for industrialization even before they were ready for it economically or technically. Even as Jeffersonian agrarianism had a strong psychological and intellectual anti-urban and anti-European bias, so early industrialism displayed a counter tendency, and, under Hamiltonian guidance, it welcomed the new technological importations and immigration from England. The psychological, as distinguished from the strictly economic, considerations of early industrialism are well illustrated in the *American Museum* of 1787. A monthly journal published in Philadelphia by Matthew Carey, an arch-protagonist of American protectionism, it reported faithfully the numerous manifestations of popular and public interest in the new industries. Among these were associations of patriotic ladies, in Hartford, Connecticut, Halifaxtown, North Carolina, and elsewhere, who pledged themselves to refrain collectively from all luxury imports until the prevailing hard times were over and "to give due preference to the manufacturers of their country." The conjunction of frugality with domestic industry and its protection became a characteristic feature of American depressions during the nineteenth century, reflecting and stressing their psychological implications.

The first wave of industrialization in the United States was barely launched, in the years of the Napoleonic wars and America's troubled relations with the belligerents, before there ensued the first in the series of nineteenth-century depressions. It is with this succession of depressions that the remaining essays in this volume are concerned. There were six of them, each sufficient in impact to leave a substantial record. Three came before and three after the Civil War. While there seemed to be a considerable degree of recurring periodicity about them, beginning respectively in 1819, 1837, 1857, and again in 1873, 1882, and 1893, their regularity must not be stressed unduly. They were, to begin with, events in the stream of history, which never flows too regularly or too systematically, despite the generalizations of the economists. Each depression was in a real sense unique, growing out of its own peculiar combination of circumstances and productive of its own particular consequences. They differed, of course, in scale and duration, in proportion to the size and development of the country, and they were affected differently by the incidence of war either in the United States or elsewhere, as well as by the occurrence of technological innovation, bad crops, the discovery of gold, and similar events of economic or other character. The business cycle had external as well as internal factors determining or directing its course. Above all there was the long secular wave of national growth, at once in geography, politics, population, and production, within which the business cycles were essentially pulsations of expansion and contraction. Historically, each period of depression is, therefore, to be examined specifically and separately in its own terms of what happened, as indeed is done in the following essays.

Undoubtedly, too, the depressions of the nineteenth century present certain common characteristics, whatever the uniqueness of each, among them certain elements of both a pragmatic and a theoretical nature. Thus, aside from the economics and history of depressions, there is also a sociology of depressions, which observes and analyzes the broader manifestations of the depressions in their social, psychological, and intellectual responses and patterns, which pervaded all aspects of life in the American community.

One major intellectual product of depression was the development of economic theory in relation to the cycle. Indeed, it became increasingly customary to interpret the economic course of events in terms of the business cycle both in Europe and America. Many theories were devised to trace and interpret the causes and conditions which seemed to carry the economy more or less regularly, time and again, from an expanding and booming phase to a contracting, deflationary stage of a business cycle. They were accompanied, moreover, by social overtones either of criticism or of apologetics.

This theoretical analysis began with Simonde de Sismondi, a Swiss economist who visited England in 1819 at a time of depression following the Napoleonic wars. He was moved by his observations to formulate a theory of business fluctuations derived from underconsumption and the plight of the working class. His *Nouveaux Principles d'Économie Politique* departed from the doctrines of Adam Smith in radical fashion and initiated a long line of similar critical interpretations that flourished particularly during or in consequence of periods of depression. An abundant literature of business-cycle theory came into existence. It was of two principal kinds, consisting first of occasional and temporal writings dealing with the specific conditions and causes of particular depressions. Productions of this sort were legion and formed an integral part of each depression in the form of articles, pamphlets, and volumes. There were, secondly, more general treatises concerned with the theory and genetics of the business cycle. They constitute an important part of economic literature during and since the nineteenth century in both Europe and America. Among the authors may be listed such significant figures as Clément Juglar, Max Wirth, Karl Marx, W. Stanley Jevons, Michael Tugan-Baranovsky, Thorstein Veblen, and a host of more recent names.[2]

However neutral and scientifically impartial these writings on the business cycle might appear to be, they all had their particular theoretical orientation and inclination toward a favored viewpoint. It is perhaps noteworthy that the culminating and perhaps most comprehensive contribution to this literature should be by an American in the early years of the twentieth century. This was Wesley C. Mitchell, who received his introduction to economics at the end of the nineteenth century, during the depression of the 1890's. He became interested in the early history of greenbacks and the monetary problems related to inflation and deflation in a modern economy. From this he moved into a life-long study of the business cycle, for which he undertook to devise and apply precise statistical measures. His work, *Business Cycles,* was first published in 1913, and was issued again in 1927.

Wesley Mitchell became, indeed, the head of a school of business-cycle economists, many of them his disciples, who wrote numerous monographs on various aspects of the business cycle under the auspices of the National Bureau of Economic Research. Founded in 1920, with Mitchell as its principal promoter and first director of research, primarily in relation to the national income, the Bureau became the source of a great outpouring of publications on the business cycle for a generation. What this literature perhaps lost in theoretical breadth, it made up in concrete description and a profusion of statistical material. In a little more than a century, the economic theory of the business cycle expanded from its beginnings with Sismondi in the depression of 1819 to its full fruition during the last great depression after 1929, under the auspices of the National Bureau of Economic Research.[3]

The depression phase of the business cycle in particular inspired a voluminous literature, offering explanation, censure, and remedy, as was evident most recently, for example, during the 1930's. It was, however, a manifestation of all nineteenth-century depressions, even the earliest. This was natural, since the activities associated with prosperity were scarcely conducive to much writing other than that of self-congratulation and exaltation. But the discomfort generated by a depression provided ample opportunity to dwell upon what had caused it and what if anything might be done about it in the future. Inexpert as much of it undoubtedly was, such writing offered a kind of catharsis for the prevailing pains and pressures. There were many views to present, almost as many as there were groups and individuals affected by depression, and the only limitation was that of existing outlets for publication. But there were oral forms of expression as well: sermons and addresses by ministers and by political and other figures comprised a considerable portion of the total volume, whatever their value. The immediacy and urgency of sentiment and explanation were perhaps the most useful aspects of this literature, pointing to a particular and relevant condition, problem, or remedy.

In addition to its literary output, depression had one other advantage, if it may be called that, over the prosperity phase of the business cycle. It affected severely many others beside the business class, which was otherwise directly involved in the excitement of speculation, expansion, and contraction. Depression left none untouched. Workers in particular were its victims to a painful degree and tended to add to the constant factor of poverty and distress. Usually inarticulate, they found some voice during a depression, their own or more likely that of sympathetic spokesmen. Ministers were more conscious of the moral implications of economic activity and, in a more religious age, participated freely in the discussion of the evils of excessive preoccupation with business and money, especially when these ceased to be profitable and became sinful. Social critics, generally indifferent to economic processes, became interested and were moved to offer their sympathetic commentaries and panaceas, often of a radical nature. This added other dimensions to the development of economic and social theories in the nineteenth century. Critical contributions disturbed what might otherwise have been the placid and smug self-satisfaction of conventional economic theory. During the nineteenth century, this was the prevailing doctrine of laissez-faire, which preached the inexorable inevitability of economic processes and the impropriety of any extensive public effort to alleviate the distress of depression. Founded on the quite irrelevant conclusions of Charles Darwin, as interpreted by Herbert Spencer, social Darwinism was especially expounded as orthodox gospel in America by the weighty pleading of William Graham Sumner, among many others.

An anomaly of social theory in nineteenth-century America lay in determining the major source and support for the note of pessimism which appeared during depressions and which added its antiphony to the pervasive mood of optimism supposedly dominant in this young and expanding country. Was the doctrine of the ineffectiveness of human effort, explicit in Sumner and other apologists for the established economic order, more truly the source of a fatalistic kind of pessimism? Or was it the censorious social critics, who, in time of depression, advanced quite radical programs of reform and change, which reached a kind of peak in the 1890's? To compound the contradiction, the latter were perhaps more truly optimistic in propounding the doctrine that human effort and public policy could produce positive improvement in modifying the pains and pressures of depression. Progress, even in time of depression, was their principal note and major contribution.

In any event, the literature of depressions was not merely a by-product of any incidental search for causes and remedies. It was in a real sense a part of the depression itself. Its patterns and complexity reflected the character, moods, and composition of the population in each period. The material had a great diversity of content and emphasis, varying from depression to depression, as well as a continuity and recurrence of theme and purpose that expressed the troubled spirit and needs of the nineteenth century as a whole. It may be added that the stresses of depression were more intricate and more demanding of analysis than the pleasant and even intoxicating sensations of boom and prosperity. There was an inclination to consider the latter as normal and permanent, and notes of caution were frequently disregarded or denounced as unsuitable croaking or the work of spoilsports. The distresses and strains of depression were, on the other hand, regarded as temporary and abnormal, to be accounted for on psychological grounds, as noted by John Mills in 1867: "The malady of the commercial crisis is not, in essence, a matter of the purse, but of the mind."[4]

Even as each depression passed away, its literary product remained part of the record. Thus, while the publication of critical and unorthodox views tended to be periodic and rhythmic in character, corresponding to the recurrence of depression, these views were also cumulative and progressive, as it were, throughout the century. The result was a certain ambivalent duality in the growth of economic and social thought. There was first the persuasive voice of self-assurance: let nature run its course; depression is merely a temporary interruption, perhaps even a curative corrective, to be accepted as a kind of bad-tasting medicine. Sounded against this was the voice of warning and incrimination, often religious and critical in inspiration. Out of it all came a considerable body of progressive and even radical thought and opinion which was as American as the more acceptable doctrine of laissez-faire.[5]

Of the approximately three-fourths of a century between 1819 and 1896, about one-third comprised the "hard times" so frequently referred to in contemporary accounts. This time was distributed among six separate periods of depression, each of which averaged roughly four years in duration. Only the depression of 1857 seemingly was shorter and less intense, in part because the South was less affected. In fact, it was able to boast of its stability and immunity to depression and proclaimed cotton as king at this time. But the approaching Civil War was to bring far-reaching economic and social consequences of inflation and subsequent deflation to the entire country. Aside from differences in duration and intensity, which were due to variations in the scale and circumstances of the national economy, there was a remarkable similarity in the sequence of events characteristic of each depression. This was true not only of the economic but even more of the social and psychological aspects of the depression, as indeed was to be expected because human responses were likely to be more comparable even under different conditions.

The first stage usually marking the transition from expansion and boom to depression and contraction was the panic. Panics figured prominently in the nineteenth century, since the means for stabilization and prevention by advance, concerted, and united action were lacking in this age of individual and virtually unregulated enterprise. In only one depression, that beginning in 1882, was there no initial panic; it came instead in the middle, in 1884. Carroll D. Wright, who was in 1884 the first United States Commissioner of Labor, noted this omission and designated the period as one of industrial depression, thereby differentiating it sharply from a financial crisis, a distinction not always clearly made at this time.[6] The panic, by its very name, imparted a quick, dramatic, and conspicuous, if not very colorful, character to the otherwise rather drab activities of the business community. Prices tumbled rapidly in both commodity and stock markets, accentuating, as it were, the shift from speculation to an orgy of selling.

The concentration of markets in New York City by 1837 tended to focus national attention on the psychological excitement and even hysteria associated with Wall Street. Already in 1837, the New York City merchant and mayor, Philip Hone, noted in his diary the acuteness of the panic in that city. Whatever its beneficent role and attraction in good times, Wall Street thus early became a convenient symbol of opprobrium and the theme of moral denunciation during depression.[7]

Panic was not confined to stock and commodity activity. Banks followed suit by contracting their loans and withdrawing funds, especially from the volatile call money market. Deposits and specie reserves became subject to draining demand, as depositors began a run on the banks. This became a characteristic feature of the panic and contributed to its intensity. In virtually all of the depressions of the nineteenth century, the banks of key cities, particularly in New York and Philadelphia, were compelled to suspend specie payments for a time, thereby violating the law and threatening to disrupt the operation of a monetary system never too solid or stable, whatever its indispensable utility to the economy. Money shortages developed, causing recourse to many substitute devices and adding to psychological uncertainty and mass fears. For want of any established program of cooperation or coordination among the banks, especially after the expiration of the national charter of the Second Bank of the United States in 1836, chaos prevailed in monetary policy. Each bank was on its own, relieved only in part by the issue of clearing house certificates, for the first time in 1857, by the Clearing House of New York City banks to facilitate intercity bank exchanges. It was from the conditions of panic and depression that American banks slowly learned and only gradually applied the necessities of monetary and banking regulation and cooperation. This ultimately led to the creation of the Federal Reserve System in 1913, which itself was the direct outgrowth of a panic occurring in 1907-1908.

Accompanying the panic phase, which tended to exaggerate and exacerbate the character of the crisis, there occurred a progressive decline of prices and the deflation of values. All forms of property were affected, although precise measurement in statistical terms is not available for most of the nineteenth century.[8] The distress of the propertied class, generated by this downward trend, therefore tended to be inflated by a pervasive and contagious psychological sense of impending disaster. Rising figures of bankruptcies and foreclosures provide, however, a measure of its reality and intensity, as do the general clamor for debtor-oriented bankruptcy laws, the abolition of imprisonment for debt, and stay and exemption laws, the last especially in agricultural areas, during periods of depressions. Unquestionably, the losses and distresses of the propertied classes, then a considerable portion of the population, were real enough and found vocal expression in complaint and a mood of pessimism, which perhaps extended the sluggishness of recovery.

But such dire effects were reinforced and multiplied by the experience of the working class in the urban and industrial communities. Here it was not merely a question of more or less profit-making, as was the case with the business class; it was a matter of actual subsistence and survival. As Wesley Mitchell observed, those without money are never too prosperous in good or bad times. Despite the mythology of a new country with a shortage of labor, the fact of the matter was that the lack of a strong and effective labor movement, joined with considerable immigration and the fragmented distribution of labor among many small and scattered industrial communities that often contained only one employer, exposed workers to a constant insecurity of employment and a downward pressure of wages and working conditions. The boasted frontier escape valve for labor was largely mythical during most of the nineteenth century. Farming on the frontier was increasingly a remote and unlikely possibility for city people. Workers scarcely enjoyed any surplus of income or savings even in good times and had little reserve for a period of depression. The more serious incidence of depression took the form of unemployment, either total or partial. Industrial depression was highly variable, affecting each industry and community diversely and unevenly. Statistics for labor are even less reliable than those for business during much of the nineteenth century. Except for Carroll D. Wright's pioneer and tentative efforts as commissioner of the Massachusetts Bureau of Labor during the 1870's, and as United States Labor Commissioner after 1885, only occasional, tentative, and usually alarming estimates of unemployment were available, which added to the psychological aggravation of the crisis.

Distress, hunger, and deprivation were real enough in the drab working quarters of nineteenth-century cities and towns, from New York City downward and outward. Much of the suffering of the silent masses was unexpressed, but some found voice in the efforts of a concerned middle class to relieve it through the establishment of bread lines, coal and clothing distributions, soup kitchens, charity funds, and various other devices. Occasional and haphazard organizations for these purposes flourished usually during the winter only, when distress and need were especially great. For example, Edward Atkinson, a businessman and amateur economist of Boston, preached the gospel of thrift and frugality. He became interested in an economic stove for the poor, and he boasted that he taught the working poor to stew and to live cheaply on little. Ironically, the associations for "improving the condition of the poor" and the "charity organization" societies, formed during years of depression, espoused the middle-class objective of reducing the calls for charity by eliminating the undesirable relief of paupers. Their emphasis was generally on "scientific" relief rather than on compassionate aid. Public relief was occasionally proposed in the form of work projects, but governments had neither the funds nor the inclination for such enterprises. The general call was for economy rather than expenditure in time of depression, whether by public or by private agencies. Public work relief became an increasing demand in the later nineteenth century, but it usually took the crude form of work-house and wood-pile labor in return for lodging and food.[9]

One effect of depression on the working poor, as they were designated during this period, was even more extensive deprivation. Slack labor conditions permitted a resort to wage cuts, which constituted the principal adjustment to declining demand and fall of prices. In the absence of significant resistance, whether by labor or business, in a strongly competitive economy, wage cutting was perhaps the only logical corrective for depression and the chief means of restoring demand, although countered by a comparable decline of disposable income. Undoubtedly, the parallel fall of prices was its major justification, but wage cuts tended to be greater, and equalizing the discrepancy between wages and prices became a problem, perhaps never completely overcome, in the period of recovery. Labor paid heavily for the dubious blessing of lower prices.

If action for the relief of distress was rare and grudging, depressions provided a great stimulus to analysis and agitation. The very rise and growth of verbal and printed exposition delineated and perhaps sharpened the reality of hardship. Aside from the apologetics of the orthodox economists, who became increasingly more numerous and articulate if not more convincing as the century progressed, there were the views of ministers, publicists, and social critics generally, which gained in vehemence and volubility what they lacked in clarity or precision of expression. A moralistic tone often permeated the discussions. In earlier years, ministers from pulpit and with pen inveighed against the sins of extravagance and greed and called men to repentance, prayer, and simple living. By the 1870's, a more sophisticated and systematic movement in Protestantism advocated the Social Gospel and urged the need for greater justice and harmony between employers and workers. One of the persistent and persuasive spokesmen for the Social Gospel was a layman, Richard Ely, who combined it with the new German economics of welfare government. He was one of the founders and the first secretary of the American Economic Association in 1885, to which he attempted to give a liberal direction. Opposed to such modern if moderate views was the orthodox laissez-faire philosophy of the Rev. Francis Wayland in the first part, and William Graham Sumner in the latter part, of the nineteenth century.

Depression in the nineteenth century provided the excuse for stressing certain pet and pat doctrines. The tariff runs through the entire century as a sure road to recovery, reaching its climax in the "full dinner pail" argument in the McKinley campaign of 1896. Money and banking, chronic, controversial issues during the entire century, attained shrill heights of diatribe during periods of depression. Surprisingly, sides were changed on this subject between the first and second halves of the century. Prior to the Civil War, "hard" money was the demand of laborers and farmers, unaccustomed to the financial manipulations of the new banks, although the Specie Circular of 1836 was undoubtedly a factor in slowing land speculation and in precipitating the panic of 1837. After the Civil War, inflationary monetary policy, whether in the form of greenbacks or free silver coinage, was adopted by the same farmers and workers, and reached its culmination in the Populist-Democratic campaign of 1896. It is noteworthy, however, that the idea of a national currency, linked with government credit and fixed low interest rates, originated with the writings of Edward Kellogg in the wake of the depression of 1837.[10] Banks and their mysterious ways remained, moreover, a constant source of distrust and dislike to these popular and populist elements. With it was associated a kind of xenophobic sentiment, fed by resentment against British bankers and the Bank of England, whose control over world trade, finance, and gold reserves kept the United States in a chronic condition of dependence, especially vulnerable during years of depression.

Beyond such relatively moderate attitudes and prescriptions lay more radical remedies for depression, entailing programs of public works, taxes on income, Henry George's single tax, and public ownership of utilities. Some even attained utopian proportions, as in the case of Edward Bellamy's *Looking Backward* and the Nationalist Clubs of the 1890's. These followed the earlier Henry George Clubs, which were organized on the basis of his *Progress and Poverty,* written between 1877 and 1879 as an "Inquiry into the Cause of Industrial Depressions. . . ." A great variety of radical relief proposals was offered at the same time to the Congressional Committee, under the chairmanship of the noted industrialist and congressman, Abram S. Hewitt, which investigated the causes of the prevailing depression. Witnesses ranged widely over the social and economic spectrum from the academic William Graham Sumner to the agrarian William Godwin Moody. The contrast was as between Sumner's rather brutal advice that society owed no man a living "except in the state prison," and the more humane proposal of William A. Carsey, Secretary of the Greenback-Labor Party, that "it is the best government that takes the best care of the people." There was the implied threat of Charles

Sotheran, chronicler of early American socialism, that the Constitution must be amended, or "the people will take it into their own hands." Others offered the remedies of an eight-hour working day, subsidized migration to the frontier, nationalized railroads, and public works.[11]

Utopian Communism and Fourierite Communities flourished in the United States during the 1840's, publicized by the journalists Albert Brisbane and Horace Greeley. By the 1870's, however, a more doctrinaire type of socialism appeared on the American scene in many forms, often imported from Europe. With it came also anarchism, even more threatening in thought and deed. The dreaded theories of Communism became a bogey of American journalism during years of deep depression. Labor organizations rose and fell, throwing a frightening shadow over a depressed and uneasy society. The years 1877, 1886, and 1894 witnessed the desperate outbreak of great strikes accompanied by violence. They raised the spectre of revolution and the counter-threat of repression, for which expanded city armories and state militias were sponsored. In the glare of the violent railroad strikes in 1877, William Grosvenor, a financial publicist, depicted extravagantly "by the light of flames at Pittsburgh a terrible trial for free institutions in this country. The Communist is here. . . . It would be simpler to elect Colonel Scott [president of the Pennsylvania Railroad] Perpetual President of the United States with the powers of a dictator. . . ."[12]

Friedrich Engels, Marx's associate and intellectual heir, saw great promise for socialism in the labor disturbances of 1886, as he wrote an American correspondent: "The great thing is to get the working class to move as a class, . . . they will soon find the right direction." Unintentionally providing some corroboration, Carroll D. Wright, first United States Commissioner of Labor, collected many theories and cures for depression in his first publication in 1886, *Industrial Depressions,* and he himself stressed the saturation of innovation and capital investment beyond society's needs and consumption capacity as a major cause.[13]

As if to give support to Wright's pessimistic thesis, there was an acceleration of depression during the latter part of the nineteenth century. It occurred in every decade and was interpreted by some, David A. Wells among others, as one prolonged depression with brief interruptions. The continuous deflation of prices, in agriculture even more than in industry, offered a sharp contrast to what was otherwise a period of great growth and generated a continuing controversy over causes and remedies. The concept of a "Great Depression" was apparently applicable to both England and Germany. In England it prompted investigations by Parliament and Royal Commission, and their conclusions stressed a progressive decline of England's industrial preeminence. The result was the rise of a tariff reform movement, which in England, as contrasted with the program of the same name in the United States, involved a reversion to higher tariffs. It produced a split in the Liberal Party and the creation of a Unionist coalition with the Tories under the sponsorship of Joseph Chamberlain.[14] Unquestionably, deflationary post-Civil War policies of tight money based on resumption of the gold standard, coupled with a certain glut of both agricultural and industrial goods that resulted from increased technological productivity and world-wide competition, generated a certain chronic malaise among American farmers and discontent associated with depression. Added to these was the trust movement that attempted to slow and stabilize the declining trends in the interests of business. This only added to general discontent and distrust.

Despite efforts to unite the various popular movements of protest into a single farmer-labor political activity, unity was not achieved. Each group went its own way, seeking remedy and relief in organization and political agitation. The Populist-Bryan campaign of 1896, fought in a year of depression, was the final manifestation. What it might have brought, had it been victorious, is speculative. It was probably too early to have resulted in much political and economic change. At best it was the breeding-ground of progressivism, which affected both major parties after 1900. A general revival of business and even farm recovery thereafter slowed, if it did not halt, the waves of discontent and agitation that had developed during the depressions of the nineteenth century.

The occurrence of a severe depression after 1929, certainly the most extensive since the 1890's if not the most acute ever, generated the usual distress and discontent. Now, however, there ensued an extensive and positive New Deal program of relief and reform, such as would have been unthinkable in the preceding century. A new era and a combination of circumstances and consequences were present that were unlike any earlier situation. Aside from significant economic stabilizers introduced under the New Deal for almost automatic correction of a decline or recession, a new philosophy was generally accepted. The increased effectiveness and power of labor were coupled with a doctrine that stability was best achieved and preserved by a wider distribution of well-being and the fruits of increased productivity among a larger proportion of the population. Even as it was, agriculture did not fully share in the new wave of prosperity following World War II, nor did the chronically depressed people in the back parts of the country and the Negroes in the cities, who began to clamor for recognition in this period of supposedly wide affluence.

The experience of past depressions, with their recurring distress and discontent and their negative policies of inaction, based on the law of nature, was no longer adequate or satisfactory. It has been followed not so much by a disappearance of swells and swings in the secular business curve, but rather it was displaced by an intensified sensitivity to the earliest signs of recession. There is prevalent now not a resigned acceptance of the cycle as if it were an inexorable law of nature, but rather an eternal watchfulness and determination to check downward dips by appropriate preventive measures. It is not yet demonstrated that the business cycle might not reassert itself, perhaps even by a recurrence of real depression. All elements of society appear, however, to have accepted psychologically and politically the concept of prevention, as well as the pursuit of stability, by a more general distribution of the products, if not the wealth, of society.

The Great Depression of the 1930's is thus directly responsible for the present attitude and policy that it must never be allowed to happen again. Back of it, however, lies a century of recurring depressions that tried the endurance and patience of people and brought forth a plethora of complaints and agitation, if few remedial results. For all their intermittent character, they are part of the continuity of American history. Out of them came a diverse and complex pattern of opinion and controversy, which ultimately provided a background of interest, demand, and potential for change. These were not unrelated to the actualities which became possible in more recent years and the current concepts of and concern with the business cycle, and its prompt correction if not total elimination.[15]

NOTES

1. An interesting and independent testimonial to the operation of the business cycle is contained in the *President's Report on Harvard University* for 1955-1956. President Pusey reports the reading of Harvard's reports for 130 years, since 1826: "Though they are rarely given explicit mention, one becomes aware of each of the periods of depression in turn, as reports written during those periods grow more tense and more sombre . . . and, contrariwise, there is ample evidence of good times, of the exhilarating growth and westward spread of industrial America . . ." (p. 16).

2. C. Juglar, *Des Crises Commerciales et Monétaires* (Paris: Guillamin et cie., 1857, 1889); M. Wirth, *Geschichte der Handelskrisen* (Frankfurt a.m.: J. D. Sauerländers Verlag, 1858, 1874, 1883, 1890); Karl Marx's theory of crises permeates much of his writing, but especially the three volumes of *Das Kapital* (Hamburg: O. Meissner, 1867-1894); M. Tugan-Baranovsky, *Studien zur Theorie und Geschichte der Handelskrisen*, German translation from a Russian edition of 1894 (Jena: G. Fischer, 1901); Thorstein Veblen, *Theory of Business Enterprise* (New York: C. Scribner's Sons, 1904), who in turn influenced Wesley Mitchell's social, as distinguished from his statistical, concern with the business cycle. An excellent review of business-cycle theory and history is contained in Alvin H. Hansen, *Business Cycles and National Income* (New York: W. W. Norton Co., 1951).

3. An extensive bibliography of business-cycle and depression literature is contained in and constitutes perhaps the most useful feature of Theodore J. Burton, *Financial Crises and Periods of Industrial and Commercial Depression* (New York: D. Appleton and Co., 1902), pp. 347-377. For Wesley Mitchell's contributions, cf. A. F. Burns, editor, *W. C. Mitchell, The Economic Scientist* (New York: National Bureau of Economic Research, 1952), which includes an extensive Mitchell bibliography. Cf. also the series of "Studies in Business Cycles," issued by the Bureau, covering both historic and contemporary cycles. For particular depressions, cf. especially M. N. Rothbard, *The Panic of 1819* (New York: Columbia University Press, 1962); G. W. Van Vleck, *The Panic of 1857* (New York: Columbia University Press, 1943); and Charles Hoffmann, *The Depression of the Nineties* (New York: Greenwood Publishing Corp., 1969); and the *Journal of Economic History*, Vol. XVI (June, 1956), pp. 137 ff.

4. Quoted in Burton, *Financial Crises* . . . , p. 29; J. Mills, "On Credit Cycles and the Origin of Commercial Panics," *Transactions* of Manchester Statistical Society (1867-1868).

5. The ambivalent evolution of American social theory is well illustrated and elaborated in Sidney Fine, *Laissez-Faire and the General Welfare State* (Ann Arbor: University of Michigan, 1956). A significant correlation of all aspects of development, economic, political, social, and intellectual, in a prolonged period of depression is presented by Hans Rosenberg, *Grosse Depression und Bismarckzeit* (Berlin: Walter de Gruyter & Co., 1967). For surveys of American business-cycle theory in the nineteenth century, cf. H. E. Miller, *Banking*

Theories in the United States before 1860 (Cambridge: Harvard University Press, 1927); and Paul Barnett, "Business Cycles and the National Income," *The Journal of Business,* Vol. XIV (New York, 1951); Joseph Dorfman, *The Economic Mind in America,* Vols. II and III (New York: Viking Press, 1946-1949).

6. Carroll D. Wright, *Industrial Depressions* (Washington, D. C.: Government Printing Office, 1886). This was the first full-length survey of depressions undertaken by the first United States Commissioner of Labor as his first official task and publication. It was, however, preceded by congressional committee investigations of the depression in progress since 1873. *Depression in Labor and Business* (45th Cong., 3rd Sess.) (Washington, D. C.: Government Printing Office, 1878); *Causes of General Depression in Labor and Business* (46th Cong., 2nd Sess.; H. R. Misc. Doc. 5.) (Washington, D. C.: Government Printing Office, 1879).

7. For the development of New York City and Wall Street as the principal national market, cf. Margaret G. Myers, *The New York Money Market,* 2 vols. (New York: Columbia University Press, 1931); Robert Sobel, *The Big Board* (New York: The Free Press, 1965).

8. Still the most useful systematic collection of statistics for the depressions of the early nineteenth century is W. B. Smith and A. H. Cole, *Fluctuations in American Business, 1790-1860* (Cambridge: Harvard University Press, 1935). Other sources include Edwin Frickey, *Production in the United States, 1860-1914* (Cambridge: Harvard University Press, 1947); A. R. Eckler, "A Measure of the Severity of Depressions, 1873-1932," *Review of Economic Statistics,* Vol. XV (1933); cf. Thomas S. Berry, *Western Prices before 1861* (Cambridge: Harvard University Press, 1943); *Long Term Economic Growth, 1860-1965,* U.S. Department of Commerce, Bureau of the Census (Washington, D.C.: Government Printing Office, 1967); *Historical Statistics of the United States, 1789-1957,* U.S. Dept of Commerce, Bureau of the Census (Revised Edition, 1960); *The Statistical History of the United States from Colonial Times* (Stamford, Conn.: Fairfield Publishers, Inc., 1966).

9. The most extensive survey of poor relief in depression is Leah H. Feder, *Unemployment Relief in Periods of Depression* (New York: Russell Sage Foundation, 1936). Other sources are the annual reports of the various charitable organizations established during the nineteenth century in the principal cities and Amos Warner, *American Charities* (New York: T. Y. Crowell and Company, 1894). For the relief problems of particular depressions, see the essays in this volume and B. J. Klebaner, "Public Relief During the Depression of 1857" (unpublished Ph.D. thesis at Columbia University).

10. Edward Kellogg, *Currency, The Evil and the Remedy* (New York: W. H. Graham, 1843). This book was first published in 1843 and re-issued in many editions thereafter. For other versions of national currency and public credit systems, cf. William Dealtry, *Money, its History, Evils, and Remedy* (Albany: B. Taylor, 1858); and John Mason, *An Inquiry into the Laws which Regulate the Circulation and Distribution of Wealth* (New York: G. P. Putnam and Co., 1856).

11. For these and other matters relating to the relief of depression, cf. *Depression in Labor and Business* (Reports of Congressional Committees, 1878 and 1879).

12. *International Review*, Vol. IV (Sept., 1877), pp. 585 ff.; Vol. V (Sept. and Nov., 1878), pp. 577 ff., pp. 734 ff.; R. Hunter, *Violence and the Labor Movement* (New York: Macmillan Company, 1914); H. A. James, *Communism in America* (New York: H. Holt and Co., 1879); John Smith, *Hard Times, A Few Suggestions to the Workers* (Chicago: Industrial Union Publishing Co., 1885); Dorfman, *The Economic Mind in America*, Vol. III, Ch. 2. For earlier manifestations of depression-inspired social movements, cf. *Socialism and Life in America*, Vol. I (Princeton: Princeton University Press, 1952), pp. 189 ff.; A. E. Bestor, *Backwoods Utopias* (Philadelphia: University of Pennsylvania Press, 1850), Ch. 3; William Charvat, "American Romanticism and the Depression of 1837," *Science and Society*, Vol. II (1937), pp. 67-82.

13. C. D. Wright, *Industrial Depressions*, pp. 76, 79, 254 ff.; Karl Marx and Friedrich Engels, *Letters to Americans* (New York: International Publishers, 1953), pp. 157, 165, 285 ff.

14. D. A. Wells, "Economic Disturbances Since 1873," *Popular Science Monthly*, Vols. XXXI-XXXIII (1887-1889), *passim; Recent Economic Changes* (New York: D. Appleton and Co., 1890) ; J. W. Jenks, "The Causes of the Fall of Prices Since 1872," *Journal of Social Science*, No. 35 (Dec., 1897), pp. 34 ff.; H. L. Beales, "The Great Depression," *Economic History Review*, Vol. V (Oct., 1934), pp. 65 ff.; E. D. Hobsbawm, "Economic Fluctuations and Some Social Movements since 1800," *Economic History Review*, second series, Vol. V (1952), pp. 1-25; W. W. Rostow, *British Economy in the Nineteenth Century* (Oxford: Clarendon Press, 1948); Hans Rosenberg, *Grosse Depression und Bismarckzeit*.

15. The depression of the 1930's produced a vast literature of exposition and remedy, which cannot be cited at any length here. For a recent treatment, as well as for a good sample of its bibliography, cf. R. T. Patterson, *The Great Boom and Panic* (Chicago: H. Regnery & Co., 1965); Dixon Wecter, *The Age of the Great Depression* (New York: Macmillan Co., 1948); J. K. Galbraith, *The Great Crash* (Boston: Houghton Mifflin Co., 1955).

CHAPTER II

The Rise and Early Development of Industrial Consciousness in the United States, 1760-1830

The following essay originally appeared in the *Journal of Economic and Business History,* Supplement, Volume IV, Number 4 (August 1932), pp. 784-811. It is reprinted here, in its entirety, with the permission of *The Business History Review* and the author. The original pagination appears in brackets at the bottom of each page.

THE RISE AND EARLY DEVELOPMENT OF INDUSTRIAL CONSCIOUSNESS IN THE UNITED STATES, 1760–1830

Changing economic phenomena are of necessity reflected in the pattern of social thought and institutions. The rise of American manufactures before 1830 was accompanied by a parallel development of industrial consciousness, which received formulation in public opinion as well as in a considerable amount of social activity. The political and economic stress of the revolutionary period afforded the first occasion for an awakened interest in domestic industry (pp. 786–788). It was, however, during the years of national organization under the Constitution that the manufacturing agitation made rapid progress (pp. 788–790). The apologetics of industry were developed in the *American Museum* by men like Tench Coxe and Matthew Carey (pp. 790–791), while the enterprise of societies modeled upon the Pennsylvania Society for the Encouragement of Manufactures stimulated the growth of industrial consciousness (pp. 795–796). Hamilton's Report on Manufactures (pp. 790, 797), together with his active interest in the Paterson Manufactory, gave an added impetus to the movement (pp. 790, 794, 797–798).

After 1800 changing political conditions converted even Jefferson to a partial advocacy of domestic manufactures (pp. 798–799). As industry itself gained momentum, its sponsors were able to organize and conduct an effective agitation for protection. By 1830 industrial consciousness had entered upon a more mature stage of development. It found expression in several social manifestations of considerable importance. The industrial fair became a characteristic feature of urban life in the East (pp. 803–805). Technical journalism was begun successfully with *The Franklin Journal*, while a promising start had been made in the field of practical education for mechanics (pp. 805–811).

IN THE early history of American manufactures it is not alone the building of factories and the introduction of machinery which constitute the rise of an industrial society in the United States. Equally important is the rise and growth of an industrial consciousness, which did not at once fit smoothly into the older social pattern. The ultimate antecedents of American industrial consciousness may possibly be traced back to the earlier colonial period, but these are necessarily slight, and the period of true beginnings can be dated roughly between 1760 and 1830.[1] It received much of its early stimu-

---

[1] Brief reference may be made here to early colonial legislation, the Boston Spinning Craze of 1718, and the public manufactories sponsored after 1748. R. M. Tryon, *Household Manufactures in the United States* (Chicago, 1917), pp. 35, 87, *passim*; William R. Bagnall,

[784]

lus from the political storm and stress which preceded and led to the winning of independence. Early industrial consciousness was, in fact, an accompaniment of that and of other related political events. Although for a long time a great deal of emphasis was placed upon household, and therefore primitive, industry, the really decisive stimulus came from the revolutionary changes in industrial technique which England was then beginning to undergo. Paradoxically, American industrial consciousness grew out of the broad wave of political and economic resentment against England, but was mainly directed almost from the start toward the transfer of English skill and technique to this country. By 1830, it had succeeded, and American technology and industrial organization were by then comparable to those of England. In the face of war and commercial restriction which confronted the United States during the greater part of this period, the need for home-made manufactures was, of course, very real. And yet the chief obstacles to the rise of industry were unfavorable economic and social conditions, which could not be argued out of existence by the most eloquent sponsors of early industry.

It was the experience of the United States that the will to manufacture was born before manufactures were started, and, according to many, even before the ability to manufacture was present. Out of this paradoxical situation sprang the principal controversy which engaged the active makers of opinion in the next generation. It was a double controversy, in which were involved both the question as to whether American manufactures were possible and also as to whether they were desirable. The controversy was perhaps mainly academic, since only trial and error could in the end determine whether manufactures were possible; and nothing could pre-

The Textile Industries of the United States, vol. i, 1639-1810 (Boston, 1893), p. 19; J. L. Bishop, *History of American Manufactures* (Philadelphia, 1864), vol. i, pp. 296 ff.; J. S. Davis, *Essays in the Earlier History of American Corporations* (Cambridge, 1917), vol. i, pp. 94 ff.; E. B. O'Callaghan, *Documentary History of the State of New York* (Albany, 1851), vol. iv, pp. 219 ff.; V. S. Clark, *History of Manufactures in the United States, 1607-1860* (Washington, 1916), vol. i, pp. 260, 399.

vent them, once they became feasible. But the very unfolding of the debate gave added impetus to the rise and growth of industrial consciousness. In the period of beginnings opinion often preceded the industrial experiment, but was also stirred by it. Each confirmed the other and brought it into better notice.

Complete pessimism as to the prospects of American manufactures was impossible, in view of the widely prevalent and pervasive zeal for useful improvement which this country shared with England in the eighteenth century. This zeal had already found early, eloquent, and concrete expression in the American Philosophical Society, originally sponsored by Franklin in 1744, and reinforced in 1769 by a fusion with the American Society for Promoting and Propagating Useful Knowledge.[2] In later years similar associations, particularly in Philadelphia, diverted some of this zest for useful improvement into the specific channel of industrial development.

In the decade of political conflict preceding the Revolution the chief weapons of American resistance were, of course, the commercial boycott and the non-intercourse association, as in fact they continued to be in another form down to 1812. The logical corollary to this was the consumption and the encouragement of domestic manufactures. Many gestures were made in that direction in this period.[3] Among others, Congress in February, 1776, adopted a resolution proposing the formation of societies in all the colonies for the promotion of manufactures.[4] In the agitation for domestic industry which developed in this revolutionary period three separate notes

---

[2] Cf. Franklin's pamphlet of 1743, "A Proposal for Promoting Useful Knowledge Among the British Plantations in America," *Writings* (A. H. Smyth, ed., New York, 1905–07), vol. ii, pp. 228–232. See also *Proceedings of the American Philosophical Society*, vol. xxii (Philadelphia, 1884), pp. 1, 11, 25, 66. For premiums offered cf. *Transactions of the American Philosophical Society* (Philadelphia, 1799), vol. iv, p. iv.

[3] C. P. Daly, *Origin and History of Institutions for the Promotion of the Useful Arts* (Albany, 1864), p. 18; W. B. Weeden, *Economic and Social History of New England* (Boston, 1890), vol. ii, pp. 731 ff.; Scharf and Westcott, *History of Philadelphia* (Philadelphia, 1884), vol. iii, p. 2227; A. M. Schlesinger, *The Colonial Merchants and the American Revolution* (New York, 1917), pp. 77, 122; *Niles' Register*, vol. xi, p. 52.

[4] *The Works of John Adams* (C. F. Adams, ed., Boston, 1850–56), vol. ii, p. 487; also *ibid.*, vol. vi, pp. 235, 252.

may be detected, and these persist for many years. The first was, of course, the note of patriotic necessity, on which agreement was for the moment virtually unanimous. The second note was that of economy, and even Franklin gave sanction to the current opinion that domestic industry would halt the drain of money out of the country.[5] This was linked up with a third notion that the use of home manufactures would encourage a simplicity of taste and check the spread of extravagance and luxuriousness.[6] While most people accepted the immediate and patriotic necessity for "Industry and Frugality," Hamilton, already at this early date, had a vision of America's "grandeur and glory" which would follow upon the development of manufactures.[7]

In these years of agitation and revolution actual industrial achievement fell far below the hopes and wishes which were entertained.[8] Bounties and premiums were offered for various products, and many projects for manufactures were in circulation.[9] At least one public enterprise was organized in order to promote American manufactures. This was the United Company of Philadelphia, which flourished between 1775 and 1778. Among its patrons and managers were Christopher Marshall, Samuel Wetherill, and Tench Coxe, who became persistent and devoted advocates of American manufactures.[1] Despite its failure, it had some significance in industrial history. A spinning jenny, the first of its kind in the United States, is reported to have been set up and used in the factory of the United Company.[2]

With the coming of peace patriotic fervor was, of course, relaxed, and the manufactures established during the war

---

[5] Bagnall, *op. cit.*, p. 60; *American Museum*, vol. v, pp. 582–583, citing the second annual report presented to the United Company of Philadelphia in 1777 by R. S. Jones, and giving all the current arguments. See also Franklin's *Writings*, vol. v, p. 316.

[6] *Ibid.*, p. 203; *American Museum*, vol. v, p. 582.

[7] *Works of Alexander Hamilton* (J. C. Hamilton, ed., New York, 1851), vol. ii, p. 12.

[8] Cf. Schlesinger's comments on what he calls the "newspaper manufactures" of the period, *op. cit.*, p. 124.

[9] *Ibid.*; *Niles' Register*, vol. xi, p. 52; Bishop, *op. cit.*, vol. i, pp. 380–384.

[1] *American Museum*, vol. v, pp. 581–584; Christopher Marshall, *Passages from the Remembrancer* (Philadelphia, 1839), pp. 16, 24, 25.

[2] Bishop, *op. cit.*, vol. i, p. 384.

felt the depressing effect of competition. Lord Sheffield's *Observations on the Commerce of the United States* foretold that England would have little to fear from American manufactures.[3] In the United States proper, Adams, Washington, Franklin, and even such an enthusiastic advocate of American industry as David Humphreys regarded its future prospects as unpromising; Jefferson was altogether hostile.[4] The very depression, however, which intervened between 1783 and 1787 produced a reawakening of manufacturing zeal. Patriotism again provided the impetus to it, while there was also a better appreciation of the fact that English superiority in technique could be overcome only by borrowing it. The new wave of industrial agitation rose to a rapid climax in the first years of the federal government. Manufactures, like the Constitution, were expected to strengthen the country and to help it achieve true independence.

One of the sources from which the fresh wave of interest in domestic industry derived inspiration was the practical predicament in which the artisans already established in the country found themselves.[5] They were feeling the pinch of depression, and they resorted to organization and propaganda in an effort to obtain recognition of their needs for protection. They represented, to be sure, the older craft tradition of industry, and what they wanted was immediate relief. But their activity added, nevertheless, to the general agitation, and their identification of their own interest with the destiny and welfare of the country as a whole contributed to a stir-

---

[3] Lord Sheffield's *Observations* (London, 1783). Tench Coxe's reply appeared in the *American Museum* in 1790 and was reprinted in his *A View of the United States of America* (Philadelphia, 1794), pp. 111ff.

[4] *American Museum*, vol. ii, p. 3; *The Writings of George Washington* (W. C. Ford, ed., New York, 1889–93), vol. xi, p. 353; *Works of John Adams*, vol. vii, p. 247, 255; Davis, *op. cit.*, vol. i, p. 361; Thomas Jefferson, *Notes on the State of Virginia* (Baltimore, 1800), p. 165.

[5] Matthew Carey, *The New Olive Branch* (Philadelphia, 1820), pp. 35–36. The extent of this industrial group and its interests is indicated in the letters of Phineas Bond, who was British consul at Philadelphia in this period. These letters were published by the Historical Manuscripts Commission in the *Annual Report of the American Historical Association for the year 1896*, vol. i (Washington, 1897), pp. 513–659. These letters are hereafter cited as "Letters of Phineas Bond." Cf. also *The Industrial and Commercial Correspondence of Alexander Hamilton* (A. C. Cole, ed., Chicago, 1928), *passim*.

ring of industrial consciousness. Beginning in 1785, the mechanics, tradesmen, and manufacturers formed societies and committees in New York, Boston, Baltimore, and Providence. They avowed charitable and fraternal aims, but their correspondence with one another stressed their desire for public relief and encouragement.[6] In 1788, for example, the Boston Association of Tradesmen and Manufacturers addressed a circular letter to similar societies in other towns, urging union and co-operation:[7]

These States are so extensive in their boundaries, so various in their climate, and so connected in their national interests, that if a plan could be adopted throughout the confederation for the exchange of the produce and manufactures of each State, we conceive it would serve to cement a general union. . . . An association formed throughout the States upon so liberal a plan, would establish many extensive branches of manufactures; and if prosecuted with spirit, would put this country above the humiliating state of lavishing her stores of wealth to promote the manufactures of Europe.

Such appeals for help were not altogether fruitless, and several States responded with special acts and resolutions. Upon the formation of the new government, the pleas were directed to the first session of Congress, which replied in part with the tariff act of 1789.[8]

Industrial consciousness, in these early years of American nationality, was, however, stimulated more effectively from a quarter which was at once more academic but also more articulate. The American gift for forming associations was fully exploited, and in addition there were meetings, resolutions, processions, and industrial experiments. Resolutions favoring the use of domestic goods were adopted in 1786 at meetings held at places as far apart as Hartford, Connecticut; Halifaxtown, North Carolina; Germantown, Pennsylvania; and Richmond, Virginia.[9] Political office-holders were

---

[6] *Annals of the General Society of Mechanics and Tradesmen, 1785–1880* (New York, 1882), pp. 9, 27; also T. W. Griffith, *Annals of Baltimore* (Baltimore, 1833), p. 115; Weeden, *op. cit.*, vol. ii, p. 850; "Letters of Phineas Bond," p. 654.

[7] *American Museum*, vol. iv, pp. 347–348.

[8] *Annals of the General Society*, p. 12; *American Museum*, vol. i, p. 19, and vol. v, p. 54; "Letters of Phineas Bond," *op. cit.*, p. 637; Edward Everett, *Address Before the American Institute of New York* (New York, 1831), pp. 22, 33; Bishop, *op. cit.*, vol. i, p. 499, and vol. ii, p. 15.

[9] *American Museum*, vol. ii, pp. 165ff.

asked to pledge themselves to wear only clothes of American manufacture in the performance of their duties.[1] The Federal Procession held at Philadelphia in 1788 to celebrate the ratification of the Constitution offered an opportunity to parade the promise of the new industrial methods. The whole Hewson family, father, mother, and four children, was carried on a float of gigantic proportions, drawn by ten horses. These pioneers of industry were shown at work on a variety of machines, from carding to printing.[2] A "Philadelphia Mechanic" was able to note with great satisfaction in a letter to the *New York Packet* in 1789 that "a passion for encouraging American manufactures has, at last, become fashionable in some parts of our country."[3]

Principally, of course, it was the press which served as the medium of agitation. Persuasive publicity could carry farther than deeds, and was, moreover, not subject to the trying test of success or failure. The industrial experiments themselves had to be translated into plausible and convincing words in order to make the proper psychological impression. In this respect the movement was fortunate in enjoying the invaluable services of Matthew Carey and Tench Coxe, the pamphleteers and propagandists of the cause. Alexander Hamilton gave it his active support, and his Report on Manufactures, coupled with his sponsorship of the New Jersey Society for Establishing Useful Manufactures, constitutes the transcendent achievement of the agitation. The movement had its capital at Philadelphia, from which came quite logically the first avowed organ of American manufactures, the *American Museum*, published by Matthew Carey between 1787 and 1792. In its twelve volumes appeared all the news regarding the current development of manufactures, while the more theoretical and optimistic speculations of Coxe, Bar-

---

[1] The members of the Massachusetts General Court entered into an association for such a purpose in 1786. *Proceedings of the Massachusetts Historical Society*, 2nd ser., vol. viii (Boston, 1894), p. 496. Cf. also the proposals in the *American Museum*, vol. iii, p. 89, and in the *New York Packet*, Jan. 13, 1789.

[2] Everett, *op. cit.*, p. 22; Bagnall, *op. cit.*, p. 110.

[3] *New York Packet*, Jan. 13, 1789.

ton, Rush, and Carey, himself, helped to elaborate the complete case for American industry, which Hamilton was to present in its final form. The writers in the *Museum* set up the conventional arguments of the opposition as if they were straw figures, and then proceeded to knock them down.

But Thomas Jefferson, whose challenge to the manufacturing agitation was the most provocative as well as the most characteristic of the period, was no straw figure to be knocked down by a mere blast of polemic enthusiasm. Jefferson's antagonism was the more invincible because it was grounded in a strong prejudice against manufactures, which he shared with many others, including Franklin.[4] Certainly his arguments, as first expressed in the *Notes on the State of Virginia*,[5] published in 1785, were iterated and reiterated many times thereafter, and as late as 1830 they were still available for use, although their point must have been dulled considerably in the meantime through impact upon changing circumstances.[6]

The particular appeal of Jefferson's position on the subject of American industry consisted in the fact that it combined and colored current economic theory with strong emotion. It grew out of the familiar physiocratic doctrine that agriculture was the only source of true wealth. This was, of course, in harmony with the conditions of American economy as it was then constituted. Further plausibility was added to it by the smooth and highly flattering abstractions of eighteenth century nature-philosophy, which Rousseau and the early romanticists had made popular.

To the general fear of the moral and social consequences of a manufacturing system were added the well-worn arguments

---

[4] Franklin's *Writings*, vol. i, p. 148, and vol. v, pp. 103, 139.

[5] Jefferson, *Notes*, pp. 165–166. Cf. also his circular letter of 1792 addressed to the American consuls abroad in *The Writings of Thomas Jefferson* (The Thomas Jefferson Memorial Association, Washington, 1903), vol. viii, pp. 350–352.

[6] Reiteration of Jefferson's arguments occurs in John Filson, *The Discovery, Settlement and Present State of Kentucky* (New York, 1793), vol. ii, p. 159; Thomas Cooper, *Some Information Respecting America* (London, 1794), pp. 77–78; and Condy Raguet, *The Principles of Free Trade* (Philadelphia, 1835), pp. 150–151.

that America was lacking in the necessary skill, labor, and capital.

The sponsors of domestic manufactures met these objections in a variety of ways, if rather evasively. The shortage of labor could be overcome by the employment of women and children, and this would be a clear gain to the country.[7] Tench Coxe believed that work would be the salvation of women, while Colonel David Humphreys became lyrical over the promise of child labor:[8]

> Teach little hands to ply mechanic toil,
> Cause failing age o'er easy tasks to smile;
> . . . .
> So shall the young find employ,
> And hearts, late nigh to perish, leap for joy.

If it was objected that the employment of women and children was demoralizing, Coxe was apparently able to satisfy himself by retorting that, in the matter of vice, seaports and courts were worse than industrial towns. An even more callous answer was given many years later, namely, that long hours of employment left little opportunity for vice. Others, however, saw the remedy in "a course of the purest, moral, and religious instruction," which a generous employer might provide, "without preventing reasonable profits."[9] Horse and mechanical power were also suggested as substitutes for hu-

---

[7] *The Writings of George Washington*, vol. xi, p. 353; Hamilton's Report on Manufactures, printed in the *Industrial and Commercial Correspondence of Alexander Hamilton*, p. 259; Moses Brown, as cited in G. S. White, *Memoir of Samuel Slater* (Philadelphia, 1836), p. 88. Brown assured Hamilton that "mills and machines may be erected in different places, in one year, sufficient to make all the cotton yarn that may be wanted in the United States."

[8] Tench Coxe, *An Essay on the Manufacturing Interest of the United States* (Philadelphia, 1804), p. 15; David Humphreys, *Poem on Industry* (Philadelphia, 1794), p. 14. Cf. also Matthew Carey, *Essays on Political Economy*, cited in A. M. Simons, *Social Forces in American History* (New York, 1911), p. 173.

[9] Coxe, *An Essay on the Manufacturing Interest of the United States*, p. vi; White, *op. cit.*, p. 126; *Niles' Register*, vol. xxv, p. 195; also *ibid.*, vol. xiii, p. 213, n. The example of Samuel Slater was cited, who founded the first Sunday school in the United States, for children in his employ, and who taught them himself. It was regarded at first as a profane innovation, and one young man, the son of a clergyman, refused an offer to conduct the school. Henry Howe, *Memoirs of American Mechanics* (New York, 1852), p. 95. In 1828, a Mr. Tufts testified before a congressional committee that manufactures were favorable to morals, since most large establishments provided education, especially in the form of Sunday classes, for the children. *The Register of Pennsylvania* (Samuel Hazard, ed.), vol. i (1827), p. 159.

man labor,[1] and it was pointed out that foreign artisans would gladly supply the necessary skill, if offered suitable incentive.[2] In 1790, Coxe actually wrote to Madison, then in Congress, suggesting an appropriation of a million acres of western land as "a fund to reward the introduction of Machinery, inventions, arts, and other things of that nature from foreign countries."[3]

The shortage of capital was admitted, but, on the other hand, means for supplying it were not lacking. Some could easily be spared from agriculture, where it was often misused, and from commerce, which was in any case over-emphasized, while mechanics were mistakenly held in low esteem.[4] Capital, like labor and skill, might also come from abroad. An ingenious scheme for raising capital originated with Coxe and was adopted by Hamilton in his Report on Manufactures.[5] It became part of the program of the New Jersey Society for Establishing Useful Manufactures, for which it was proposed to mobilize the newly funded national debt. The capital stock of the company was to be paid for in public debt certificates, on which, it was believed, a loan could be raised at Amsterdam at less than 6 per cent.[6] Coxe was an unfailing source for other suggestions. Industrial capital might be provided by means of a large public lottery, or even by an outright State loan, which would prove profitable to Pennsylvania in a very short time.[7] In a letter of April 15, 1791, Coxe, already assistant secretary of the Treasury, attempted to convert Jefferson to the merits of a plan by

---

[1] Tench Coxe, in an address delivered in 1787 (*A View of the United States*, p. 42). Already in 1785, Silas Deane had observed that labor in England was not cheap, but that its efficiency was increased by the use of machinery. He offered to introduce the steam engine into the United States, if given encouragement (*Collections of the New York Historical Society*, New York, 1891, vol. xxiii, p. 460).

[2] Coxe, *A View of the United States of America*, pp. 42, 47; *American Museum*, vol. iv, p. 342; *DeBow's Commercial Review*, vol. vii, pp. 348f. See also the *Pennsylvania Gazette*, Jan. 30, 1772.

[3] Cited in Davis, *op. cit.*, vol. i, p. 355.

[4] *American Museum*, vol. i, pp. 17–19.

[5] *Ibid.*, vol. ix, pp. 179ff.; Coxe, *A View of the United States*, pp. 165f.; *The Industrial and Commercial Correspondence of Alexander Hamilton*, pp. 272f.

[6] Davis, *op. cit.*, vol. i, p. 351.

[7] Coxe, *A View of the United States of America*, p. 385.

which a grant of 64,000 acres of land in the newly established federal district was to be devoted to the development of manufactures.

Already in 1787, Coxe had argued that the manufacturers were a "judicious body of men," who loved their country. They would be satisfied with a modest degree of encouragement.[8] Patriots were, however, reminded that in the recent war "none then but tories were clothed in purple and fine linen."[9] And now only domestic manufactures could appease "this untimely passion for European luxuries."[1]

The manufacturing agitation in these early years of American nationality used more than verbal argument to confute Jefferson. There was also a considerable amount of public enterprise and industrial experiment to prove that manufactures were possible. Many of the early ventures into industry were, of course, undertaken privately, stimulated by the prospect of profit, which was meager and rare enough at first. But even such purely business undertakings as the Beverly Manufactory or the Paterson establishment were endowed with a generous and genuine measure of public interest. They applied to the State for encouragement and frequently received it. In the case of the New Jersey Society in particular, Hamilton's close connection with it is anomalous unless he is credited with something more than mere friendship for Duer and his fellow-speculators, who almost ruined it in the first year of its existence. Hamilton owned no stock in the company, and he was an officer in the national government; yet he was almost the chief sponsor and manager of what from the beginning was dubbed the National Manufactory.[2] For several years after 1787 every industrial undertaking, whether public or private, was identified with the national interest and helped to stimulate and arouse industrial consciousness in the country.

---

[8] *Ibid.*, pp. 6, 16, 21. The manufacturers, he insisted, did not intend to enter into conflict with "our great leading interest."

[9] *American Museum*, vol. i, p. 18.

[1] *Ibid.*, vol. ii, p. 254; vol. iv, p. 344.

[2] Davis, *op. cit.*, vol. i, pp. 349, 367.

The growing zeal for American manufactures expressed itself through associations, which became a characteristic feature of urban activity after 1787. These were of two kinds, or rather they presented two main aspects. They were agencies of propaganda, offering premiums, circulating information, and stimulating interest. But they might also raise a special fund and venture into manufacturing proper. In this respect they are scarcely to be distinguished from those enterprises which were purely private and profit-seeking. Even the test of success or failure does not clearly separate the public from the private establishment, since failure was more often than not the fate of each type.

Of these public associations the first and most completely characteristic was the Pennsylvania Society for the Encouragement of Manufactures and the Useful Arts. Founded in August, 1787, it had Benjamin Franklin as its official patron and General Thomas Mifflin, Tench Coxe, Matthew Carey, and Samuel Wetherill as its principal sponsors. It flourished until about 1790, then languished, and was revived again in 1803, with Benjamin Rush as president, Coxe, Wistar, and Anthony Morris as vice-presidents, while Wetherill was once more chairman of the manufacturing committee. In 1787, membership was open to all citizens upon the payment of 10 shillings annually. Within the general membership there was a smaller group, composed of those who had contributed £10 toward the manufacturing fund. Shares were transferable, and the capital was to be invested in equipping a factory. By 1788 the manufacturing fund amounted to more than £1,300, to which the State contributed £1,000. In April, 1788, the factory was ready for operation. In March, 1790, however, it was burned, and the venture came to an end. There was suspicion at the time that the fire was incendiary, and the State offered a reward for the discovery of the guilty person.[3]

Similar societies were established in other States. In New

---

[3] *American Museum*, vol. ii, p. 167; "Letters of Phineas Bond," pp. 553f., 583; Samuel atchelder, *Introduction and Early Progress of the Cotton Manufacture in the United States* Boston, 1863), p. 34; Scharf and Westcott, *History of Philadelphia*, vol. i, p. 515.

York a Manufacturing Society was founded in 1789. Here also a fund was raised, with which the New York Manufactory was started. Samuel Slater was employed here for a short time prior to his removal to Providence in 1790.[4] Another ambitious venture was projected in Baltimore under the name of the Baltimore Manufacturing Company, and workmen were advertised for.[5] In Delaware also a society was proposed for the purpose of encouraging manufactures by means of premiums.[6] And even in the South and the newer West, Coxe reported that several manufacturing associations were on foot. In the Ohio country a fund of "about 25000 dollars had been raised . . . to carry on the cotton manufacture," while in the western district of South Carolina forty farmers and planters had combined for the promotion of manufactures and agriculture.[7] In 1789, Washington noted that manufactures were, with inland navigation, "the greatest and most important objects of internal concern, which at present occupy the attention of the public mind."[8] In the same year, Washington was serving as an intermediary in a negotiation between the governor of Virginia and an English manufacturer who was willing to set up the woolen industry in that State.[9] Not until 1791 did Washington refuse to take further part in the matter, since "it certainly would not carry an aspect very favorable to the dignity of the United States, for the President in clandestine manner to entice the subjects of another nation to violate its laws."[1] In 1794, Henry Wansey, an English manufacturer, was promised the use of slaves "almost for nothing," if he would establish a cotton manufactory at Richmond.[2]

---

[4] *American Museum*, vol. v, p. 325; the *New York Packet*, Feb. 17, 1789; *DeBow's Commercial Review*, vol. vii, p. 352; Bishop, *op. cit.*, vol. i, p. 402.

[5] *American Museum*, vol. v, p. 591; Bagnall, *op. cit.*, pp. 131-132; Griffith, *op. cit.*, p. 128.

[6] *American Museum*, vol. v, p. 174; "Letters of Phineas Bond," p. 654.

[7] Coxe, *A View of the United States of America*, pp. 303-305.

[8] *The Writings of George Washington*, vol. xi, p. 358.

[9] *Ibid.*, vol. xi, p. 445.

[1] *Ibid.*, vol. xii, pp. 6-7.

[2] Henry Wansey, *An Excursion to the United States* (2nd ed., London, 1798), p. 179.

In his Report on Manufactures, Hamilton gave currency, on a national scale, to this zeal for American manufactures. He referred with approval to the enterprise of the Pennsylvania Society and deplored only its lack of funds. He proposed to nationalize its work and suggested the creation of a national board of commissioners, who would draw upon a national fund for the importation of machinery and artisans and for the reward of discovery and invention.[3] Still more does his active participation in the founding of the Paterson Manufactory constitute the very climax of the manufacturing movement in this period. Organized in 1791 under the name of the Society for Establishing Useful Manufactures, it was active industrially, despite its initial difficulties, until 1797, although as an industrial experiment it was never successful.[4] Its very size and scope brought it into public notice; with a capital of more than a quarter of a million dollars, it was the largest industrial venture as yet attempted in the country. Possessing an interstate character, conceived in New York, with a charter from New Jersey, and with stockholders from several of the eastern States, it was from the start regarded as a national enterprise. It was to be not merely a factory, but an entire community, the first of those industrial towns which were to mark successive stages in the evolution of the industrial revolution in America, a predecessor of Lowell, Lawrence, and Manchester. This idea also originated with Tench Coxe, who had already proposed the Susquehanna as a suitable site for an industrial village, and who had foretold that in time there would be many such towns, each located in the center of its market and drawing its food and materials from the countryside.[5] It was no accident that since 1790 Coxe had been assistant secretary of the Treasury, and Hamilton's chief aid. The New Jersey Society was their joint

---

[3] *The Industrial and Commercial Correspondence of Alexander Hamilton*, pp. 319–320.

[4] The best account of the New Jersey company is in Davis, *op. cit.*, vol. i, pp. 351ff. See also Bagnall, *op. cit.*, p. 181.

[5] *American Museum*, vol. xi, pp. 179–180. Also "A Plan for Encouraging Agriculture and Increasing the Value of Farms in the Midland and more Western Counties of Pennsylvania . . . ," published in Coxe, *A View of the United States of America*, pp. 384ff.

product, coinciding so happily and perhaps deliberately with the publication of the Report on Manufactures.[6]

Both the general acclaim and the censure which the National Manufactory provoked at the outset served to focus public attention on the subject of manufactures. Paradoxically, no sooner were American manufactures in prospect of becoming a reality than there was evoked the specter, which haunted American social thought all through the nineteenth century, of the industrial corporation, large, privileged, devouring, and discriminatory. The New Jersey Society became the target of criticism for those who feared that it endangered the livelihood of the mechanic and petty manufacturer. It supplied, of course, fuel for the antifederalist campaign against Hamilton and the "new system of monopolies."[7] The most complete criticism came from Dr. George Logan, who addressed five letters to the yeomanry of the United States.[8] Logan was no outright opponent of manufactures; in 1792 he was president of the Germantown Society for Promoting Domestic Manufactures, and in 1800 he sponsored the Lancaster Society for Promoting Agriculture, Manufactures, and the Useful Arts. In the latter year he published a general appeal for the encouragement of domestic manufactures.[9] His chief fears were that American towns were filled with British traders and agents and that foreign manufactures were threatening to destroy the American character. Home industry was necessary, but, like Jefferson and Cooper, he disliked the manufacturing system of Europe.

Political and economic conditions, however, were converting agrarians like Logan and even Jefferson into advocates of a modified policy of home industry. After 1800, the Napoleonic wars offered ample opportunity for American commerce and shipping, but at the same time the Continental System and British measures of retaliation were rapidly creating a

---

[6] Davis, *op. cit.*, vol. i, p. 356.   [7] *Ibid.*, pp. 388, 430-431.

[8] George Logan, *Five Letters Addressed to the Yeomanry of the United States* (Philadelphia, 1793). Reprinted in the *American Museum*, vol. xii, pp. 159ff., 213ff.

[9] George Logan, *A Letter to the Citizens of Pennsylvania on the Necessity of Promoting Agriculture, Manufactures, and the Useful Arts* (Lancaster, 1800).

crisis in the relations between Europe and the United States. As president, Jefferson bore the brunt of responsibility, and he was compelled to restate his former objections to manufacturing. He compromised with the impending Industrial Revolution, but he would have placed two main limitations upon it. There was the evident necessity for a greater degree of independence in relation to Europe. The United States could, therefore, do with enough manufactures to supply domestic needs and to work up the raw materials raised in the country. But there must be no more.¹ As early as 1805, Jefferson complained that his former views had been misunderstood. They were intended to apply only to the great cities of Europe and not to this country at the present time. As yet American manufacturers were "as much at their ease, as independent and moral as our agricultural inhabitants."²

The second limitation Jefferson would have imposed upon the development of American industry had its roots in a hope and a wish rather than in reality. He was eager to domesticate the Industrial Revolution. He gloated over the fact that the English machinery had been reduced "for most things to the compass of a private family, and every family of any size is now getting machines on a small scale for their household purposes."³ On his own estate he had set up textile machinery, with which 2 women and 2 girls were able to supply all his domestic needs, amounting to 2,000 yards of cloth a year.⁴ He followed with enthusiasm the growth of domestic manufactures; and, with the optimistic faith of an idealist living in the far-off South, he was able to shut his eyes to the fact that this was the very period in which the factory and the new industrial technique were being acclimatized in the North.⁵

Certainly between 1800 and 1815, machine industry made

---

¹ *The Writings of Thomas Jefferson*, vol. xii, p. 235; Bishop, *op. cit.*, vol. ii, p. 138.

² *The Writings of Thomas Jefferson*, vol. xi, p. 55.

³ *Ibid.*, vol. xiii, p. 170. For the apparent promise of domestic manufactures in this period, cf. Tryon, *op. cit.*, pp. 144ff., 284.

⁴ *The Writings of Thomas Jefferson*, vol. xiii, pp. 170–171.

⁵ *Ibid.*, vol. xi, pp. 397, 427; vol. xii, pp. 235, 271; vol. xiii, pp. 38, 122; vol. xiv, pp. 318, 389.

notable progress in the United States.[6] By 1815 the economic interest of American manufacturers had become large enough to play an increasingly prominent part in national politics. Between 1816 and 1833 it both won and lost the battle for protection. Associations were now formed for the particular purpose of agitating the cause of adequate protection for industry, and partisan propaganda was organized and circulated on a national scale. In 1816 the American Society was founded in New York, which later developed into the American Institute, "for the purpose of encouraging and promoting domestic industry in this state and the United States."[7] In 1817 the Connecticut Society was formed, and in 1819, the Philadelphia Society for the Promotion of Useful Industry by Protective Laws.[8] In 1820 the National Institution for the Promotion of Industry grew out of preliminary conventions of the Friends of American Industry. Its membership included such outstanding figures in the new world of manufactures as Peter Colt, E. I. Dupont, P. H. Schenk, and, of course, that veteran propagandist, Matthew Carey. For a year it sponsored the publication of the *Patron of Industry*, an outspoken organ of protection.[9] The agitation culminated in the convention of the Friends of Domestic Industry, held at New York in 1831. It issued an appeal for protection, which was based upon an extensive and detailed account of the state of American manufactures.[1]

The rise of the protectionist controversy, with its abstruse theorizing and rationalizing, clearly belongs to the more restricted field of tariff history, except insofar as it is an index

---

[6] Batchelder, *op. cit.*, pp. 53ff.; Bagnall, *op. cit.*, pp. 488, 525, 536. An early survey of the new industry appears in the *Emporium of Useful Arts and Sciences*, vol. i (May, 1812), pp. 75ff.

[7] Daly, *op. cit.*, p. 28.

[8] *Loc. cit.* In 1816 the American Society issued an "Address to the People of the United States," of which 5,000 copies were distributed (*Niles' Register*, vol. xi, pp. 366ff.). Cf. also Isaac Briggs' activity as a propagandist (*ibid.*, vol. xii, pp. 166, 311; vol. xiii, p. 212). Matthew Carey recounts his own efforts in his *Autobiography in Thirty-Two Letters* (Philadelphia, 1837), pp. 103f. Also Batchelder, *op. cit.*, p. 58.

[9] *Patron of Industry* (June 28, 1820), vol. i, no. 1.

[1] *Convention of the Friends of Domestic Industry Held at New York, October, 1831* (Baltimore, 1831).

of the advanced state of industrial consciousness. More mature practices and methods for centering attention upon the prospects of American industry were being developed; and, in fact, the pattern of social life was being adjusted to the needs of a growing industrial society. The more naïve methods characteristic of the earlier period were, however, still available; and the familiar appeal to patriotic necessity, in particular, retained considerable effectiveness, both before and after the war with England. Thus, in 1808, a Manufacturers' Festival was held at Philadelphia. There was a dinner, with Colonel David Humphreys as the guest of honor, and among the toasts drunk was one to "The Best Mode of Warfare for our Country—the artillery of carding and spinning machinery, and the musketry of shuttles and sledges."[2] The encouragement of industry was again a matter for public enterprise. The State of New York offered premiums for household woolen manufactures.[3] In Philadelphia a Premium Society was functioning in 1808, and an attempt was made to organize a Manufacturing Society.[4] Baltimore was more successful; the Union Manufacturing Company was sponsored by William Patterson. Some 672 people subscribed to its capital stock of $350,000, and both city and State took shares in it. In 1812 two mills were in operation, with a total of 8,300 spindles, comprising the largest cotton factory then in existence, and it prospered during the war years.[5]

A special complaint of the period was that American manufactures were hard to sell. There were two prevailing prejudices against them: they were inferior to and dearer than imported goods.[6] In New England federalist merchants opposed to the war policy refused to sell them.[7] Already in 1805

---

[2] Scharf and Westcott, *op. cit.*, vol. i, p. 532.

[3] *Transactions of the Albany Institute*, vol. iv, p. 123. New York spent $20,000 for such premiums between 1808 and 1814, in collaboration with the Society of Useful Arts, and it returned to this policy in 1819 (Daly, *op. cit.*, pp. 20, 25).

[4] Scharf and Westcott, *op. cit.*, vol. i, p. 531; vol. iii, p. 2231. The managing committee included the old guard, Wetherill, Coxe, and Carey.

[5] Bagnall, *op. cit.*, pp. 488ff.

[6] *Niles' Register*, vol. i, p. 462.

[7] Bagnall, *op. cit.*, p. 603; N. Appleton, *Introduction of the Power Loom and the Origin of Lowell* (Lowell, 1858), p. 11.

the Philadelphia Domestic Society was formed with a capital of $10,000. Dividends were to be a secondary consideration; its main purpose was to provide a warehouse and salesroom for American manufactures. It was hoped that about 500 weavers might be kept in employment in that way; and, in fact, during the first 6 years, profits were as high as 8 per cent.[8] At Baltimore, the Athenian Society existed for a similar purpose, with a capital of $12,000, and in 1811 it did a business of more than $50,000.[9] After the war American warehouses began to multiply, addressing themselves to the business of selling American manufactures.[1] One firm advertised American-made hosiery for sale, appealing especially to those who had "patriotism enough to pay twelve and a half cents more for American than for imported stockings."[2]

The hard times of 1819 gave further occasion for the time-honored appeal to patriotic sentiment. The Society of Tammany,[3] the Society for the Promotion of Agriculture, Manufactures, and Domestic Economy, in Cincinnati,[4] and the Lycurgus Society at Yale University, all recommended frugality and an increased patronage of American manufactures. American business men were quick to take advantage of the opportunity; and, on the same page with the announcement of the Lycurgus Society, the *Patron of Industry* carried several advertisements offering cloth suitable for the purpose expressed in the resolution.[5] Even twisting the lion's tail and John Bull-baiting were resorted to as a means of stimulating industrial consciousness. It was reported that associations of English manufacturers had been formed for the purpose of flooding the American markets with cheap goods. They were prepared to sacrifice £300,000.[6] The over-zealous Niles ac-

---

[8] Scharf and Westcott, *op. cit.*, vol. iii, p. 2302; James Mease, *The Picture of Philadelphia* (Philadelphia, 1811), p. 264.

[9] *Niles' Register*, vol. i, p. 461.

[1] Cf. the advertisements in the *Patron of Industry*, March 3, 1821, which are typical.

[2] *Ibid.*, June 29, 1820.

[3] Bishop, *op. cit.*, vol. ii, p. 252.

[4] James Flint, *Letters from America* (Edinburgh, 1822), p. 244.

[5] *Patron of Industry*, Sept. 2, 1820.

[6] *Niles' Register*, vol. iii, p. 9 and vol. xviii, p. 151.

cused the British of using incendiary methods as a means of destroying American manufactures.[7]

By this time, however, industrial consciousness was receiving more mature and more positive expression. In the decade of the 1820's, the industrial fair and exhibit was developed into a permanent and regular institution for the proud display of actual achievement and for the stimulation of interest in future prospects. It originated as an adjunct to the agricultural fair, and it came as a logical consequence of the zeal for encouraging manufactures by means of premiums and other rewards. Already in 1807, Elkanah Watson made himself the sponsor of the agricultural exhibit, in which agricultural improvement was linked up with manufactures. He placed a pair of merino sheep on display under a tree in the public square at Pittsfield, Massachusetts, and from the wool of these prize sheep he had a piece of broadcloth made up by the "best artists in the country." Samples of the cloth were then sent to all parts of the country, and Watson's own claim was that this "was the origin of the present woolen factories, producing cloths which will vie with the best European."[8] Watson later founded the Berkshire County Agricultural Society, which held its first fair in 1811. In the grand procession with which the fair opened manufactures had a place of prominence.[9] At the Pittsfield fair in 1813, premiums were offered for domestic manufactures as well as for agricultural products, and the exhibit included both kinds.[1]

The State of New York adopted a similar policy of encouraging household manufactures in 1819. It set aside $10,000 a year for premiums to be distributed in all the counties; and, as a consequence, New York County held a fair in 1821 for the display of goods and the award of prizes.[2] In other States such exhibits were also being held. In 1823 the Brighton Cattle Show and Exhibition of Domestic Manufactures was an-

---

[7] *Ibid.*, vol. v, p. 9.

[8] E. Watson, *History of the Rise, Progress, and Existing Condition of the Berkshire Agricultural Society* (Albany, 1819), p. 10.

[9] *Ibid.*, pp. 13, 16.

[1] Daly, *op. cit.*, p. 23. [2] *Ibid.*, p. 25.

nounced. There was also a New Hampshire show and fair in the same year, at which "there was fine exhibit of cattle and a great many manufactured articles."[3]

During this period, however, the industrial exhibit was acquiring a strictly urban character almost simultaneously in Boston, New York, and Philadelphia. In 1818, the Massachusetts Charitable Mechanic Association held its first exhibit of goods for the award of prizes. A larger one was held in the following year, and in 1821 a still more extensive one.[4] The society then abandoned the practice, but returned to it in 1837, when the "First Exhibition" was announced. The net profits in that year were $700, and thereafter displays were arranged for at irregular intervals down to 1860.[5] In the meantime, in New York, as early as 1823, the newly organized Mechanic and Scientific Institution planned an industrial fair, which, it was hoped, would arouse pride and stimulate ambition, so that "under proper regulations, we may soon compete with foreigners in the manufacture of all useful articles."[6] The fair, held in October, 1824, was completely successful. Manufacturers from other States participated and carried away some of the premiums. A banquet formed part of the celebration, with Governor Clinton in attendance.[7]

In the same year, the Franklin Institute, recently established at Philadelphia, launched the first of a series of annual industrial fairs, which became increasingly popular.[8] The New York Mechanic and Scientific Institution did not survive its first fair; but, in 1828, the American Institute sponsored the first of its annual fairs, which in time acquired a national character.[9] In 1836 the Institute established a per-

---

[3] *Niles' Register*, vol. xxv, p. 82.

[4] *Annals of the Massachusetts Charitable Mechanic Association* (Boston, 1892), p. 9.

[5] *Loc. cit.*, In 1825, the mayor of Boston called a meeting of manufacturers to arrange for a public sale and annual fair for domestic manufactures (*Niles' Register*, vol. xxix, p. 181).

[6] *Plan for Extending the New York Mechanic and Scientific Institution* (New York, 1824), p. 16; Daly, *op. cit.*, p. 30.

[7] *Niles' Register*, vol. xxv, p. 42; vol. xxvii (Nov. 27, 1824), p. 1.

[8] *Ibid.*, vol. xxix, p. 129.

[9] In 1831, a new Mechanics' Institute was founded at New York, which offered 120 premiums at its first mechanical fair in 1835. Daly, *op. cit.*, p. 30; *Mechanics' Magazine*

manent repository for the collection and exhibition of models and machines. It also maintained a free reading room for the public, and it published a monthly journal of its activities.[1]

Long before this, however, an industrial fair, on a truly national scale, had been held at Washington. The first impulse to this enterprise was supplied by a meeting of "mechanics, manufacturers, and friends of American Manufactures," which was held in 1824 at Philadelphia under the direction of Matthew Carey. It was agreed upon to enter into a correspondence with other cities for the purpose of organizing an exhibition of American goods near Congress. The Philadelphia plan was adopted at meetings held in Baltimore and New York, and in February, 1825, the fair opened in the "noblest room" in the Capitol. In spite of the short notice, the exhibit was extensive, and visitors were astonished at the scope of American industry.[2] In 1846 was held another exhibit, which was described at the time as the First National Fair. A million dollars' worth of goods was shown as "a grand testimonial to the power of American manufactures." Intended as a counter-blast to the lobbying activities of British manufacturers and their allies at Washington, the fair of 1846 almost turned out to be a boomerang, since it occasioned a cry among free-traders that American manufactures could now stand on their own feet and needed no further protection.[3]

In 1843, the American Institute, which had become an important instrument for the systematic diffusion of industrial consciousness, introduced an innovation. Its members were to hold weekly conversational meetings for the discussion of selected topics in both their scientific and practical aspects.[4] The method may have been new, but the underlying motive was not. It was only another manifestation of that zest for

---

and Register of Inventions and Improvements, vol. vi, no. 5 (New York, Nov., 1835), pp. 249ff.; Bishop, *op. cit.*, vol. ii, p. 338; *Transactions of the American Institute* (Albany, 1842–72), Second Report, Appendix A, pp. 4–5.

   [1] *Ibid.*, p. 12.   [2] *Niles' Register,* vol. xxvii, pp. 243, 337, 401.

   [3] *Ibid.*, vol. xxviii, p. 42; *Fisher's National Magazine and Industrial Record*, vol. iii (New York, 1846), pp. 66, 155.

   [4] *Transactions of the American Institute*, Third Report, pp. 6, 142.

useful knowledge which had characterized the manufacturing movement from the start. It was, in fact, an expression of that improving spirit which was so pervasive a phenomenon of American life already in the eighteenth century. By 1830, it had begun to crystallize and was assuming organized and permanent form along two main lines. One was the rise of technical journalism; the other concerned the beginnings of practical education, with special reference to the needs of the mechanic, the hero of the new Industrial Revolution.

The zeal for useful knowledge was scarcely divorced at first from the more academic interest in pure science. The American Philosophical Society combined both in its early activities.[5] But with the rise of the manufacturing agitation came the realization that not only men and machines but also skill and useful information must be imported from Europe and made available in America. The *American Museum* made itself, to some extent, an organ for the dissemination of useful industrial knowledge in the years between 1787 and 1792. From Philadelphia also came the idea that the new federal government should help in the diffusion of useful knowledge. Already in 1787, as part of his proposal for a federal university, Dr. Benjamin Rush suggested that a professorship of economy should be established and that its incumbent should make it his business to "unfold the principles and practice of agriculture, and manufactures of all kinds, and to enable him to make his lectures more extensively useful, congress should support a travelling correspondent for him, who should visit all the nations of Europe, and transmit to him from time to time, all the discoveries and improvements that are made in agriculture and manufactures."[6] Nothing came of this proposal; but many years later, in 1825, another Pennsylvania society interested in the promotion of internal improvements actually sent William Strickland abroad for a

---

[5] Cf. above, p. 786, n. 2. By contrast, the American Academy of Arts and Sciences, established at Boston in 1779, was interested in pure science from the start (*Memoirs of the American Academy of Arts and Sciences*, 1785-1926).

[6] *American Museum*, vol. i, p. 10; also vol. iv, p. 442.

year and commissioned him to collect information about the manufacture of iron and the building of railroads.[7]

The publication of useful knowledge was haphazard and only occasional at first, but by 1830 it was developing into a regular and periodic function of journals specially designed for the purpose. As early as 1808, Jefferson approved a project of Dr. James Mease to publish an account of the manufactures of Philadelphia, adding that other cities should do this as well and regretting that the federal government was unable to support such a venture financially.[8] Not long after, Mease became the editor of the *Archives of Useful Knowledge*, one of several works of a practical nature.[9] In the same period, between 1812 and 1814, the *Emporium of Useful Arts and Sciences* appeared as a monthly publication under the editorship, first of Dr. J. R. Coxe, and then of Thomas Cooper. In it were reprinted many articles from English journals, dealing with such topics as the steam engine, and the properties and manufacture of iron, copper, brass, and tin.[1]

But the age of popularized technical knowledge was really ushered in with the appearance at New York of the *American Mechanics' Magazine* as a weekly on February 5, 1825. Its preface revealed its close connection with the existing industrial consciousness: ". . . The deep interest which exists in various sections of our country relative to the extension and prosperity of our manufactures renders correct information concerning them exceedingly desirable and this is intended to do so."[2] Originally it was intended to be merely a copy of the London *Mechanics' Magazine;* after a year, however, it was taken over by and merged with *The Franklin Journal*

---

[7] Strickland's reports received considerable currency through publication in *The Franklin Journal*, vol. i, pp. 12, 71, 134.

[8] *The Writings of Thomas Jefferson*, vol. xii, p. 216.

[9] The *Archives* were published in three volumes (Philadelphia, 1810–13). Already in 1804, Mease had published an enlarged American edition of A. F. M. Willich's *Domestic Encyclopaedia, or a Dictionary of Facts and Useful Knowledge*, and in 1811, a *Picture of Philadelphia, giving an Account of its Origin, Increase, and Improvements in Arts, Sciences, and Manufactures*.

[1] Five volumes of the *Emporium of Useful Arts and Sciences* were published altogether between May, 1812, and April, 1814.

[2] *American Mechanics' Magazine* (James V. Seaman, publisher), vol. i, p. 1.

and American Mechanics' Magazine. As the official organ of the newly established Franklin Institute at Philadelphia, it became the first successful technical journal in the United States. Its appeal was very different from that of the almost contemporary *American Journal of Science*, which had been founded by Benjamin Silliman in 1818. While the latter was purely scientific, *The Franklin Journal* was addressed to the artisan and manufacturer and was intended to usher out "the age of secrets in arts and trades."[3] In July, 1826, the editor confessed that his chief difficulty was in making his material intelligible to the mechanic. A special section was inaugurated under the heading of the *Artisan*, which was "to aid in elevating them to that station, which, from their numbers, the value of their services, and the genius of our institutions, they ought to occupy."[4] The editor offered no apology for reprinting articles; he had published copious extracts from Nicholson's *Operative Mechanic*, and he was able to recommend an improved American edition of that famous English work.[5]

The Franklin Journal had its followers, of course, in the new field of technical journalism, although few of these were as long lived or as successful. In 1830, Boston saw the brief appearance of the *Mechanics' Magazine and Journal of Public Internal Improvement*, which was addressed to "a class of the community, with whom science has heretofore been but little concerned."[6] In the same year, the first issue of a bi-weekly was published at New York under the name of the *Mechanics' and Farmers' Magazine*, which lapsed, however, when the American Institute pleaded poverty in refusing to accept it as an official organ.[7] In 1835, however, the Institute brought out a journal, which disavowed all concern with politics; it was to be devoted to the "Interests of Agriculture, Com-

---

[3] *The Franklin Journal*, vol. i, p. 2.

[4] *Ibid.*, vol. ii, p. vi.

[5] *Ibid.*, vol. i, p. 47; vol. ii, p. 126. Another special feature was a monthly list of new patents issued in England and America.

[6] *Mechanics' Magazine*, vol. i, p. 1.

[7] *Mechanics' and Farmers' Magazine*, vol. i, no. 1 (June 15, 1830).

merce, Manufactures, and the Arts."[8] But already since 1833
another *Mechanics' Magazine and Register of Inventions and
Improvements* had been appearing at New York, and in 1836
it became the *Journal of the Mechanics' Institute*. Its purpose
was to give expression to the "unprecedented spirit of inquiry and thirst for knowledge. . . ."[9] From the start the
journal was devoted to the cause of mechanics' institutions
and of self-improvement through practical education.

A beginning in this field had, in fact, already been made,
in both New York and Philadelphia. The rise of technical
education by 1830 is significant as a further manifestation of
the urban and industrial consciousness which was rapidly al-
tering the pattern of American thought. As early as 1819, the
Massachusetts Charitable Mechanic Association had considered the matter of establishing lectures on scientific subjects,
but no money for the purpose was appropriated until 1828,
and the lectures began in the following year.[1] In 1822, the
General Society of Mechanics and Tradesmen of New York
commended by resolution the "novel and interesting spectacle of literature mingling with labor, and of a master mechanic and apprentices devoting their leisure evenings to
literary improvement. . . ." By 1824, this first evening class
in English grammar had developed into a regular school, with
an attendance of 117 pupils, of whom 53 received free tuition.[2]

This was perhaps only an ordinary school conducted under the auspices of an association of mechanics. Technical
education of a kind for mechanics proper was, however, in-

---

[8] *Journal of the American Institute*, vol. i, p. 2. Four volumes were published altogether.
The first labor journals, which began to make their appearance in 1827, are not included
here, since they belong more appropriately to the early history of class consciousness,
which was, of course, a further consequence of industrial consciousness.

[9] *Mechanics' Magazine and Register of Inventions and Improvements*, vol. i, p. iii. Nine
volumes were published, and in 1837 it was merged with the *Railroad Journal*.

[1] *Annals of the Massachusetts Charitable Mechanic Association*, p. 5. In 1820 the Association became the beneficiary of the philanthropy of William Wood, a Boston merchant,
and acquired the first mechanics' apprentices' library in the United States (*ibid.*, p. 6).
Wood also helped to establish the mechanics' library of the New York Society of Mechanics
and Tradesmen (*Annals*, pp. 282–283).

[2] *Annals of the Massachusetts Charitable Mechanic Association*, pp. 60, 69, 70.

augurated by the New York Mechanic and Scientific Institution in 1822, almost simultaneously with the formation of similar establishments at Edinburgh and London.[3] The program of the new society, three-fourths of whose managers were to be practical mechanics or manufacturers, was indeed too ambitious for complete realization. It included lectures on "the principles of mechanical and chemical philosophy" as well as many other related subjects, and its purpose was to "foster the Mechanic and Useful Arts, and to enlighten the minds and to stimulate the genius of those who practise them."[4] There was a project to raise a fund for a building.[5] This lapsed, however, together with the society itself, in 1824. But already in 1822, lecture courses had been given, for which the hall was filled, and two professors had been named, one in mechanical philosophy and the other in "the terminology and diseases incident to mechanics."[6]

If the Mechanic and Scientific Institution of New York was the first failure of the movement for popular and technical education, the Franklin Institute of Philadelphia was its first lasting success. Launched as a non-political, purely educational enterprise at a general meeting on February 5, 1824, on the recommendation of a smaller committee, it offered free public lectures by volunteers in April, while paid professors gave courses in chemistry as applied to the arts, natural philosophy, and architecture. In the following year, mechanics and natural history were added. To the latter course ladies were admitted, and a hundred of them are reported to have attended the lectures. Classes in drawing and mathematics were added, and a practical workshop was suggested.[7] By 1826 it was discovered that the chief defect was

---

[3] *Report on a Plan for Extending and More Perfectly Establishing the Mechanic and Scientific Institution* (New York, 1824), pp. 6–8. The Andersonian Institution at Glasgow had preceded them all in 1800.

[4] *Charter, Constitution, and By-Laws of the New York Mechanic and Scientific Institution* (New York, 1823), p. 14. There were also to be a laboratory and scientific library, while premiums were to be offered at periodic exhibitions of manufactures. See also *Niles' Register*, vol. xxv, p. 82.

[5] *Report on a Plan for Extending and More Perfectly Establishing the Mechanic and Scientific Institution*, p. 24.

[6] *Ibid.*, pp. 19–20.   [7] *The Franklin Journal*, vol. i, pp. 70, 130–134, 254.

the want of preparatory instruction, and a high school department was proposed and opened in October, with an enrollment of 300.[8]

In the same year, also, a public meeting was held to consider the establishment of a Polytechnic and Scientific College, in which the classics would be dispensed with as a requirement. The tuition was to be low enough to place it within "the power of the industrious mechanic." The courses were to be adapted to the needs of "the agriculturist, the mechanic, or manufacturer, the architect, the civil engineer, and other man of business." Two objections are reported to have been raised against the project. One was that it was too "aristocraticall;" the other came from the university and was presumably based on the ground that it was too democratic.[9] But, already on November 5, 1824, Stephen Van Rensselaer had informed the Reverend Samuel Blatchford that he had established a school at the north end of Troy, "for the purpose of instructing persons, who may choose to apply themselves, in the *application of science to the common purposes of life.*"[1]

The movement for popular education of a practical and technical nature was no more to be checked than the spread of the new industry itself. By 1830 the two were linked together as cause and effect, and both were being reflected in new patterns of thought and behavior. With these there were other manifestations of the newly developed industrial consciousness. There was concern over the prospective social benefits and ills of manufactures. There was an eagerness to display industrial achievement. And above all, there was the pervasive zeal for improvement and for the spread of useful knowledge, which organized technical journalism and practical education were beginning to satisfy.[2]

---

[8] *Ibid.*, p. 254; vol. ii, p. 269.   [9] *Ibid.*, p. 190.

[1] P. C. Ricketts, *History of Rensselaer Polytechnic Institute* (2nd ed., New York, 1914), p. 9. The founder's original intention was to "qualify teachers for instructing the sons and daughters of farmers and mechanics . . . in the application of experimental chemistry, philosophy . . . to agriculture, the arts . . . and manufactures."

[2] Cf. Carroll D. Wright, *Historical View of Wages and Prices, 1752–1860* (Boston, 1885), p. 20.

CHAPTER III

The Depression of 1819-1822
A Social History

The following essay originally appeared in the *American Historical Review*, Volume XXXIX, Number 1 (October 1933), pp. 28-47. It is reprinted here, in its entirety, with the permission of the American Historical Association and the author. The original pagination appears in brackets at the bottom of each page.

THE DEPRESSION OF 1819–1822, A SOCIAL HISTORY

In 1819, the United States, in common with all Europe, experienced a severe shock to its economic and social well-being. Not only was there a general and drastic decline in property values, but fully as significant were the radical changes in social mood and outlook which found expression in widespread agitation and, finally, in political action. Perhaps even more than in indexes of prices and bank clearings the history of a people is reflected in the alternating moods of buoyant expansiveness and earth-bound depression. In this early precedent are illustrated all the major features of what has become a recurring phenomenon of American social and economic history.

There was, in the first place, the preceding period of extravagant speculation and apparent prosperity. The long cycle of wars, both in Europe and America, ending only in 1815, had favored the erection of an unstable and overdeveloped structure of credits and debits. Every type of economic activity had flourished, including industry, which grew into the proportions of a boom after 1808, under the stimulus of an exclusive home market. Upon the financial façade, in particular, was lavished all the aspiration of a people who were projecting an accidental and temporary good fortune into the indefinite future. The close of the war cycle brought only a momentary lull in the strong breeze of prosperity. It shifted rather than abated its course. While the new industry felt the chill air of British competition, both commerce and agriculture continued to prosper, and the expansion of banking went on with uninterrupted vigor. The prevailing condition was admirably described in the report of a committee of the Pennsylvania legislature, prepared in 1820.[1]

The plenty of money, as it was called, was so profuse, that the managers of the Banks were fearful that they could not find a demand for all they could fabricate, and it was no infrequent occurrence to hear solicitations urged to individuals to become borrowers, under promises of indulgences the most tempting.

[1] William M. Gouge, *A Short History of Paper Money and Banking in the United States* (Philadelphia, 1833), p. 66. For the current bank expansion, see W. G. Sumner, *A History of Banking in the United States* (New York, 1896), p. 74; John Austin Stevens, *Albert Gallatin* (Boston, 1884), pp. 267, 270. On the prosperity generally, J. Leander Bishop, *A History of American Manufactures* (Philadelphia, 1868), II. 235, 244; John Bach McMaster, *A History of the People of the United States* (New York, 1911), IV. 321, 344, 484.

[28]

The few warnings and protests went largely unheeded, and even Niles, the shrewdest observer and reporter of the times, quickly changed to a note of optimism. In 1817 he was able to detect signs of returning normality.[2]

> We are settling down better than was hoped for. . . . Let us go on then, . . . the trial of war and the trial of peace have passed. It remains that we . . . march steadily on to the high destinies that await our country.

The really great trial, however, was still ahead. It was precipitated by a sharp crisis in the affairs of the second Bank of the United States. Established in 1816, it had not fulfilled its intended purpose of checking the current bank inflation. The center of a large and spectacular speculation in its own stock, it had indeed added to the inflation. In August, 1818, the Bank management decided upon a policy of contraction. The resulting pressure upon specie brought about a suspension of payments in many places and by many banks. An outcry against the Bank led to a congressional investigation which turned up evidence both of mismanagement and dishonesty. There was a movement to repeal its charter, and several lean years followed.[3]

The collapse of the financial façade was the signal for, rather than the entire cause of, the rapid spread of distress and the mental attitudes characteristic of depression. Business bankruptcies multiplied; prices fell; unemployment increased. A mood of complaint and rebellious protest grew upon the American community, and legislatures became the arena of what might be described as depression politics. Calhoun was greatly impressed with its seriousness in discussing the situation with John Quincy Adams in 1820:

> There has been within these two years an immense revolution of fortunes in every part of the Union; enormous numbers of persons utterly ruined; multitudes in deep distress; and a general mass of disaffection to the government, not concentrated in any particular direction, but ready to seize upon any event and looking out anywhere for a leader. . . .

That leadership was subsequently found in Andrew Jackson.[4] Similar Cassandra-like predictions of impending doom had begun early, and Niles in particular made himself both the prophet and the historian of

[2] *Niles' Register,* Apr. 13, Aug. 16, 1816; Mar. 15, 1817.

[3] *Ibid.,* Nov. 23, 1816; Nov. 29, 1817; Gouge, pp. 86, 93 ff., 102; Ralph C. H. Catterall, *The Second Bank of the United States* (Chicago, 1903), pp. 30, 73, 91.

[4] *Memoirs of John Quincy Adams,* Charles Francis Adams, ed. (Philadelphia, 1875), V. 128 f.; Frederick Jackson Turner, *The Rise of the New West* (New York, 1906), p. 148.

the depression. Already in April, 1816, he had warned that if only "half of the evil that is anticipated by intelligent gentlemen be felt, we shall have 'such times' as the present generation has never seen".[5]

The prophecy came true, even if allowance is made for a note of exaggeration in the current accounts of the hard times.[6] But exaggeration is itself an earmark of depression and a product of its pervasive pessimism. In 1819 Mathew Carey estimated that three million people, approximately one-third of the population, were directly affected.[7] From far-away Cincinnati came a report describing the "distress as beyond conception. Marshall and Sheriff Sales are almost daily".[8] Western New York, where the Erie Canal, even then in process of construction, held out the promise of future prosperity, was, nevertheless, in deep despair. At the annual meeting of the Genesee Agricultural Society, in October, 1820, at Batavia, its president, Samuel Hopkins, proclaimed himself an "alarmist". "My first wish would be . . . to speak in a tone that should rouse the tenants of every log-house in these counties, and make them stand aghast at the prospect of families naked—children freezing in the winter's storm—and the fathers without coats or shoes to enable them to perform the necessary labours of the inclement season." With wheat at thirty-seven and a half cents a bushel, and flour selling for $2.19 a barrel at New York, conditions were "without a parallel".

Last year we talked of the difficulties of paying for our lands; this year the question is, how to exist. The struggle is not now for property; from this time onwards we shall have to contend for clothing, and a few other necessaries, without which we must become a miserable, and, I fear, a barbarous people. . . . There can be no industry without a motive: and it appears to me there is great danger that our people will soon limit their exertions to the raising of food for their families . . . there cannot be much ambition or hope; education will decay, and the decencies of social life be neglected. . . .[9]

In city and country the distress was equally acute. Unemployment was widespread, and pauperism an urban problem commanding serious attention for the first time in American history. At Philadelphia, an investigating committee named at a general meeting in August, 1819,

[5] *Niles' Register*, Apr. 13, 1816.

[6] The charge of exaggeration was leveled against the protectionists in particular, on the ground that they had an axe to grind. *Cf. The American* (New York, Sept. 1, 1819).

[7] M. Carey, Address to the Farmers of the United States, in *Essays in Political Economy* (Philadelphia, 1822), p. 417.

[8] Letter printed in the Rochester *Telegraph*, Oct. 3, 1820.

[9] Carey, p. 419.

reported that in thirty industries, studied in detail, employment had decreased from 9672 in 1816 to 2137 in 1819; weekly wages were down from $58,000 to $12,000. The total reduction in employment could not be less than 11,592. Niles was able to add up a total of 50,000 as either unemployed or irregularly employed in the three cities of New York, Philadelphia, and Baltimore alone. Baltimore had lost 10,000 people since 1815, and he was afraid that the "distress of the people has reached an alarming extent, and there is no considerate man in our large cities and towns that looks to the approaching winter, without anticipating scenes of misery such as he never before witnessed".[10] James Flint estimated that half a million people were unemployed in the country as a whole.[11] From Lexington, Kentucky, the report came to the *Carolina Centinel* that mechanics were without work and that factories representing a capital of half a million dollars were idle. In this section, wrote a correspondent to the same journal: "A deeper gloom hangs over us than was ever witnessed by the oldest man. The last war was sunshine, compared with these times. . . . It is not my business to disguise the facts. . . . The present season requires plain, manly, unsophisticated truth." The *Centinel* also printed the account of a John Daely of Poughkeepsie, New York, who pleaded guilty to the charge of stealing a horse, giving as his reason:

The Times were so hard he could get no work, and could hit upon no other plan so ready and certain to provide him with a home and steady employment. He is a strong healthy young man; and was to his great gratification sentenced to the state prison for eight years.[12]

Relief for the unemployed and the urban poor was an urgent necessity. Baltimore provided no less than twelve soup stations for its poor during 1820. At Philadelphia also daily distribution of soup took place at the rate of a pint to a person. At New York soup houses were established through the generosity of the butchers, and collections were raised in the city's churches. In 1819 the New York Society for the Prevention of Pauperism was alarmed at the growing numbers of paupers, estimating them at 8000, in a city of 120,000; in the following year it reported that between 12,000 and 13,000 were receiving poor relief. From Cincinnati Flint wrote that many were leaving for the backwoods to raise

10 *Niles' Register,* Aug. 7, Sept. 4, Oct. 23, 1819; Sept. 16, 1820. *Cf.* also Carey, The New Olive Branch, *op. cit.,* p. 319; McMaster, IV. 532.

11 James Flint, *Letters from America* (Edinburgh, 1822), letter of Aug. 15, 1820 p. 248.

12 *Carolina Centinel,* June 12, Nov. 20, 1820.

food, while the newspapers were appealing for old clothes for the poor and for shoes to enable poor children to attend Sunday school.[13] Both at Philadelphia and at New York newly organized societies made studies of the growth of pauperism, analyzing causes and proposing remedies. The sad example of the English poor law was invoked as a warning. Nevertheless, self-sufficing individualism was in need of a prop, and it was partly supplied in the form of a recipe brought from Liverpool for a "cheap, wholesome, and savoury food", which could be made from a pound of rice and mutton suet gravy at a cost of three pence for a family of six.[14]

The propertied classes also suffered great hardships in this period of depression. Property values declined sharply along with earning capacity; added to this was the burden of old debts which could be liquidated only by means of forced sheriff's sales, and this depressed prices still further. A committee of the Pennsylvania senate reported that during 1819 there were 14,537 actions for debt in the state; not counting those for smaller amounts before justices of the peace. In Philadelphia County alone there were 1808 commitments to prison for debt. The value of real and personal property in New York State, as recorded at the comptroller's office, declined from 315 million dollars in 1818 to 256 millions in 1820. In Pennsylvania, land which had been boomed to $150 an acre in 1815 dropped to $35 in 1819.[15] At Baltimore rents declined from forty to fifty per cent., and a third of the property was held by the banks; Niles was sickened "to the heart to see the lists of persons who are published weekly in the Baltimore papers, as making application for the benefit of the insolvent laws of Maryland".[16]

Similar conditions prevailed east, west, and south. At Richmond, Virginia, property depreciated from a half to three-fourths, and half of it was mortgaged to the banks. At Alexandria, a wharf and storehouses which had cost $17,000 brought only $1250 at auction in 1820; at Augusta, Georgia, cotton, for which an offer of twenty-four cents a pound had

---

13 Flint, pp. 202, 211; Carey, pp. 319, 431; Rochester *Telegraph,* Mar. 7, 1820; Second and fourth annual reports of the Society for the Prevention of Pauperism (New York, 1820 and 1821); McMaster, IV. 349, 535; Thomas W. Griffiths, *Annals of Baltimore* (Baltimore, 1833), p. 231; James Grant Wilson, *Memorial History of the City of New York* (New York, 1893), III. 307.

14 *The American,* Oct. 2, 13, 1819; McMaster, IV. 526 ff. *Cf.* also the first five reports of the Society for the Prevention of Pauperism (1820–1822), *passim.*

15 *Niles' Register,* Feb. 24, 1821; Carey, p. 321; Murray Shipley Wildman, *Money Inflation in the United States* (New York, 1905), p. 90.

16 *Niles' Register,* June 26, 1819.

been refused, could not fetch fifteen. In Massachusetts commercial capital was reported to have taken a loss of twenty-five per cent. during 1819, while the volume of revenue bonds for which the government had entered suits against the debtor merchants increased from less than two million dollars to more than three millions in the course of the year. This was one-fifth of all the bonds outstanding. In the South the Bank of the United States finally took a loss of over two million dollars on bad debts; in the West its losses were smaller because it was able to hold on until values recovered. In the meantime, it owned every kind of property, as Senator Benton of Missouri put it:

I know towns, yea, cities . . . where this bank already appears as an engrossing proprietor. All the flourishing cities of the West are mortgaged to this money power. . . . They are in the jaws of the monster! A lump of butter in the mouth of a dog! One gulp, one swallow, and all is gone! [17]

European creditors lost 100 million dollars through the operation of American insolvency laws, and this, Niles dryly concluded, was our chief profit on the booming trade of the last five years.[18]

John Quincy Adams believed that the low point had been reached at the close of 1820, but a sluggish condition persisted for several years thereafter. As late as August, 1822, while "dashing failures" were no longer taking place, there were still enough "to serve us for half a century. Conditions are such that almost everybody is wondering how other people live." In Boston failures were still numerous in 1822, one hundred occurring during May, June, and July, to an amount exceeding three million dollars, while 3500 persons were imprisoned for debt between 1820 and 1822. Kentucky was compelled to adopt a new stay law for debts in 1821, since the first one had expired and the process of foreclosure was threatening to begin all over again. By 1821 prices were in a complete state of collapse; corn was at ten cents a bushel at Cincinnati; wheat was less than twenty-five cents, and whisky could not sell at fifteen cents a gallon.[19] The banks, to be sure, were crammed with money; government bonds were at a ten per cent. premium, while even the stock of the Bank of the United States had regained lost ground and was back to 119, although paying only five per cent. Niles noted and

[17] *Ibid.,* May 8, 1819; Apr. 22, June 24, 1820; Richmond *Enquirer,* June 1, 1819; Adam Hodgson, *Remarks during a Journey through North America* (New York, 1823), pp. 37 ff. *Cf.* also *Abridgment of the Debates of Congress* (New York, 1860), VI. 622; Catterall, p. 67.

[18] *Niles' Register,* Sept. 16, 1820.

[19] *Ibid.,* Apr. 7, 1821; Jan. 5, Aug. 3, Nov. 2, 1822; Adams, *Memoirs,* V. 409; McMaster, IV. 547; Wildman, p. 99.

deplored the rise of "a system of speculation (we might call it gambling)", which bade fair to equal the stockjobbing at London, and for which idle capital was to blame. He marveled at the paradoxical situation, but argued that the timidity of capital must be overcome and people put back to work. Any other "scheme to relieve the general distress must be mischievous".[20]

The prolonged years of distress naturally provoked a large amount of thinking and even more writing both to explain and to account for the depression. Often the exposition was linked up with a favorite measure of relief, and one was, therefore, intended to justify the other. The prevailing distress was, for example, a boon to the comparatively young protectionist movement, and its sponsors almost reveled in the opportunity to agitate and to forward their particular cause. Other explanations came from moralizing philsophers, who were not so much incorrect as they were vague and obvious; certainly what may have been fresh and new then has since become banal and trite, with endless repetition. All of them, however, belong in the pattern of thought which is characteristic of a period of depression.

A practical man of affairs like Stephen Girard, the greatest private banker of his day, was brief and obvious in attributing the calamity partly "to the great facilities which our Company Chartered Banks have afforded to several of our merchants, traders, and mechanics, who with their fictitious capital have acted imprudently".[21] Everybody blamed the banks, of course, but the exact nature of their offense was best described by an anonymous writer in the *Carolina Centinel,* who incidentally displayed an excellent understanding of banking theory for that early date. Banks should lend only "for a short time to real capitalists". They should lend only part of the necessary capital, such as may be used for immediate needs:

> But instead of this minimum, our numerous banks have sometimes stretched their loans to the utmost . . . . They have created accommodation paper, to enable one man to buy real estate; another to build houses and to buy furniture; a third to buy whole crops of tobacco and flour . . . a fourth to purchase the fixed capital of large manufactories . . . . We wanted to take short cuts to fortune. . . .

Shrewdly also, this writer, justly calling himself Economicus, pointed to causes even deeper than improper banking practice. There had been

20 *Niles' Register,* Aug. 26, 1820; Mar. 17, June 2, 9, 1821.
21 John Bach McMaster, *The Life and Times of Stephen Girard* (Philadelphia, 1918), II. 356.

[34]

a long war, which "adds to the debt, not to the wealth of a nation".
Not only the war, but also the peace which followed had led to large-
scale borrowing—three hundred million francs by France for indemni-
ties, great sums by Prussia, Russia, Austria, and Sweden for their military establishments. The English manufacturers had overreached themselves, and our trade also had been expanded with the aid of loans
According to Niles these had amounted to 172 million dollars in five
years. To all this there was a necessary limit and termination.[22]

Others also saw clearly that the past wars were the ultimate cause
of the present difficulty. As a people we "had fattened upon the distresses
of Europe. So easy was money to be obtained that many, very many of
us, had anticipated years of growth. . . . We have grasped at the emolu-
ments of futurity, calculating upon a promulgation of the miseries of the
old world as a sure guarantee of the prosperity of the new. . . ." [23]

Such speculations bordered very closely on, and, in fact, generally
passed over into the moral; on this theme many changes were rung.
Few particulars were specified, but the spirit of extravagance, imported
from Europe, received general arraignment, and the call was sounded
to return to the simpler ways of our ancestors. Industry and frugality,
words weighted with revolutionary authority, were given fresh currency.
A series of essays on Domestic Economy, under the pseudonym of
Howard, appeared in the *National Advocate* at this time, and were
widely reprinted in the country press. They dwelt on the vices of the
day, attacked that "unincorporated fraternity" of shavers and brokers in
Wall Street, and harked back to the better ways of a simpler generation,
when ladies did not buy cashmere shawls at $1100, Leghorn hats at $70,
nor did they spend fifty dollars on cake for a single party.[24] The Society
of Tammany sponsored a public *Address,* in which the recent state of
the nation was described as that of "the overgrown and pampered
youth . . . vaulting and bounding to ruin". The present visitation was
regarded as "the Act of Providence to arrest our hasty strides to national
destruction". One after another, it impeached the principal evils, among
them, that spirit for speculation which derived "from this factitious and
preternatural accession of money . . . ." It called to account the brokers

[22] *The Carolina Centinel,* June 12, 1819; *Niles' Register,* Apr. 23, 1821.

[23] Rochester *Telegraph,* Dec. 1, 1818. *Cf.* also Albany *Gazette,* July 12, 1819;
Oliver Wolcott, *Remarks on the Present State of the Currency, Credit, and National Industry* (New York, 1820), pp. 4 ff.

[24] *Niles' Register,* Oct. 26, 1816; Jan. 31, 1818; Wolcott, p. 36; *National Advocate*
(New York), Nov. 7, Dec. 14, 1818; Jan. 27, 1819.

[35]

"who have fastened upon society like leeches, who eat out its substance and live upon its distresses . . ."; in particular it condemned "the general propensity for shows and public exhibitions, which absorb the time and money, steal on the credulity, and give a wrong turn to the morals of the people".[25]

Not only had past prosperity been demoralizing, but the present distresses were liable to have a similar effect. The alarm was sounded by a director of the Bank of the United States in a letter which received circulation in both the English and the American press. Bankruptcies were so numerous as to "take away the odium . . . and the barriers of honesty are broken down by a perpetual legislation suited to the condition of insolvent debtors . . . . Credit is become very rare . . . . Besides our commercial distresses we are suffering great alarm in this city from incendiaries . . . . Mail robberies and piracies are quite the order of the day. . . ."[26]

Among the banks one in particular was offered up for sacrifice. The Bank of the United States had been investigated and found wanting; its very efforts at reconstruction produced additional hardships and, to the debtors at least, seemed inopportune, if not criminal. Hence even Niles, who otherwise favored the program of thorough purgation and opposed radical measures of debtor relief, lent himself to the attack upon this symbol of oppression. He defended the right and obligation of the various states to tax it out of existence if necessary. He was even prepared to accuse the Bank of bringing on the present distress deliberately in order to compel Congress to act in its favor by creating a new national currency.[27] With the tide of indignation rising high against the Bank, any defense was of little avail, although ably presented by John Serjeant in Congress. He could point out reasonably enough that all speculation was alike, equally good or bad:

The variety is infinite, and in no country greater than in this. Everything about us invites to speculation . . . . Not an axe sounds in the forest, without adding to the sum of national wealth. I should like, then, to know, in what the discrimination consists, which makes one kind of speculation offensive, and another innocent, if both are permitted by law . . . . What is

25 *Address of the Society of Tammany . . . to its Absent Members* (New York, 1819), pp. 6 ff.

26 Reprinted in Gouge, pp. 122 ff.

27 *Niles' Register*, Mar. 7, 14, 1818; *cf.* especially the series of articles on the Paper System, appearing in the *Register* during 1818; also Dec. 5, 1818. *Cf.* John Randolph's warning, issued in 1816, against "this grand mammoth, which is set up to worship in this Christian land". Gouge, p. 81.

the difference between speculating in land, and speculating in merchandise, or the stocks? [28]

While the banks offered themselves as a ready symbol for the double purpose of explanation and accusation, others looked elsewhere for the true causes. Mathew Carey believed that the symptom was being mistaken for the cause; it was as if a patient were to be accused of eating a horse, because a horse collar was found in his bed. The banking evil was exaggerated; the real difficulty was the unbalanced state of our foreign trade, which in turn was the outgrowth of an unbalanced national economy. There were too many people on the land, multiplying products for which the foreign demand was diminishing, while we did not make enough for ourselves. Three million out of eight million free people in the United States were raising breadstuffs in seven states, but European markets totalling sixty million people had either been closed or were being closed to them. Russian wheat from Odessa had become an increasing factor in the competition for European markets. Even American cotton no longer enjoyed its virtual monopoly; the rise in prices before 1816 had produced a greater call for East Indian and Brazilian cotton. American cotton was a drug in the world market, and prices had fallen from thirty-three to sixteen and one-half cents a pound between January and June, 1819. The South was admonished to look at home for its outlet.[29]

Every opinion could apparently be countered by its opposite. If Carey and Niles deplored the redundancy of the rural population, in the West it was believed that too many had been drawn into the cities, while man was intended to live by tilling the land. In no other nation had "the thirst for the acquisition of riches without labour taken such deep root as among ourselves". But an exodus was preparing, and the West was ready to welcome it.[30] If, on the one hand, the belief that speculation was an evil product of the city was a tenet of the national creed, there was also the valid objection that a vicious speculation had grown up on the land as well, encouraged by the liberal credit feature of the national land policy. This was creating a debtor interest in the West, which might disrupt the Union.[31]

[28] *Select Speeches of John Serjeant of Pennsylvania* (Philadelphia, 1832), p. 164.

[29] Carey, *Essays*, pp. 323 ff. (The New Olive Branch); pp. 470 ff. (The Farmer's and Planter's Friend); and pp. 399, 492 (Address to Congress). *Cf.* the figures of the world cotton trade in *Niles' Register*, Jan. 30, 1819.

[30] The Cincinnati *Inquisitor Advertiser*, June 8, 1819.

[31] *Niles' Register*, Sept. 4, 1819. Between 1815 and 1819 the amount of the debt on land bought from the government increased from three to nearly eighteen million dollars. Benjamin Horace Hibbard, *A History of the Public Land Policies* (New York, 1924), p. 97.

The most dangerous factor in the situation was undoubtedly the lengthening chain of entangled debts which stretched from the merchants and manufacturers in England to the American seaboard and from there westward and southward. At the far end of it a "wild son of Tennessee who has been with Jackson, can ill brook that his bit of land, perhaps his rifle, should be torn from him by a neighbouring shopkeeper, that the proceeds may travel eastward, where the 'sceptre' of money has fixed itself. . . . This subject is a painful one, but. . . . We have no patience with those who tell us coldly that things will correct themselves . . . . We cannot believe that the remedy consists in folding our arms".[32] But the matter of a proper remedy was no less painful, presenting indeed a dilemma, which the congressional committee on manufactures clearly perceived and described in 1821. The people were looking to the government for relief, and the latter reversed the operation, "the resources of both exhausted; both marching to poverty . . . in the same road, on the same principles; their expenses exceeding their receipts".[33]

For the relief of distress due to depression there were ample advice, much agitation, and even some actual achievement. The advice was at times quite detached and reasonable; the action taken under the pressure of urgent need often took flight in palliative in the guise of panacea. The country survived both. There were those who offered neither advice nor remedy, but believed rather that the distress was not serious. This was particularly characteristic of the official attitude. Mathew Carey complained that when he first began to depict conditions in 1819 he was censured for it; the misery he described was denied; and, in any case, it was objected that such writing was pernicious in discouraging immigration. Carey, however, persisted, protesting:

> I respectfully ask those fastidious gentlemen, whether 'numerous families being deprived of the common necessaries of life'—the 'prisons overflowing with insolvent debtors'—and 'vast numbers of industrious farmers being driven from their homes, and forced to seek in the uncultivated forests of the west, that shelter of which they had been deprived in their native state', be not as complete proofs of misery as can be exhibited?

Carey also complained of congressional obduracy in refusing relief, while in a series of messages the President long continued to ignore or

---

32 *The American* (New York), Aug. 28, 1819.

33 Quoted on the title-page of Carey's *Address to the Farmers of the United States,* separately and in the *Essays.*

to minimize the existing depression.[34] In his message of December, 1819, Monroe made passing allusion to the contraction of credit and the industrial depression. A year later, he waxed eloquent over "the prosperous and happy condition of our country . . . it is impossible to behold so gratifying, so glorious a spectacle, without being penetrated with the most profound and grateful acknowledgments to the Supreme Author of All Good for such manifold and inestimable blessings". To be sure, there had been "pressures on certain interests . . . but they detract but little from the force of the remark already made", and the President was, therefore, unable to "regard these pressures . . . as otherwise than in the light of mild and instructive admonitions, warning us of dangers to be shunned in the future; teaching us lessons of economy . . .".[35] At that moment the government was not paying its way in a time of world peace and was, in fact, adding to the public debt.

Privately, of course, the administration was greatly concerned over the "alarming situation", which John Quincy Adams discussed both with the President and with the Secretary of the Treasury. It was admitted that distress was "universal in every part of the country. The revenue . . . must very sensibly and very soon be affected by this state of things, for which there seems to be no remedy but time and patience." Adams agreed with the President that

> They must work out their own termination. Government can do nothing, at least nothing by any measure yet proposed, but transfer discontents, and propitiate one class . . . by disgusting another. . . . As it is, the arbiters of weal and woe, the healers and destroyers, Time and Chance, must bring the catastrophe or the cure. . . . 'Thy will be done.' [36]

The official fatalism of the "Time and Patience" school was echoed in the New York *Gazette,* which denounced the "rant in most of our prints, about our distresses". From the present derangement important lessons were to be learned. "Trade will regulate itself. Banks will soon become more useful, and merchants more wise . . . . There is no real distress in the country, and we hope to hear no more of it." [37] In the face of such an attitude, Niles was justly critical of the general apathy

---

[34] Carey, *Essays,* p. 421 (Address to the Farmers); p. 309 (The New Olive Branch); and p. 196 (Addresses, new series).

[35] J. D. Richardson, *A Compilation of the Messages and Papers of the Presidents* (Washington, 1899), II. 55, 72 ff. *Cf.* the sharp satire this message provoked in the Philadelphia *Weekly Aurora,* Nov. 20, 1820.

[36] Adams, *Memoirs,* IV. 375, 498; V. 129.

[37] Reprinted in the Cincinnati *Inquisitor,* Jan. 12, 1819; *cf.* the sharp rebuke appearing in the *National Advocate,* Dec. 10, 1818.

and indifference which prevailed. Every effort at supplying a remedy was condemned as a form of radicalism, and his conclusion was that "it has grown out of the powerful excitements caused by the late war, and the general depression of mind and business which followed it". We were helpless and rudderless.[38]

Niles himself was far from radical. He was opposed to the inflation of the currency; a thorough purgation, however unpalatable, was the only real cure possible. Aside from increased protection for industry, his main reliance was upon the hope that "honest men would get into fashion . . . [replacing] speculating madmen and visionary schemers". There also circulated such familiar slogans as "Take Courage" and "Keep Cool". The country was sound and would recognize the propriety of "going back to the simplicity of our forefathers and exchanging our disease for health . . . our dissipation for temperance and our vice for virtue . . .".[39] The Order of Tammany proclaimed a new age and called for "a fundamental change in morals and habits".[40] But the hard times also produced a real suggestion of class disaffection and even a threat of class conflict. A writer calling himself One of the People addressed a "Morsel of Advisement to the Rich", in which he warned them that the common people greatly outnumbered them. These were times "to try your souls". They could continue to extort and to oppress, "but if you do so, a woful chance will it prove in the end". They would do better to show themselves "rich in good works . . . . Thus will ye take the surest way to preserve your treasures from being moth-eaten, and will lay a good foundation against the time to come." [41]

More concretely, however, the problem was to restore prosperity. Economicus, an anonymous writer in the press, began by defining the term and then offered some sound advice for its restoration. Prosperity was "nothing but a lively exchange of commodities". To bring it about, those who could afford it should be encouraged to live and spend more liberally. Tradesmen must be content with lower prices and smaller profits; laborers also should accept lower wages, adjusted to the new level of prices, which had declined by about a third. Self-help was good, but the government must "throw a rope to sustain us till the tide changes".[42]

38 *Niles' Register*, Feb. 10, 1821.

39 *Ibid.*, Jan. 9, June 5, 12, 1819; Sept. 16, 1820; also the Rochester *Telegraph*, July 6, 1819.

40 *Address of the Order of Tammany*, p. 13.

41 Rochester *Telegraph*, July 28, 1819.

42 *Ibid.*, Oct. 31, 1820; *The American* (New York), Aug. 28, 1819.

The time was particularly opportune for the protectionists, for whom there was no ill wind but blew some good. They launched an extensive campaign of propaganda, by means of meeting, memorial, association, and print, to convert both the public and Congress to the doctrine that relief could only be found in a new system of taxation and industrial protection. Four main points emerged in their program; they included higher import duties and the cash payment of customs dues, a Federal tax on public auctions, and a return to the war policy of internal excise taxes to supply the deficiency in the revenue. Local associations were formed in the larger Eastern cities, and in 1820 a national convention of the Friends of Domestic Industry was held at New York. Veteran agitators like Mathew Carey, whose activity in this respect reached back to the beginnings of American industry, were now reënforced by the zeal of younger contemporaries like Niles at Baltimore; for a year New York was the seat of a strictly protectionist journal, *The Patron of Industry*.[43] The sentiment even penetrated into Boston, where it was admitted that the commercial boom was at an end and that prosperity was "bottomed upon the success of agriculture and manufactures, which begin to excite interest in proportion to the decline of commerce".[44]

The protectionists added to the clamor for an early convocation of Congress in 1819 in order to deal with the emergency, and eventually they had their day there, which was, in fact, prolonged for several years.[45] Their first victory was the recognition of manufactures as a major interest in national politics. A separate committee on manufactures was set up in Congress, divorced from the committee on commerce. Under the chairmanship of Mr. Baldwin of Pennsylvania, it went zealously to work and submitted three bills to Congress early in 1820, which promised to "cover our country with smiles in less than six months". Baldwin referred to the mass of popular petitions on the subject and defended the legislation as a necessary outcome of depression.

When a nation thus complains, we are not to inquire if women and children cry. Pennsylvania speaks in a still more decided tone. . . . Five years ago she was the richest in the union . . . But . . . she has yielded to the pressure of general distress, and, for the first time in her history, has been obliged to resort to a stop law, to save the property and persons of her citizens.

[43] Bishop, II. 256; *cf.* my article on the Rise and Early Development of Industrial Consciousness in the United States, *Journal of Economic and Business History*, IV. (August, 1932, Supplement), 800, 802.

[44] Cited from the Boston *Yankee*, in *Niles' Register*, Nov. 13, 1819.

[45] *The American* (New York), June 16, 1819; *Niles' Register*, May 22, 1819.

The Senate blocked the tariff bill in 1820, and a second effort was also frustrated in 1821. Not until 1824 did the protectionists win a real congressional victory.[46]

A second matter which pressed for immediate action was the national revenue. Before 1819 the government receipts, particularly those derived from foreign trade, had been large. In 1816 the customs had yielded thirty-six million dollars; by 1821 they were reduced to thirteen millions. As late as 1818 the total revenue had been more than twenty-six million dollars, which was reduced progressively to some twenty-one millions in 1819, fifteen millions in 1820, and it did not recover until 1822, when it again reached twenty million dollars. In 1820 the deficit was met by an authorized loan of three million dollars, and in the following year a second loan of five millions was needed.[47] In addition, an annual fund of some five million dollars which had been used prior to 1819 for the redemption of the debt was now no longer available, and Niles predicted a further deficiency of fifteen million dollars in 1825 and 1826 when forty-one millions of the debt fell due. He believed that the customs revenues were a "broken staff" and that new internal taxes were necessary, since economies could not be made to yield more than two million dollars.[48]

Retrenchment and economy became familiar terms; a plea for the reduction of expenses was made at a meeting at Harrisburg, Pennsylvania, as early as October, 1819.[49] In 1820 a Southern congressman ironically proposed the total abolition of the navy in the interest of economy, since in any case we were about to become a nation of weavers and would need no defense. A special committee of Congress proposed a number of ways in which the costs of government could be reduced. Unnecessary offices were to be abolished; salaries lowered to the level of 1809, and the military establishment cut from 10,000 to 6000, while half the naval force was to be recalled from active service. A few of these were finally enacted in 1821, and a total saving of two million dollars effected. The Secretary of War was reported to have cut into his pension

[46] *Niles' Register*, Apr. 1, May 6, June 3, 1820; Jan. 20, 1821; *Abridgment of the Debates of Congress*, VI. 603; McMaster, IV. 515, 521; F. W. Taussig, *The Tariff History of the United States* (New York, 1923), pp. 68, 74.

[47] *Niles' Register*, Dec. 22, 1821; *Abridgment of the Debates of Congress*, VII. 409, 609; Turner, p. 140; Davis Rich Dewey, *Financial History of the United States* (New York, 1924), p. 167.

[48] *Niles' Register*, July 1, 1820; Dec. 22, 1821; Apr. 27, 1822.

[49] *Ibid.*, Nov. 13, 1819; Adams, *Memoirs*, V. 231.

roll, reducing its 16,000 names by half.[50]   The various states also were under public pressure to economize; and, in the case notably of New York and Connecticut, they even anticipated Congress in their program of retrenchment.   In 1820 the New York State salary bill effected a saving of $22,000 a year. In New York City the mayor's salary, among others, was reduced from $5000 to $3000 a year.   In Connecticut the annual budget was brought down from $100,000 in 1818 to $63,000 in 1820 and to $53,000 (in round figures) by 1822.[51]

One other large measure of relief assumed national proportions. This was in the interest of Federal land purchasers.   In 1820 the Secretary of the Treasury reported to Congress that since 1789 the government had sold land to a value of forty-four million dollars, of which about half was still unpaid.   One form of immediate relief was to allow debtors to pay with any bank notes which were "in good credit in the district".   Another was to permit the purchasers in default to consolidate their holdings by keeping as much land as was covered by the payments already made at the new price of $1.25 an acre and surrendering the remainder without the penalty of complete forfeiture.   This policy was continued through 1824.[52]   The depression also afforded an opportunity to establish a new landmark in the evolution of the Federal land policy. The act of 1820 lowered the price from two dollars an acre to a dollar and a quarter, but it also abolished the credit provision in the act of 1800, requiring full payment in cash, and setting the minimum quantity of land which could be purchased at eighty acres.[53]

The more radical issues of debtor relief made little progress in national politics; in this respect certain state legislatures proved more responsive and in the end were held in check mainly by the Federal judiciary.   Demands enough were made for some kind of national action as regards the currency, either to release it from its specie basis or to declare an embargo on specie exports, both of which proposals created alarm and provoked opposition, from Niles, for example, "as a mere

[50] *Niles' Register*, May 6, 1820; Feb. 10, 1821; *Abridgment of the Debates of Congress*, VII. 54; *cf.* also T. H. Benton, *Thirty Years' View, or a History of the Working of the American Government for Thirty Years* (New York, 1854), p. 11; James Schouler, *History of the United States* (New York, 1885), III. 174 f., 190.

[51] Rochester *Telegraph*, Aug. 31, 1819; Feb. 15, Apr. 4, 1820; *Niles' Register*, Apr. 14, July 7, 1821.

[52] *Niles' Register*, May 8, 1819; Dec. 9, 1820; Turner, p. 141; Benton, p. 11; *Abridgment of the Debates of Congress*, VI. 457; VII. 627; Hibbard, p. 94.

[53] *Abridgment of the Debates of Congress*, VI. 455 ff.; Turner, pp. 141–142; Hibbard, pp. 97 ff.

nostrum ... to cure incurable disorders".[54] In Kentucky and Tennessee public meetings adopted resolutions which demanded the abolition of all banks and the establishment of a paper currency.[55] Congress, in the main, ignored the clamor; it did, however, take up a bill for the Federal regulation of bankruptcy in 1820 and again in the two succeeding years. It failed each time, in spite of the able advocacy of John Serjeant, supported by Niles, who looked to it for the protection of the creditor against the roguery encouraged by the various state insolvency acts. An earnest effort to abolish Federal imprisonment for debt also failed at this time.[56]

Since the relation of debtor to creditor fell for the most part within state jurisdiction, it was to the state legislature that the clamor for relief addressed itself, and here it received its most sympathetic hearing. In Benton's summary,

> Stop laws—property laws—replevin laws—stay laws—loan office laws—the intervention of the legislature between the creditor and the debtor: this was the business of legislation in three-fourths of the States of the Union—of all south and west of New England .... Distress the universal cry of the people: Relief, the universal demand thundered at the doors of all legislatures, State and federal.[57]

There was a humanitarian as well as an economic motive in this legislation, for the distress of the debtor in this period of depression strengthened the movement for the abolition of imprisonment for debt, and some progress was actually made in that direction. Already in 1817 New York State had abolished imprisonment for debtors owing less than $25. By 1823 a number of other states had mitigated the hardships of the law in various degrees. Vermont and New Hampshire exempted persons owing petty debts, as did Pennsylvania, which also freed women from imprisonment. Kentucky, Ohio, and North Carolina abolished it for debtors who turned over their property, while the newer states, such as Indiana, Mississippi, Illinois, and Alabama embodied a similar provision in their constitutions.[58]

The relief mainly needed in the emergency, however, was economic,

54 *Niles' Register*, Dec. 5, 1818; *The American* (New York), July 3, Aug. 18, 1819. The Albany *Gazette* (June 14, 1819) warned that such proposals would only produce "a windy debate, some futile expedients . . . and a heavy run upon the treasury".

55 *Niles' Register*, Jan. 30, May 13, July 24, 1819.

56 *Niles' Register*, Apr. 8, 1820; Feb. 10, Mar. 3, 24, 1821; Feb. 2, Mar. 6, 1822; Feb. 8, 1823. *Cf. Abridgment of the Debates of Congress*, VII. 233, 280; F. R. Noel, *A History of the Bankruptcy Clause of the Constitution* (Gettysburg, 1918), pp. 134 ff.

57 Benton, pp. 5 ff.

58 *Niles' Register*, Feb. 26, 1820; Feb. 9, 1822; Jan. 18, 1823; McMaster, IV. 533 ff.

in order to save the debtors' assets, such as they were, from the demoralizing prices established at forced sales under the wholesale application of the insolvency laws. In New York State the complaint was made that the law was too hard on the poor debtor; in 1820 the mechanics of Ontario County petitioned the legislature to protect their tools and implements against executions, especially for the default of rent. In the New York senate a bill was offered to require an appraisal of the debtor's property by three disinterested persons before sale. A committee of the assembly even recommended that the comptroller sell the bank stock owned by the state and lend the proceeds on real estate.[59] What was only proposed in New York, and more, was actually adopted in other states, particularly in the West. Tennessee enacted a stay law in 1819, which required the creditor to accept the notes of the state bank, and others at par with them, or else wait two years for his judgment in court. A similar law was adopted in Illinois in 1821. Both states followed through the logic of their stay legislation by establishing state banks and authorizing them to lend their notes on real estate. These notes were also expected to supply the shortage of ready money.[60]

Kentucky adopted a full program of debtor relief and could serve as a model to other states in this respect. After the Bank of Kentucky suspended payments at the close of 1819, the legislature promptly enacted a stay law, and in 1820 set up a new Bank of the Commonwealth, which was to issue notes up to three million dollars. Without capital or stockholders or specie, its sole assets were a state grant of $7000 for the printing of notes. If a creditor refused to accept the notes, he might be made to wait two years for an execution. After 1823, when the state court of appeals nullified the legislation, a political battle of serious proportions developed between the debtor and creditor parties for the control of the judiciary. For several years two rival courts of appeal competed for jurisdiction; in the end the old court party won.[61]

Other states followed the example of Kentucky. Indiana had a stay law in 1822. Missouri began its career as a state by establishing a loan office for the relief of debtors. With Ohio and Tennessee it also adopted the principle of appraisement, by which property offered for sale under

[59] *Niles' Register,* Jan. 22, 1820; *The National Advocate,* Mar. 25, 1818; also the Rochester *Telegraph,* Apr. 13, 1819; Mar. 21, 1820.

[60] *Niles' Register,* Sept. 2, Dec. 27, 1820; Mar. 31, Sept. 15, 1821; Sumner, pp. 146, 157.

[61] *Niles' Register,* Nov. 25, 1820; Feb. 17, 1821; Sumner, pp. 120, 131, 137; Turner, p. 139; McMaster, IV. 508. Also Samuel Perkins, *Historical Sketches of the United States* (New York, 1830), p. 270.

an execution must bring a minimum price as established by impartial appraisers. Even in Pennsylvania the governor recommended such legislation, including a provision for a loan office to lend up to two million dollars. It was, however, rejected by a committee of the legislature.[62]

All this legislation gave rise to a great clamor and clash of opinion when the judiciary attacked it and invalidated it in several states, among them Kentucky, Tennessee, Maryland, and Missouri. The controversy assumed large national proportions when it was focussed upon the issue of the Bank of the United States and its liability to the taxes which Maryland, Ohio, and Kentucky attempted to impose and to collect. Early in March, 1819, coinciding closely with the exposure of the Bank scandal by the congressional committee of investigation, the Supreme Court, in McCulloch *v.* Maryland, denied the states the right to tax the Bank. Following this came the collision of state and Federal jurisdiction in Ohio, involving the same issue. A terrific logomachy ensued, which eventually crystallized into a proposal to amend the Constitution. In January, 1822, Senator Johnson of Kentucky submitted and defended a resolution providing that appellate jurisdiction in all cases affecting a state or a state law should thereafter belong to the Senate. The initial proposal he attributed to Pennsylvania, as a sequel to the Olmstead cases. Pennsylvania had yielded at that time, however, in the interest of public order, and had refused to use force. But now the McCulloch case was a further instance of judicial tryanny, which needed curbing. Virginia, to be sure, went so far as to claim the right to decide such issues for herself, but this, Johnson argued, would produce anarchy, and a higher tribunal was, therefore, more appropriate.[63]

Thus was the logic of the depression of 1819 carried to a climax. What had begun as a contraction of money and credit, accompanied by a general decline of prices and property values, led finally, by an unbroken chain of economic circumstance and political agitation, to a questioning of the Constitution itself, particularly in reference to the newly developed power of judicial interpretation. It was appropriate

[62] Philadelphia *Weekly Aurora*, Mar. 27, 1820; *Niles' Register*, Aug. 11, 1821; Sumner, pp. 150, 156, 161; McMaster, IV. 494, 510.

[63] *Niles' Register*, Mar. 20, 1819; Aug. 4, 1821; Sept. 15, 1821; Feb. 23, June 8, 1822. *Cf.* also Schouler, III. 119; Sumner, p. 129; Wildman, p. 108; McMaster, IV. 496, 499; V. 406, 412. Senator Johnson continued to propose amendments to the same end in the next few years, supported by other men from Kentucky. *Abridgment of the Debates of Congress*, VII. 145, 152; Charles Warren, *Congress, the Constitution, and the Supreme Court* (Boston, 1925), p. 218.

that, while Massachusetts condemned such procedure, Ohio and Kentucky approved it, appealing to the authority of Virginia, which at this time missed passing similar resolutions by a small margin.[64]   Neither this, nor the more immediate economic issue of money and credit, was settled then, of course; both remained available for agitation in succeeding periods of depression, thus giving a kind of continuity to what has otherwise been an occasional but recurring phenomenon of American social and economic history.   In the wake of this early depression came an intensification of class consciousness, as between the rich and the poor, the creditors and the debtors, those who lived by honest labor and those who engaged in vicious speculation.   A permanent by-product of the period illustrating this contrast was the savings bank.   At a time when banks were being discredited as the seats of vicious and grasping speculation, a place of safe-keeping was created, without stocks or notes, for the money of the mechanic and the small tradesman.   It was to encourage thrift in such people.   Started as early as December, 1816, at Philadelphia, the Savings Fund Society was quickly followed by the Provident Institution for Savings at Boston, and in July, 1819, by the Savings Bank at New York.   The New York institution was sponsored by the Society for the Prevention of Pauperism; it accepted deposits of as little as one dollar, and it paid interest at five per cent. on amounts of five dollars or more.   It was at once hailed as a "moral institution", seeking no profit, and boasting William Bayard as its president, with Colden, Pintard, and Livingston among its trustees.   At the end of its first year, in 1820, the New York bank had an aggregate of $313,000 in deposits, and its accounts numbered 2995.[65]

[64] *Niles' Register*, Feb. 23, 1823; McMaster, IV. 502.

[65] Albany *Gazette*, June 24, 1819; *The American*, July 3, 1819; June 29, 1820; *The National Advocate*, July 9, 1819; *Second Annual Report* of the Society for the Prevention of Pauperism, pp. 14–15.   *Cf.* also Bishop, II. 230; O. C. Lightner, *The History of Business Depressions* (New York, 1922), p. 112.

CHAPTER IV

The Social History of an American Depression, 1837-1843

The following essay originally appeared in the *American History Review*, Volume XL, Number 4 (July 1935), pp. 662-687. It is reprinted here, in its entirety, with the permission of the American Historical Association and the author. The original pagination appears in brackets at the bottom of each page.

THE SOCIAL HISTORY OF AN AMERICAN DEPRESSION,
1837–1843

THE year 1835 was once characterized as the most prosperous the United States had ever known. To Harriet Martineau it seemed "as if the commercial credit of New York could stand any shock short of an earthquake", since it had recovered so rapidly from the losses of the Great Fire in that year.[1] Within two years, however, not only New York but the whole country was convulsed by a shock as devastating as any earthquake could have been. Its depressing effects were felt for several years, and even 1843 was described as "one of the gloomiest years in our industrial history". Between 1837 and 1843 American society was passing through the deep hollow of a great economic cycle, and the air became heavy with doubt and distress. Contemporary opinion regarded it as no mere "pressure in the money market", but, on the contrary, as "a national pay day. The Nation has been drawing on the Future, and the Future dishonors the draft. The forcing process is then applied, widespread ruin is the result, and a long period of paralysis ensues."

As early as 1840 the estimated losses due to depression were added up to a total of six billion dollars, but even more important were those losses incapable of measurement, as one writer pointed out:

> Let every individual calculate for himself what he, personally, has lost, what chances have been sacrificed by him, what he might have done, and what he might have been, if the prosperity of the country had not been arrested. . . .

And before prosperity was restored, he predicted a "reckoning of misfortune . . . sufficiently astounding".[2]

Depression came quickly and catastrophically, ushered in by panic; but there had been ample warning. Already in April, 1836, Niles had sounded the alarm, which was repeated in succeeding months, as disaster approached. The notes of warning alternated, however, with the call

---

1 '37 and '57: a Brief Popular Account of all the Financial Panics (New York, 1857), p. 16; A. M. Sakolski, The Great American Land Bubble (New York, 1932), pp. 232 ff.; Harriet Martineau, Society in America (New York, 1837), II, 270, 274.

2 Arthur H. Cole, "Wholesale Prices in the United States", The Review of Economic Statistics, VIII (Apr., 1926), 76 ff.; also "Statistical Background of the Crisis Period", ibid., X (Nov., 1928), 191; '37 and '57, p. 1; Calvin Colton, The Junius Tracts (New York, 1844), no. II, p. 16.

to renewed confidence in the continuance of the era of universal prosperity. Even in the midst of the general gloom and panic during the early months of 1837, the wish fathered the thought that the worst would soon be over. It was "now time for people to thank God and take courage. Down with the panic makers, and down with the prevalent distrust. . . . A bright sun will soon dispel the remaining darkness, and days of prosperity and glory will be ours." Two years later, Greeley was still mourning over the "corpse of poor, defunct Speculation" as the unfortunate victim of undeserved slander.[3]

The collapse of business and banking, early in 1837, was, however, only the beginning of a long and severe process of purgation. The purging extended beyond the complicated and congested mass of credits and debits which was the major proof of preceding prosperity. Every class in the community was affected, and economic interests were deeply stirred. As distress spread, political strife became embittered. Social thought, as well as public sentiment, came under the whiplash of depression. The whole pattern of American life thus mirrored the prevailing mood and state of depression.

The propertied classes felt the immediate pinch of the general depreciation of values, and were especially articulate in voicing their grievances. Their plight is recorded poignantly, year after year, in the diary of a man like Philip Hone, merchant, mayor, and *bon vivant* of New York. During 1838 he wrote that half his friends were, like himself, deeply in debt, with no prospect of getting out. A year later, Hone reported that he was now out of debt, but at the cost of two thirds of his fortune. Living was high, and Hone wondered "how the poor man manages to get a dinner for his family". In closing a volume of his diary, in June, 1840, he grieved that he had three grown sons out of work. "Business of all kinds is completely at a stand . . . and the whole body politic sick and infirm, and calling aloud for a remedy". He took comfort chiefly in the fact that a new national administration was in sight.[4]

---

[3] *Niles' Register*, Apr. 23, May 14, 1836; Apr. 8, 1837; *A Collection of the Political Writings of William Leggett*, Theodore Sedgwick, ed. (New York, 1840), II, 86, 96; *'37 and '57*, pp. 18, 23; *Georgia Constitutionalist*, Apr. 4, 1837; Alexander Trotter, *Observations on the Financial Position and Credit of . . . the States* (London, 1839), p. 43; Captain Marryat, *A Diary in America* (Philadelphia, 1839), p. 16; *The New Yorker*, Oct. 15, 29, 1836; Mar. 4, 18, 1837; Oct. 12, 1839. For a more detailed account of the panic of 1837, *cf.* W. G. Sumner, *A History of Banking in the United States* (New York, 1896), pp. 266, 294, 335; and particularly R. C. McGrane, *The Panic of 1837* (Chicago, 1924), *passim*.

[4] *The Diary of Philip Hone*, Allan Nevins, ed. (New York, 1927), I, 294, 378, 385, 485 f. For the general collapse of values, *cf. Hunt's Merchants' Magazine*, I (Aug., 1839),

Not only individuals, but whole communities were involved in the general collapse. There was the case of Buffalo, which Captain Marryat found in a stagnant state, following a period of phenomenal growth. Its leading promoter and benefactor, Benjamin Rathbun, was in jail, while all of his vast enterprises were involved in a series of fraudulent endorsements. With the collapse of prices, the tide of bankruptcy rose, engulfing nearly everything and everyone. "Failures, numberless and without limit, and hardly create a sensation." In the few months of its operation the Federal Bankruptcy Act of 1842 finally wiped out four hundred and fifty million dollars of debts, affecting one million creditors. Philadelphia derived amusement from a spurious message of the governor, which recommended the project of a special railway to Texas for defaulters.[5]

Labor, as well as property, suffered from the prolonged process of contraction and liquidation, although it is impossible, of course, to measure comparably the degree and kind of loss which each class incurred. Labor's loss came chiefly from want of employment and from lowered wages, which created an immediate problem of relief, particularly in the larger Eastern cities. Labor, however, was also subjected to other more general stresses. Class consciousness was intensified, while current doctrines of class antagonism received a sharper definition in theory, and even some application in practice.

The hardships of labor began to command early notice. Already in April, 1837, a call was issued for a meeting of the unemployed in Greenwich Village in order to petition the city for work. An early estimate reported that fifty thousand were unemployed, and two hundred thousand without adequate means of support in New York City. In August, a New York journal carried the story that five hundred men had applied in a single day, in answer to an advertisement for twenty spade laborers to do country work at four dollars a month and board. While announcing somewhat prematurely that the country was now at the bottom of the hill, Greeley added that fully "one-fourth of all connected with the mercantile and manufacturing interests are out of business, with dreary prospects for the coming winter".[6]

185; New York *Spectator*, Apr. 27, 1837; New York *Journal of Commerce*, Jan. 4, 1840; McGrane, pp. 112 ff.

[5] Marryat's *Diary*, p. 48; *Niles' Register*, Aug. 13, 1836; Aug. 12, 1837; May 2, 1840; Horace Greeley, *Recollections of a Busy Life* (New York, 1868), pp. 94 ff.; *Journal of the American Institute*, IV (May, 1839), 506; *Journal of Commerce*, Jan. 11, 1840; Trotter, *Observations*, p. 43; D. Morier Evans, *The History of the Commercial Crisis, 1857* (London, 1859), p. 139.

[6] *New Era*, Apr. 20, 22, 1837; *Niles' Register*, June 10, Aug. 12, 1837; Feb. 15, 1840;

Similar conditions prevailed at other points in the country. A correspondent wrote that two thousand were out of work at Lynn, while wages were reduced to half the earlier rates. In Boston as in Lowell the mills were lifeless, many going only "in mercy to the workmen and all were living on their savings". In the fall of 1837, nine tenths of the factories in the Eastern states were said to be closed. In New York "the markets begin to look gaunt, and the theatres are deserted . . . Winter and starvation are yet some months off".[7]

As winter approached, house renters in New York were planning mass action against the coming quarter rent day. The landlords were advised to wait and to take what they could get, while the unemployed should go rent free. The Erie Railroad offered to employ three thousand men, if the city would lend its credit for supplies. An editorial in the *New Era,* under the caption of "The Poor! The Poor!", warned that some foresight was necessary, or "a civil volcano may explode". Greeley's comment was: " 'Hard Times!' is the the cry from Madawaska to Galena." He advised the wealthy and the benevolent-minded to provide work for all who wanted it. To the workers he offered the caution to keep their jobs if they had any. Those without work should stay away from the cities. The South presented little hope, and "the West doubtless offers the fairest inducement to the emigrant. . . . But even Western emigration may be overdone." New York was too crowded, and the city factory had been overbuilt, but there was room within the pale of civilization, and it was not necessary to go "beyond sun-down". In any event, Greeley's advice was, "Fly, scatter through the country, go to the Great West, anything rather than remain here. . . ." The thousands already migrating westward might, however, have to move as far as the Rockies in order to escape the malice of the "Van Buren party".[8]

As predicted, the first winter of the depression was a hard one, taxing the resources of the larger communities in the organization of relief. The problem was relatively new, and relief was largely haphazard. In New York there was a central committee for the relief of the suffering poor, which sponsored lectures and concerts as a means of raising money, but it was generally complained that hordes of beggars thronged the streets and knocked at doors. All that could be done was to see that

New Yorker, Apr. 22, May 27, 1837; Publius, *Remarks on the Currency of the United States* (New York, 1840), p. 47.

[7] Richmond *Enquirer,* May 19, Aug. 29, 1837; *Niles' Register,* June 10, Aug. 12, Sept. 16, 1837; *New Yorker,* Apr. 22, June 10, 1837; McGrane, p. 131.

[8] *New Yorker,* Apr. 22, June 3, July 8, 15, 22, Aug. 25, Oct. 7, 1837; New York *Spectator,* Apr. 11, June 5, 1837.

none froze or starved. Once winter was over, the poor were expected to "subsist on the milder state of the atmosphere". Greeley's sympathy went out especially to the respectable mechanics, "whose cry was, not for the bread and fuel of charity, but for Work! ... Work! ...".[9]

Only in certain New York wards, such as the sixth and the seventh, was the organization of relief relatively effective. Here a central executive committee regulated the solicitation of gifts, and everything was strictly accounted for. Orders for food and fuel were drawn upon a common store in the ward, while in the smaller districts visitors were assigned to every block or two. But even this was not enough, and Greeley, whose personal interest in relief was more than casually journalistic, recommended a permanent organization of all the charitable people in the city, as well as a union with similar associations all over the country, "for the extinction of mendicity and suffering from want". Primarily its purpose should be to provide work, and an intelligence office ought to be set up for this.[10]

Greeley's experience with the depression left deep scars upon him and directed his attention permanently to theories of general social reform. He also returned frequently to the specific problem of relief for unemployment. In this he was like a prophet crying in the wilderness. He pleaded for the continuance of public works, which alone kept wages from falling lower. Even if mistakes had been made, it was necessary to go on, especially since prices were down. A year later Greeley again turned to his favorite theme, "to furnish honorable and suitable Employment to every waiting, wanting son and daughter of Adam within its limits". He advocated the creation of an "Exchange of Labor", where purchaser and seller might meet, but it must not be allowed to depress other labor. Greeley had arrived at the doctrine of Man's Right to Work, and insisted that it was only the sound "principle of Mutual Insurance". During the last four years, he added, the loss from unemployment and misdirection of labor had averaged one hundred million dollars a year, and was, therefore, a vital question, "of more importance than any ruling political topic . . .".[11]

[9] *New Yorker*, Jan. 20, 1838; New York *Spectator*, Jan. 4, 18, Feb. 26, 1838; *New Era*, June 11, 1838; '*37 and '57*, p. 30; *Arcturus*, I (Apr., 1841), 303 ff.

[10] *New Yorker*, Jan. 20, 1838; New York *Spectator*, Jan. 4, 1838. New York's experience at this time with the problem of relief supplied the incentive for and finally led to the organization, in 1843, of the New York Association for Improving the Condition of the Poor, which undertook to put philanthropy on a regular and scientific basis in succeeding years (*Twelfth Annual Report*, 1855, p. 34; *Seventeenth Report*, pp. 13 ff.).

[11] *New Yorker*, Feb. 29, May 2, 1840; July 17, 24, 31, 1841; Charles Sotheran, *Horace Greeley* (New York, 1892), p. 48.

Philadelphia, like New York, had its problem of relief, for which it resorted to the familiar method of the soup house. At a public meeting in 1837, a committee reported that prices were high and suffering great. It was recommended that the state set up public granaries and coal yards, where the miner and farmer could be assured a fair price, and the consumer might buy "at cost". Another committee of sixty was appointed to beg for the poor, who were "dying of want".[12] In Boston the Society for the Prevention of Pauperism became alarmed at the spread of beggary and, in 1838, set up an office for finding work or inducing the unemployed to leave the city. Even in 1844, when work was said to be abundant, the Employment Society had a list of some seven hundred, for whom it was unable to obtain work. At this early date the thought was dawning that some permanent unemployment was perhaps unavoidable in the larger city. In 1845 the estimate was made for New York that "there are at no time less than twenty thousand persons vainly seeking work in this city". Three hundred thousand others lived on approximately a dollar a week per person.[13]

Greeley's plea that the depression must not be allowed to injure labor was, of course, unheeded. In the boom years preceding 1837, labor activity had increased greatly; unions and strikes were the order of the day. The inevitable reaction had followed, and a symptom of it was suggested in the advertisement of a hat manufacturer who offered his services, with those of his workmen, "all of whom are little affected with ... the moral gangrene of Trades' Union principles". They worked without "the inconveniences, injustice . . . regular combinations, and periodical strikes . . .". The depression favored the further progress of the reaction. In 1837, a journal welcomed the offer of the trade societies to reduce wages, but added that "the labor of voting was quite lost". Wages would come down in any event, and it was hoped that "the employers will to the full adopt the English policy and employ no men who do not forever abjure the unions. . . . The rules of the unions as to hours, pay, and everything else ought to be thoroughly broken up." At a time when there was little work to be had, the advice seemed rather gratuitous that "to work only ten hours in the summer and eight hours in winter is to waste life".[14]

[12] *Niles' Register,* Feb. 25, 1837; Thomas Brothers, *The United States of North America as They Are* (London, 1840), p. 66; J. S. Buckingham, *America* (New York, 1841), I, 113.

[13] *North American Review,* LXI (July, 1845), 13 ff.; R. C. Waterston, *An Address on Pauperism* (Boston, 1844), pp. 10 ff.; *The Harbinger,* Aug. 2, 1845.

[14] *New Yorker,* July 24, 1841; *'37 and '57,* p. 9; John R. Commons, *History of Labour in the United States* (New York, 1921), I, 456; McGrane, p. 134.

The ills of depression were obviously many, and they called for prompt diagnosis and some cure. Here, however, a familiar dilemma presented itself, such as has, in fact, appeared in every American depression. The doctor was also the patient, and neither the diagnosis nor the proposed remedy could, therefore, have the necessary degree of dispassionate and clearheaded deliberation. The ailments, moreover, were at a crisis and could scarcely wait; yet there were many clashing interests. Already in 1840, it was aptly remarked, in reference to the current controversy over banking, that the question had "very little attraction for the generality of men, except at moments of difficulty and distress, moments when they are least of all qualified to form a sound and discriminating judgment . . .".

[Now, however, like drowning men, they catch at any straw, and] readily adopt any theory which tends to relieve them from all responsibility for the misfortunes which they suffer, and which holds out . . . the splendid vision of a sudden restoration of that prosperity and wealth which they feel to be slipping from their grasp.[15]

Many were the straws thus grasped at in these years; and, if their ability to support and to supply cause or cure was small, they are at least useful in pointing the direction of the wind. It matters little now whether the diagnoses offered were good or true; the important thing is that they represent contemporary judgment. Taken together they constitute a complex pattern of speculation and controversy reflecting the manifold social interests involved.

Of causes to account for the depression there was a prolific abundance, ranging from the trivial and purely incidental to the most impressively profound. What was often only a mere circumstance in the general situation was magnified into a central and vital cause. In this almost mythical age of rugged individualism, the sins of government were too often regarded as an adequate explanation of all social ills. Many of the alleged causes served merely as weapons in the fierce battle of incrimination and recrimination. On the one side, it was charged that the failure to recharter the Bank, the distribution of the Surplus, and particularly the Specie Circular had brought on the catastrophe.[16] As against that, the panic of 1837 was laid to a deliberate conspiracy of the

[15] *Merchants' Magazine*, IV (Mar., 1841), 245.

[16] *New Yorker*, May 6, 1837, for a long list of 21 causes, covering nearly everything. New York *Spectator*, Apr. 4, 1837; Trotter, *Observations*, p. 35; *'37 and '57*, pp. 5 ff.; Edward G. Bourne, *The History of the Surplus Revenue of 1837* (New York, 1885), p. 13.

opposition.. Already in the fall of 1836, the Whigs were accused of calling on the merchants to close their stores and offices and to go into the streets as missionaries. Webster's appearance in New York at a critical moment, early in 1837, was "the first formal public step which was to inaugurate the new distress, and organize the proceedings for shutting up the banks . . .". Its ulterior purpose was to coerce the government into submission to the Bank "and its confederate politicians".[17]

The prevailing distress obviously called for a scapegoat upon which public passion might vent itself, and the Democratic administration was not the only victim available for sacrifice. England, in one way or another, was joined with it. Here also what was merely a circumstance was magnified into a major cause and became a theme for angry recrimination. It was held that England was greatly to blame for America's indebtedness, and the obligation, therefore, rested upon her to wait, or worse might follow: "Sustain what you have built." As conservative a man as Philip Hone complained that, in spite of our independence, we were plunged into a new thraldom: "All we undertake to do is predicated on the chance of borrowing money from John Bull . . . and the Bank of England becomes the arbiter of the fate of the American merchant". The more radical view is, therefore, understandable; the issues at stake were patriotism and independence. "General Jackson . . . was fighting in the same cause in which he fought at New Orleans, and against the same enemy." [18]

A shrewd insight into the world's financial interrelations, sensitive to the faintest note of disturbance even in remote China, offered a truer, because less bitter, basis for diagnosis. But this idea also lent itself to the purposes of the partisan and the agitator. The moralist inveighed against the wasteful extravagance and the love of tawdry display which swelled American imports and thus exposed us to the mercies of the international balance of trade. In a more practical way, the protectionist rose to his opportunity in casting the responsibility for the prevailing distress upon the policy of the Compromise Tariff. The American Institute of New York was prepared to lead the country back to prosperity by a return to protection. It promptly issued a call for a Business Men's Convention which met at Philadelphia during the summer of 1837. A four-day meeting of delegates, said to represent all parties and half the

17 Leggett's *Writings,* II, 97; Thomas H. Benton, *Thirty Years' View* (New York, 1854), II, 12 ff.; New York *Spectator,* June 8, 1837.

18 *Georgia Constitutionalist,* Apr. 12, 1837; Hone's *Diary,* I, 408; *Boston Quarterly Review,* II (Oct., 1839), 493. For a more just statement of England's responsibility, *cf.* J. W. Gilbart, *A History of Banking in America* (London, 1837), pp. 141 ff., 187.

country's business, adopted resolutions deploring the recent haste "to be rich" and the excess of imports and foreign debt. It recommended a return to industry and economy and the payment of duties in cash.[19]

The agitation for the revival of protection mounted and culminated, in 1841, in the formation of a Home League Association, which addressed an appeal to the people to consider "the difficulties prevailing among the productive classes . . . since 1836, and the still greater difficulties apprehended after the final reductions of duties, in 1842 . . .". The American worker must not be reduced to the European level, "underfed and overworked". Local home leagues sprang up in many places, and conventions were held, which issued fresh appeals. The crisis was affecting thousands of people, who were now idle "because no man has hired them". Clay's great authority supported the theory that free trade was always linked with depression, while protection brought prosperity. The agitation promised to bear fruit as the issue was carried into Congress. In 1842 Hone welcomed the tariff bill then pending as the "last hope of our suffering people", but was afraid it would be vetoed. After months of manipulation, however, it passed, and its reviving effects on business were soon widely proclaimed. American labor, in particular, had been rescued from "sinking rapidly into the gripping fist of European despotism, by the approximation of its prices to the European standard . . .". The tariff of 1842 was now to put it "on the true American basis, with the prospect of a fair reward".[20]

Every specific explanation of the depression thus tended to develop into a case of special pleading. On one diagnosis, however, there was nearly general agreement among doctors and patients. It had a moral aspect which offered ample opportunity for indignation and severe castigation. From the President down, it was admitted there had been an "overaction in all departments of business . . . the rapid growth among all classes . . . of luxurious habits . . . detrimental alike to the industry, the resources, and the morals of our people". The government could do something; but, in the main, nature must take its course, and it was not

[19] *Niles' Register*, Oct. 12, 26, Nov. 9, 1839; Richmond *Enquirer*, May 26, 1837; *Journal of the American Institute*, II (Apr., 1837), 338, 396, 438, 492, 609 ff.; *New Yorker*, June 10, Aug. 5, Nov. 25, 1837.

[20] *Niles' Register*, Nov. 9, 1839; *Proceedings of the National Convention for the Protection of American Interests* (New York, 1842), pp. 7 ff.; *Address of the Home League* (New York, 1841), pp. 1 ff.; William H. Handey, *Political Equilibrium* (Hagerstown, 1842), pp. 92, 142; Hone's *Diary*, II, 615; Colton, *Junius Tracts*, no. III, p. 13; John Bach McMaster, *A History of the People of the United States* (New York, 1918), VI, 65; Victor S. Clark, *History of Manufactures* (New York, 1929), I, 285; F. W. Taussig, *The Tariff History of the United States* (7th ed., New York, 1923), p. 113.

the business of government to offer relief. The governor of Pennsylvania condemned even more strongly "that desire which is now so ravenous of acquiring wealth without labour". The "gambling spirit" was responsible for most of the frauds which are being discovered. These have not even startled the public.

They heard the stories with the most stoical indifference; and if any exclamations were uttered, they conveyed rather a sentiment of commiseration for the criminals, than one of detestation for their stupendous crimes.[21]

To the clergy also the depression offered the opportunity for moralizing upon the evils of speculation. It was God's punishment for our greed and recklessness. Even ministers and religious institutions had embarked upon wild speculations, justifying them as a "means to great usefulness". Now, as a result, false social principles were abroad, and there was a lack of respect for property. The judgments of the courts were disregarded; incendiarism and lawlessness were widespread. The remedy must, of course, come from a spiritual reform. There must be patience in suffering without resort to violence, for there are more important things than wealth: "Lay up treasure in Heaven. All this may be done on a small income . . . Godliness with contentment is a great gain." The depression might even bear good fruit. To be sure, there has been some depreciation, but

The world stands the same. . . . We are much richer in experience, much more humble, much more frugal, and much more prudent already; and, if the reformation proves permanent, then will even the pressure have proved a good speculation.

Only Brownson, preaching on the text "Babylon is Falling", announced the start of a revolution. Two armies, arrayed under different banners, were "waiting but the signal to rush to the terrible encounter, if indeed the battle have not already begun".[22]

Speculation, however, had its rare apologists, in the very midst of the havoc which was laid at its door. A philosophically minded foreign observer traced its roots to the American character. Less apt than the European for penny trade, the American launches upon daring enter-

---

[21] *United States Magazine and Democratic Review*, IV (Jan., 1838), 3 ff.; Brothers, *The United States*, p. 85; Leggett, II, 87. *Cf.* also one of the earliest satires on Wall Street in *A Week in Wall Street*, by One Who Knows [Frederick Jackson] (New York, 1841).

[22] Leonard Bacon, *The Duties Connected with the Present Distress* (New Haven, 1837), pp. 4 ff.; B. P. Aydelott, *Our Country's Evils and Their Remedy* (Cincinnati, 1843), pp. 9 ff.; *Journal of Commerce*, Mar. 17, 1840; Buckingham, I, 122; O. A. Brownson, *Babylon is Falling* (Boston, 1837), p. 6.

prise. The American credit system was personal and more democratic, hence more speculative. Another traveler believed that a frequent periodic "blow-up" was unavoidable in America; it occurred here once in about every seven to ten years, as against one in every twenty years in England. But even the crash had its utility; it served as a warning, slowing up expansion; and, after subtracting losses, the net gain was still considerable. Greeley likewise argued there was no reason "to be doleful about the matter". Speculation was a phase of the natural growth of the country; it did not produce the scarcity of money. On the contrary, the scarcity checked speculation and further growth. Even its "miscalculation is on the right side". The shrewdest, if not the most eloquent, defense of speculation came from Richard Hildreth, who remarked sensibly that when it succeeds, we call it enterprise. Only when it fails, does opinion stamp it as a bubble. Thus do fashions change; the real difficulty lies in human nature, which always dodges responsibility for its mistakes. "Public opinion rushes from one extreme of blunder to another. It seldom stops half way". Government cannot regulate opinion; it must be the other way around. The best safety valve would be greater freedom from such things as the usury laws and from politics itself.[23]

With the search for the true causes of depression went, of course, the desire to find and apply the right remedy. This released a vast amount of both deliberation and agitation. Much of it was a kind of aimless milling, expressing at most the vague discomfort which derived from real distress. Some of it broadened into the general stream of class disaffection and class conflict, while a large part of it flowed into the channels of concrete program and specific relief. Of these the most important was the chronic issue of banking and currency, but there were also the lesser ones, including the usury laws, imprisonment for debt, stay and exemption laws. For several years both state and national politics were centered upon the problem of relief in its many, often trivial forms. The evils of a preceding boom and inflation had their counterpart in the evils of the depression, in which old animosities were sharpened and new ones created. The underlying riddle, which puzzled everyone, was aptly framed by the author of a pamphlet, under the title of *Common Sense,* and "Especially Addressed to the Most Suffering Portion of our Fellow Citizens . . . the Mechanics". How is it, asked

[23] F. J. Grund, *The Americans* (London, 1837), II, 111 ff.; Marryat's *Diary,* p. 18; *New Yorker,* Apr. 1, 1837; Oct. 12, 1839. R. Hildreth, *Banks, Banking, and Paper Currencies* (Boston, 1840), pp. 160 ff.; also *Letter . . . on Banking and the Currency* (Boston, 1840), p. 9.

this self-styled Mechanic, that a country as rich as ours is "yet pinched for the common necessaries of life? A vigorous, healthy, and intellectual population, yet bowed down with gloom and despair . . . with ruin and starvation before their eyes?"[24]

The cloven hoof of the partisan, however, soon appeared in its proposal that only a restored Bank of the United States "can relieve us". Only the Bank made all men equal, saving them from shavers and brokers. The controversy over banks and currency embraced, as was clearly understood at the time, the general question of price inflation or deflation. Curiously enough, the relation of the creditor and debtor classes to this issue was not the conventional one, nor was their attitude wholly consistent. The radicals, presumably reflecting the debtors' position, clamored for hard money and were against banks and credit, at least in their present familiar form. In vain did the other side, favoring the credit system and its extension, point out that more, and not less money, was needed to save the debtors from disaster. They protested that "the cures of the ignorant are themselves diseases". Hard money and the treasury system would depreciate labor and property by at least two thirds. "All the gain would be to the rich, and all the loss to the poor." Debtors would be forced to pay three times as much, and this country would cease to be the haven of the poor man. Greeley added his dread warning that to destroy the credit system was to throw a million men out of work, enabling "grasping wealth to secure [labor] for a bare trifle . . .". He urged "all sober and reasonable men" to unite "against the quack notions of the day". Protect and extend the credit system, and high prices will bring high wages. A year later Greeley argued that a metallic money "may be made a far more perfect instrument of monopoly and oppression". He was prolific in recommendation and suggestion. The national government might issue and distribute one hundred million dollars in Treasury notes bearing one per cent and receivable for all public dues. New York State should incorporate a gigantic loan and trust company, and thus add fifty million dollars to the circulation, on the security of real-estate mortgages.[25]

None of these arguments and pleas seemed to weigh against the wide distrust of banks and their irredeemable paper money. Even the Hamiltonian advocate of a new national bank admitted that the banks must not be allowed in the future "to grind the very substance from the in-

---

[24] *Common Sense* (Philadelphia, 1837), pp. 1 ff.

[25] *Georgia Constitutionalist*, Apr. 12, 1837; *New Yorker*, Mar. 4, 11, May 6, July 22, 1837; Feb. 24, Mar. 10, 24, 1838; *Merchants' Magazine*, I (Dec., 1839), 505 ff.; *Journal of Commerce*, Jan. 22, 1840.

debted". A more radical critic warned the workers not to be "deceived about banks and the credit system. Banks to help farmers appear to me something like feudal lords to defend the people." They have only "enabled speculators . . . to seize upon all the great branches of national industry . . . wrest them from the hands of the real manufacturer and put them into the hands of corporations . . .". One of these victims of the engrossing process in industry, Thomas Brothers, was bitter against the new "go-ahead men", but added that even they "are no other than mere slave-drivers to the bankers . . .".[26]

The case against banks and paper currency rested on both moral and practical grounds. To Ingersoll, who prepared a minority report against banks for the constitutional convention in Pennsylvania, which refused it publication, "the paper money mongers are at once suicides and fratricides. They destroy money, morals, law, order, industry, liberty, equality and property." The ancient prejudice of country against city was invoked.

The countryman, with his dirty acres, is richer than the tradesman on paper pinions . . . . and if country people could but unite against the disorganizers, as they greatly outnumber them, they could put them down with ease at once.

A mass meeting in New York condemned the paper system as neither honest nor Christian.[27]

The credit system did not even supply a steady and reliable medium, as was its boast. On the contrary, its practical effect was "mischievous and ruinous to the permanent prosperity of the country . . .". It kept "the whole country in a complete state of uncertainty and derangement". Actually it was an "anti-credit system", which is generous with loans when money is at three per cent a year, but "demands them back with more than Shylock sternness, when it is at three *per cent* a month . . .". Elsewhere Brownson urged that credit should not be allowed to extend beyond the rock bottom of actual resources. He admitted that such a policy would bear hard on debtors, but they could have justice done them. He proposed calculating the percentage of currency appreciation due to the deflation, which could then be subtracted from the debts. The creditor would have exactly what he lent, but no more. Brownson argued that such deflation, while bold, was yet sound. "It is better to take a

[26] *Merchants' Magazine*, I (Sept., 1839), 220; *The New Era*, Mar. 10, 1837; *Georgia Constitutionalist*, Mar. 4, 1837; Brothers, pp. 70 ff.

[27] *New Yorker*, Mar. 25, June 10, 19, 1837; Richmond *Enquirer*, June 6, 1837; *Niles' Register*, Aug. 17, 1839.

medicine, which will expel a lingering disease and restore us to health....
It is better to feel the full shock of the evil at once . . .".[28]

This factor of fluctuating uncertainty in the credit system also troubled as conservative an economist as H. C. Carey, who examined it in a series of articles during 1840. He concluded that "restriction cannot give steadiness", but was, in fact, responsible for increased unsteadiness. The remedy lay in complete freedom of association, subject only to a requirement of "perfect publicity . . . of all associations claiming to limit their liability . . .". This solution of full freedom of association, with its implication of more rather than fewer banks, also appealed to the radical anti-monopolist, who insisted on adding, however, a further requirement of unlimited liability. Such inconsistency of attitude was the symptom of a mental confusion, which earned the pointed censure of a contemporary critic.

[In spite of our bitter experience with a banking system which many condemn as] the very worst of all possible banking systems . . . yet how fondly do we see the minds of a large portion of the people clinging to it as the ark of our salvation. . . . Banks, more banks,—is the constant clamor at every session of every legislature.[29]

The movement for free banking developed in New York, and led to the enactment of a law for that purpose in 1838. Its opponents complained that the existing banks were adequate for all needs, and that the new ones were merely an incentive to fresh speculation. It was reported that Wall Street was much excited over the measure, and that one third of New York's real estate was free to be turned into new bank capital. Within two years it will "produce expansion, speculations, fortunes, and efforts, such as few at this day can realize". This dire prediction did not come true in New York, but in Michigan a similar free banking law produced disastrous results after 1837. In the next two years it seemed as if "every village plot with a house . . . if it had a hollow stump as a vault, was the site of a bank". By 1839 forty-two of these new banks had passed into insolvency, and a million dollars in worthless notes had entered into circulation.[30] In the face of the strong sentiment for free banking the demand for a new national bank had too clear an implica-

28 *Boston Quarterly*, III (Jan., 1840), 85; Brownson, *Our Future Policy* (Boston, 1841), p. 44; Theophilus Fisk, *The Bank Bubble Burst* (Charleston, 1837), p. 28.

29 *U. S. Democratic Review*, II (Apr., 1838), 7; *Merchants' Magazine*, III (Dec., 1840), 482 ff.; Leggett's *Writings*, I, 104; II, 314.

30 New York *Spectator*, Apr. 7, 1837; *Georgia Constitutionalist*, Apr. 28, 1838; D. D. Barnard, *Speeches in the Assembly of New York* (Albany, 1838), pp. 143, 178; McMaster, VI, 405; Sumner, pp. 312, 403.

tion of monopoly to make any headway. Although a writer, signing himself Aladdin, claimed for Boston a prior right to such a bank as late as 1841, there was no longer any magic in the idea; it had become purely academic.[31]

Under the pressure of general distress alarming symptoms of mass disaffection appeared, and the threat of social disorder loomed large at the moment. There never was a time like this, wrote an observer in 1837. From everywhere "comes rumor after rumor of riot, insurrection, and tumult". The public is ready to explode, "and it matters not what is applied to the train—abolition, Grahamism, high prices of food, bank frauds, or gambling. . . ". He trembled for the security of the country, should its chief props, respect for the law, the belief in God, and the like, be removed. The plan of action proposed was to fight the infidels and the agitators, among other ways, by means of a "Cheap Repository" of tracts, on the model of Hannah More's, for enlightening the people.[32]

In 1841, another writer called "Ours . . . the age of suicide and mysterious disappearance". The restless spirit of the time gathered men into "noisy and tumultuous masses—shouting for change, reform, and progress. The world lives abroad. . . . The domestic feeling—households—are in a measure abrogated . . .". As for the remedy, there was a great need for "apostles of peace and tranquility". There were too many "alarmists and preachers of agitation. . . . It is necessary that the heart of the age should be soothed and calmed . . .".[33]

The prevailing "hostility to indebtedness" was a source of apprehension to many, and it was especially deplored that even in respectable quarters there was "an amiable sympathy with what is called 'the masses'". Already the tangible consequences have been such things as the repudiation of state debts, rebellion in Rhode Island, and a repudiation of debts and rents in New York State. The cry of feudalism was spreading to the western territories, where land offices have been in danger of attack. The anti-rent disputes, troubling upper New York State after 1839, shocked Philip Hone, who described them as "of a piece with the vile disorganizing spirit which overspreads the land like a cloud and daily increases in darkness".[34]

31 *Proceedings of the Friends of a National Bank* (Boston, 1841), pp. 6 ff.; Sumner, p. 355.

32 *The Knickerbocker*, IX (May, 1837), 488, 493.

33 *Arcturus*, I (Feb., 1841), 133 ff.

34 D. D. Barnard, *The Anti-Rent Movement in New York* (Albany, 1846), pp. 1 ff.; Hone's *Diary*, I, 435 f.; McMaster, VI, 521; VII, 186; Edward P. Cheyney, *The Anti-Rent Agitation* (Philadelphia, 1887), pp. 25 ff.

There was an alarming tendency toward urban disorder as well, for even Hone noted the near-famine prices in the New York food markets early in 1837 and wondered, "What is to become of the laboring classes?" A series of meetings held in New York during 1837 under Loco-foco auspices revealed the scope and direction of current mass discontent. The very first of these meetings culminated in an attack on several flour stores and created particular alarm. The others were limited to the usual resolutions and addresses but inspired fear in those more timid.

[In language reminiscent of Carlyle, one of these gatherings was described as] standing in ominous darkness, save for the lurid light shed upon their cadaverous-looking faces from twenty or thirty flambeaux. . . . Over their heads, floating in the dark and poisoned breeze, were a variety of banners . . . underneath these stood the managers and orators, who were straining their lungs to swell the sounds of their cracked voices. . . . We might and should probably have laughed, but for the recollection of the lamp-posts, the . . . Jacobins, and the Guillotine.[35]

Actually the resolutions adopted at these meetings were tame enough. They demanded salary reductions in the city government and economy generally; they asked for employment on public works, and they recommended that the destitute immigrants and others be removed to the country. Their strongest resentment was voiced against the "legalized robberies" of the credit system; at the fifth in the series of meetings, it was proposed "to let credit alone", neither to enforce nor to annul debts by law, but to let them rest on honor only. Such a free system of credit would be "simple, efficient, and just". Finally, a call was issued, amid great cheers, for a "New Constitution, based . . . upon the broad and eternal basis of Right". In September, 1837, a Loco-foco convention at Utica adopted a program of constitutional revision, in which the principal issues were embodied. There should be no forcible collection of debts, nor was the state itself to incur a new debt without the people's sanction. These, with other recommendations covering the incorporation of banks and the principle of unlimited liability, became the main features of the movement for constitutional revision which spread into a number of states in succeeding years.[36]

Loco-focoism thus reached its climax in New York in a year of

[35] Hone's *Diary*, I, 243; *New Yorker*, Feb. 18, Mar. 18, 1837; *Niles' Register*, July 1, 1837; New York *Spectator*, Nov. 9, 1837; F. Byrdsall, *The History of the Loco-Foco or Equal Rights Party* (New York, 1842), pp. 99 ff.

[36] Richmond *Enquirer*, May 16, 1837; Byrdsall, pp. 109, 141 ff., 162, 174, 188; *Constitutional Reform*, Thomas P. Kettell, ed. (New York, 1846), *passim.;* Dixon Ryan Fox, *The Decline of Aristocracy in the Politics of New York* (New York, 1919), pp. 397 ff.: McGrane, p. 153.

severe depression; its final triumph perhaps was to see the name extended and applied thereafter to the whole Democratic party, although
its die-hard leaders protested that it should continue an independent
existence as the ideal of Christian democracy. The alarming spread of
what was loosely labelled Loco-focoism was, however, reported from
other sections of the country. In Cincinnati it was some "English natives,
mustard dealers, Penny petticoat lecturers, of questionable sex, and a few
American natives", who organized a celebration of Tom Paine's anni-
versary. The Charleston *Courier* rejoiced that an incendiary call for a
mass meeting against the banks had failed. The respectable and the
orderly had taken possession of the proceedings. Elsewhere, however,
in Virginia, at Philadelphia and at Baltimore, such meetings had been
more successful, and the "Panacea Loco-fociensis" had been approved.
From the Southwest came reports of more serious disorder. In Mississippi sheriffs had been removed by force, and a courthouse had been
attacked. The *Scioto Gazette* rebuked all those who were engaged

in the diabolical work of arraying one portion of the community against
another, the poor against the rich, the laborer with the hands, against the
laborer with the head . . . as though the farmer of this year may not be a
lawyer next, or the mechanic may not also be a banker.[37]

In the reaction which followed, nativism, a persistent factor in American
social and political life, gathered fresh strength and entered upon a
period of new growth. A nativist association at Germantown, in 1837,
protested that the paupers and malcontents of Europe were spreading
radicalism. During the next few years, petitions to Congress, from
many quarters, expressed a fear for the safety of republican institutions
and complained that a foreign party was being formed. It was charged
that the election of 1844 had been decided by an appeal to Europe against
America.[38]

Such broad social grievances requiring large general remedies could
not, of course, provide adequately for the particular stresses and strains
which had developed. Here more specific measures of relief were
needed, and many were adopted in proportion as group pressures began
to make themselves felt. A close-knit group like the New York mer-

[37] Cincinnati *Daily Gazette*, May 5, 1838; *Scioto Gazette*, Sept. 20, 1838; Richmond
Enquirer, May 26, June 6, 30, July 18, 1837; *New Yorker*, March 25, 1837; McMaster,
VI, 398.

[38] McMaster, VI, 367; VII, 369 ff., 385 ff.; also by the same author, *The Acquisition
of Political, Social, and Industrial Rights of Man in America* (Cleveland, 1903), p. 104;
J. Thomas Scharf and Thompson Westcott, *History of Philadelphia* (Philadelphia, 1884),
I, 663 ff.

chants was quick to formulate its demands in concrete form. Already in May, 1837, they asked the state to lend its credit to distressed merchants up to six million dollars for a period of ten years. A committee was also dispatched to Washington to demand a special session of Congress, the revocation of the Specie Circular, and the suspension of suits against defaulters on customs bonds. When Congress met in special session in September, it granted relief to merchants, among other provisions, by extending their customs bonds until 1839.[39] In the meantime, on all sides "Relief was the cry—regulation of the currency—a National Bank!" Party conflicts were waged keenly with weapons forged in the existing state of depression. It was the misfortune of the Van Buren administration that its career began just before the panic broke. Thereafter it labored under a great handicap; "the single cry of the opposition is 'turn out the rogues'", which in the end succeeded. To their own needs and to those of others the legislatures of states and nation addressed themselves, pouring forth a mass of relief legislation, which defies complete enumeration or even classification.[40]

The immediate danger of financial stringency in the Federal government was averted by an issue of ten million dollars in one-year Treasury notes, while the distribution of the fourth installment of the now theoretical surplus was postponed, never to be made. The issue of the Independent Treasury was brought to the front, and remained crucial for several years. Federal finances generally entered upon a period of growing deficiency as revenues fell from a peak of forty-eight millions in 1836 to fifteen millions in 1838 and an estimated twenty-three millions in 1839. In four years the Van Buren administration was charged with an accumulated deficit of fifty millions, and the Secretary of the Treasury made the desperate, if rather academic, suggestion that the states return a part of the surplus on deposit with them. An apologist for the government shrewdly observed that retrenchment had not failed for want of an earnest desire to "reduce expenses, and thus gain the credit with the people of loving economy". But "expenditures do go on, and will go on increasing", and the beginning of a new national debt was unavoidable.[41]

[39] *New Yorker*, Apr. 29, 1837; *Georgia Constitutionalist*, Apr. 22, 1837; McMaster, VI, 395; *U. S. Democratic Review*, IV (Jan., 1838), 17.

[40] *Scioto Gazette*, Apr. 19, 1838; Junius, *The Crisis* (New York, 1840), p. 14; *U. S. Democratic Review*, IV (Jan., 1838), 1 ff.; V, 350; *Niles' Register*, May 20, 1837.

[41] *U. S. Democratic Review*, IV, 49; *Jeffersonian* [Albany], Sept. 8, 29, 1838; *New Yorker*, Dec. 28, 1839; Feb. 22, 1840; *Kendall's Expositor*, Oct. 21, 1841; *Niles' Register*, Feb. 9, 1839; *Merchants' Magazine*, I (Sept., Dec., 1839), 271, 498; Colton, *The Junius Tracts*, no. I, p. 10; *Memoirs of John Quincy Adams*, Charles Francis Adams, ed. (Philadelphia, 1876), IX, 376; Bourne, p. 41; McGrane, p. 209.

Under a new administration, in 1841, a special session of Congress authorized a loan of twelve million dollars, and five millions more in 1842. Special duties were added to provide more revenue. A critic appraised the policy of "Whig Retrenchment and Reform" as meaning more taxes, more expenditures, a new debt, and continuing deficits. A more friendly writer, however, reviewed the solid achievements of what he described as the diligent and disciplined body of honest men comprising the Twenty-seventh Congress (1841–1843), which had really tried to restore prosperity by enacting a record number of bills in three sessions of unprecedented length. In all there were 514 laws, including a new tariff and a Federal bankruptcy act.[42]

Like the Federal government, few states escaped without a deficit in their ordinary budgets. Pennsylvania had a shortage of one million dollars in 1839, and resorted to rather questionable methods in raising a loan to cover arrears. New York, with better credit, was able to borrow three millions in 1841. Massachusetts pledged itself to meet future expenses by means of "taxation and retrenchment". Maryland adopted new taxes in 1841; Kentucky, Indiana, and Illinois increased their land taxes by as much as fifty per cent.[43] Many of the states were further embarrassed by the heavy burden of their debts, which in 1840 amounted to nearly two hundred million dollars. More than half of it was held abroad, and the suspension of specie in 1837 presented the immediate question of how current interest was to be paid. Pennsylvania and Maryland at first demurred but eventually fell into line and agreed to pay in specie or its equivalent, by adding the prevailing premium.[44]

Especially serious, however, was the fact that after a time some of the states could not meet the interest requirements at all; between 1841 and 1842 eight states went into default, and two or three even repudiated part of their debts. For several years default and repudiation supplied the occasion for international recrimination and embittered public opinion on both sides. As early as 1840 the Senate lectured the states on their extravagance and rejected the proposal to transfer the state debts to the Federal government. Various schemes of this kind received currency,

[42] *New Yorker,* Mar. 27, 1841; Colton, pp. 12 ff.; *Kendall's Expositor,* July 14, Aug. 4, Oct. 6, 21, Nov. 18, 1841; McMaster, VII, 57, 65.

[43] Albert Gallatin, *Suggestions on the Banks and Currency of the Several United States* (New York, 1841), pp. 48 ff.; *Kendall's Expositor,* Mar. 17, May 5, 1841; *The American Almanac* (Boston, 1842), pp. 100 ff.

[44] *American Almanac* for 1842, p. 97; Trotter, pp. 105, 350; R. C. McGrane, "Some Aspects of American State Debts in the Forties", *Am. Hist. Rev.,* XXXVIII (July, 1933), 673; William A. Scott, *The Repudiation of State Debts* (New York, 1893), p. 277.

however, but were met with the objection, among others, that only the Rothschilds and the Barings would really be relieved by them. As late as 1843 the movement for Federal assumption of state debts was again stopped in the Senate.[45]

In the meantime, however, even Federal credit suffered abroad. In 1842, the Treasury was unable to negotiate a loan in Europe, and the agent reported that the bankers did not now dare to offer American bonds to their clients. Partly it was because the bankers hoped to force the government into assuming the state debts, but also "partly, perhaps, from real doubts of the solidity of our institutions, and, partly, probably, with a view to make us all feel discredit . . . sensibly". In vain did one writer protest that such discredit was not deserved. The Federal government had virtually no debt; two thirds of the states were paying theirs, but Europe persisted in misunderstanding us, even in such a matter as the recent failure of the Bank of the United States. Europe now believed it was a national establishment, only because they "wish it to be believed so . . . ".[46]

With its roots back in 1837, a broad movement for the revision of state constitutions was traced by a contemporary chronicler to "one single cause—the improvidence of the Legislature in contracting debts on behalf of the State". In New York, although far from being the worst offender, the spirit of reform grew "after the State had been threatened with bankruptcy". Other forces contributed to it, of course, and by 1847 states as far apart as New York and Louisiana, Iowa and New Jersey, Texas and Missouri had framed new constitutions. It was predicted that before long this cycle of constitutional revision would have reached one third of the states. With many variations in detail, the new constitutions agreed particularly in curbing the economic powers of the legislature. In general, it might not lend its credit to or acquire stock in any private enterprise, nor could the legislature incur a new debt beyond a certain amount, often set as low as fifty thousand dollars, without the people's sanction and without ample provision for its repayment. In addition, stringent rules were imposed upon the legislature in the incorporation of banks and other enterprises. Where not forbidden entirely, banks were to bear full, unlimited liability; in New York, how-

[45] *North American Review*, LVIII (Jan., 1844), 122; *Journal of Commerce*, Feb. 13, 1840; *Kendall's Expositor*, Mar. 30, 1841; *Am. Hist. Rev.*, XXXVIII, 680 ff.; Scott, pp. 228, 248; McMaster, VI, 352 ff.; VII, 43; Leland Hamilton Jenks, *The Migration of British Capital* (New York, 1927), pp. 100 ff.

[46] Thomas G. Cary, *Letter to a Lady in France* (Boston, 1844), pp. 10 ff.; Scott, p. 258; Sydney Smith, *Letters on American Debts* (New York, 1844), *passim*.

ever, only double liability. New York also abolished all feudal tenures.
The most advanced of these new constitutions, in Louisiana, received
the tribute that "up to this day, it is doubtless the wisest political Constitution in force over any nation or people in the world".[47]

The private citizen, as well as the state, needed protection against
past abuse and present hardship. If the banks were permitted to suspend
specie payments, some form of stay for the ordinary debtor would be
only a just equivalent. Besides authorizing a five million dollar loan for
the benefit of debtors, Alabama provided for the deferred repayment of
bank debts. Illinois had a similar stay law, while Virginia required the
creditor to accept current bank notes, or wait. In a number of states the
collection of debts was linked up with the principle of appraisal. In
Ohio, Indiana, Michigan, Mississippi, and Illinois property could not
be sold at a forced sale, unless it brought a minimum price, usually two
thirds of the appraised value. When the Supreme Court declared the
Illinois appraisal law unconstitutional, in 1843, a local meeting recommended that the verdict should be resisted.[48] The debtor's right to the
exemption of a portion of his property from a forced sale was also reinforced and extended in many states. Under a law of 1842, New York
allowed the householder and mechanic to retain furniture and tools
worth one hundred and fifty dollars. Michigan protected the lumber-
man's oxen, the farmer's implements, and the housewife's furniture
against seizure for debt. Mississippi exempted as much as one hundred
and sixty acres, together with the necessary livestock and provisions.[49]

Imprisonment for debt was a grievance of long standing, but the
movement for its abolition received a fresh impetus after 1837. Between
1837 and 1842, Ohio, Vermont, Indiana, New Hampshire, Louisiana,
Connecticut, and Mississippi left fraud as the only legal ground for
imprisoning the debtor. An act of 1840 placed the non-resident debtor
on the same basis as the resident of New York in respect to imprisonment. In 1839 Congress instructed the Federal courts to conform to the
law of the state in which suit was made as regards the imprisonment
of debtors. There was even a proposal that a constitutional amendment

[47] *Constitutional Reform, passim;* Arthur May Mowry, *The Dorr War* (Providence,
1901), pp. 335, 375; McMaster, VII, 182 ff.

[48] William M. Gouge, *An Enquiry into . . . the Fiscal Concerns of the United States*
(Philadelphia, 1837), p. 40; *New Yorker,* May 20, 1837; Richmond *Enquirer,* July 4, 7,
11, Aug. 4, 1837; Feb. 6, 1838; Cincinnati *Daily Gazette,* Apr. 14, 1838; McMaster, VI,
624 ff.; VII, 44 ff.

[49] McMaster, VII, 47.

take the remnant of that barbarous power away from the states altogether.[50] As in 1819, during an earlier depression, so now there was a new effort to bring the whole process of bankruptcy under a Federal law. It was urged that the eagle of prosperity, having soared, "has since fallen, with broken pinions, to the earth". Many had failed, through no fault of theirs. Only men with hearts of stone, who want their pound of flesh, oppose this reform, as they have also opposed the abolition of imprisonment for debt. "Such men were born an age too late."[51]

First offered as an emergency measure by the Van Buren administration, the Federal bankruptcy bill was held up until 1841. It was then revived under Whig auspices and passed, but was repealed in the following year. It lasted long enough, however, to afford a large measure of relief; according to one estimate, twenty-eight thousand debtors freed themselves from nearly a half billion dollars of debt at an average cost of little more than ten per cent in assets surrendered.[52]

Still another question affecting debtors, theoretically if not practically, aroused considerable controversy at this time. The New York legislature rejected a proposal to repeal the existing usury laws and, in fact, adopted a more stringent act in 1837. In the discussion which accompanied it, credit was given primarily to a timely pamphlet by John Whipple, who refuted Jeremy Bentham's *Defence of Usury*. Whipple's essay became the classic American defense of the usury laws, and was reprinted during later periods of depression. Whipple warned that free trade in money would lead to extortion, and "if we do not in twenty years produce a revolution against property, then there is nothing in history and experience".[53] In 1840 the attack on the usury laws spread to Massachusetts and Pennsylvania, where it was argued that free trade in money was most needed in hard times in order to ease credit; otherwise the industrious person was driven to the usurer. Unfortunately, however, the

[American community had] a strange and mawkish sensibility for every rogue who comes under the lash of the law . . . and for every debtor who is pressed for the performance of his promises. The ingenuity of the present time is exerted to prevent murderers and robbers from being made too

[50] *New Yorker*, June 17, 1837; Feb. 16, 1839; Cincinnati *Daily Gazette*, Mar. 26, 1838; *Kendall's Expositor*, Mar. 17, 1841; *Journal of Commerce*, Apr. 25, 29, 1840; *Merchants' Magazine*, IV (Jan., June, 1841), 73, 544; *Constitutional Reform*, p. 13, McMaster, VII, 153.

[51] *Merchants' Magazine*, IV (Jan., 1841), 26 ff., 33.

[52] *Ibid.*, I (Dec., 1839), 501; XXXVII (Dec. 1857), 675; *New Yorker*, May 30, 1840; McMaster, VII, 48.

[53] *New Yorker*, Jan. 28, Apr. 1, 15, May 6, 1837; Leggett's *Writings*, II, 275; John Whipple, *Free Trade in Money* (New York, 1878), pp. 1, 14.

uncomfortable in their confinement; and to encourage debtors in a total and reckless disregard of their . . . engagements. . . .[54]

Not only genuine group needs but political partisanship as well waxed strong in this period of depression and exploited it in the strategy of campaigning. Already in 1838, a Whig journal, in reviewing the course of events since Jackson had announced he was leaving the people "prosperous and happy", reported gleefully the turn in both the economic and political tide. Elections were everywhere going against Van Buren. Only a complete change in the government could bring real relief, and with this sentiment the ground was prepared for the colorful and unprecedented campaign of 1840. In the Whig victory of this year, a contemporary writer believed that the most effective cause "has undoubtedly been the depressed prices of agricultural produce and labour". The promise of returning prosperity was heralded in the magic slogan of an election transparency:

> Little Van's policy, fifty cents a day and French soup;
> Harrison's policy, two dollars a day and roast beef.

Hope was also held out to those who still had "masses of property bought at speculative prices . . . through the process of a re-inflation of the bubble . . .". The administration, on the other hand, had spoken out "in accents of severity and rebuke . . . that they must resign themselves to their past losses. . . . Who can be surprised at the result?"[55] When prosperity did not come promptly, at the mere bidding of the Whigs, they were exposed in their turn to the taunt that the promised "better times" were actually "bitter times". Instead of roast beef and two-dollar wages, it was now only "ten cents a day and bean soup". A Democratic reaction was reported to have set in.[56]

In the campaign of 1840 the Whigs were charged with spending "fabulous" sums, supplied by the banks, and used in ways "such as history blushes to record". One of these uses was undoubtedly a deliberate effort to woo the laborer and mechanic with such pamphlets as "Facts for the Laboring Man. By a Laboring Man". It became the fashion to play the democrat, and even Webster, addressing merchants in Wall Street, was indignant that anyone should have called him an aristocrat. At Saratoga he boasted of the ancestral log cabin in New

54 *Merchants' Magazine*, II (Jan., May, 1840), 30, 387 ff.; III (Aug., 1840), 120; *Journal of Commerce*, Jan. 13, 1840; Whipple, pp. xiv, 3.

55 *Jeffersonian*, July 14, 21, Nov. 17, 1838; Greeley's *Recollections*, pp. 124 ff.; Hone's *Diary*, I, 493, 512; *U. S. Democratic Review*, VIII (Nov., 1840), 392.

56 *Kendall's Expositor*, Oct. 6, 1841; McMaster, VII, 1; Greeley's *Recollections*, p. 160.

Hampshire and demanded the American standard for the laborer.[57] With some inconsistency, therefore, the same Whig pamphleteer who courted the laborer and debtor in his *Crisis of the Country,* also dragged the red herring of Jacobinism across the political trail in his *Sequel to the Crisis.* Already in 1838 Greeley had issued a warning against the recent increase of converts to "ultra radicalism", and he himself was soon to be won over to Albert Brisbane's version of Fourierism and social reform. In 1840, however, it was charged that not only had the administration nearly broken "the spirits of the most elastic and buoyant people on earth . . . but civilization itself . . . is to be broken down, and Christianity rooted from the land!" [58]

The provocation to this indictment came from an article in a current periodical which contained one of the earliest and most trenchant statements of the doctrine of class conflict ever made in this country. Its author, Brownson, whose tortuous career was to run from radicalism to reaction, later defended himself that, "born and reared in the class of proletaries", he had only said what he knew and felt, and would stand by it, "at least, until the laboring classes . . . rise up and accuse us of misrepresenting them". His purpose had been to explode certain American myths. One was that in America every man may become rich, but nobody has grown rich by his own labor. Somewhat prematurely, Brownson announced that "the wilderness has receded, and already the new lands are beyond the reach of the mere laborer, and the employer has him at his mercy". Precisely at this time George Evans was beginning his agrarian agitation for free land, which was to culminate in the Homestead Act. Brownson also insisted that to the worker bread was more important than Channing's program of education and moral elevation. "It is no pleasant thing to go seeking work and finding none . . .". Priests and pedagogues have had their chance and can do nothing. "They merely cry peace, peace, and that too when there is no peace, and can be none." The master too is "in these times . . . shedding crocodile tears over the deplorable condition of the poor laborer, while he docks his wages twenty-five per cent . . .". And so, finally, "You must abolish the system or accept its consequences".

[57] Benton's *View,* II, 205; *Arcturus,* I (Jan., 1841), 75 ff., *Scioto Gazette,* Sept. 20, 1838; A. B. Norton, *Reminiscences of the Log Cabin Campaign* (Mount Vernon, 1888), p. 322; *Mr. Webster's Speech at Saratoga* (Boston, 1840), pp. 3 ff.

[58] *New Yorker,* Oct. 6, 1838; Greeley's *Recollections,* p. 145; Sotheran, *Horace Greeley,* p. 121; Junius, *The Sequel to the Crisis* (New York, 1840), p. 1; Norton, p. 242. *Cf.* Greeley's plaint against the "Croaking Cosmopolites", always "sneering at the patriotic feeling of (Americans)", and predicting the "downfall of her institutions" (*New Yorker,* Feb. 15, 1840).

[But it will not be done] without war and bloodshed. We or our children will have to meet this crisis. The old war between the King and the Barons is well nigh ended, and so is that between the Barons and the Manufacturers . . . and now commences the new struggle between the operative and the employer, between wealth and labor. What or when the end will be only God knows.[59]

In a second article Brownson enlarged upon the idea of change by violence. While he hoped his prophecy might prove to be false, he, nevertheless, believed that

If a general war should now break out, it will involve all quarters of the globe, and it will be in the end more than a war between nations. It will resolve itself into a social war, a war between . . . the people and their masters. It will be a terrible war! Already does it lower on the horizon. . . . Stay it, ye who can.[60]

While less extreme, the Workingmen of Charlestown, Massachusetts, were addressing similar warnings "to their Brethren throughout the Union". Their distress was due to the paradox of an overproduction which forced their wages down. There was nothing to hope for from the politicians or the reformers. "Our salvation must . . . come from ourselves." The workers must organize and become a power in the state.[61] In this respect also Brownson offered the workers practical political advice. The election of 1840 had been a victory for property; the party of 'Man' could not prevail over property unless it took advantage of the division in the opposite camp. He, therefore, urged a political union of labor with the Slave South, on the basis of a strict constitutionalism. Now, more than ever, was the time to rally to the ultimate goal of abolishing the "proletaries" and establishing equality. Brownson censured "the laissez-faire doctrine, so much in vogue . . .". But the state, rather than the Federal government, must be relied upon to "maintain between all the members of society that equality . . . which does not exist among men by nature".[62]

The decade of the 1840's passed beyond such doctrines and eventually plunged into Utopian thought and experimentation. These included among others, agrarianism and Fourierism, as well as an elaborate, if embryonic, proposal for a kind of social planning, on a national scale, which the author, Clinton Roosevelt, presented as *The Science of Gov-*

59 Commons, *History of Labour*, I, 522; *Boston Quarterly Review*, III (July and Oct., 1840), 362 ff., 460.

60 *Boston Quarterly Review*, III, 508.

61 *Ibid.*, IV (Jan., 1841), 119 ff.

62 Brownson, *Our Future Policy*, pp. 10 ff.

ernment.[63] All these belong, of course, to another and a different theme, and yet cannot wholly be separated from the background of preceding depression. The latter had begun in 1837 when the pressure of an inflated prosperity proved too great, and certain strains and stresses developed in the American economic and social structure. The immediate and acute emergency created the need for repair work, which was supplied by a mass of relief legislation. But depression was also reflected in the thought and action of both classes and masses. It produced a harvest of ideas which seem not so much immature as premature, at least when a more normal state of social well-being was restored. They perhaps brought a forewarning of America's later ripening and aging. Certainly there was more romance than reality in the reminiscence of one who harked back to this very period as one "of innocence and integrity ... and equality . . . when there were no millionaires and no Standard Oil or other combines. . . . When the rich helped the poor, and the poor helped the great." [64]

[63] Byrdsall, p. 92; Clinton Roosevelt, *The Science of Government* (New York, 1841), *passim.*

[64] Norton, p. 15.

CHAPTER V

The Influence of Depression upon American Opinion, 1857-1859

The following essay originally appeared in *The Journal of Economic History*, Volume II, Number 1 (May 1942), pp. 1-23. It is reprinted here, in its entirety, with the permission of the Economic History Association and the author. The original pagination appears in brackets at the bottom of each page.

The Influence of Depression Upon American Opinion, 1857-1859

I

ON August 26, 1857, just two days after the New York branch of the Ohio Life Insurance and Trust Company suspended payment, the *New York Herald* predicted that the financial difficulties then beginning were certain to acquire the proportions of a great crisis. It boasted, moreover, that it had foreseen and warned of this impending calamity for the preceding twelve months, but its warnings had been spurned.[1] The *Herald's* vaunted prescience perhaps stemmed chiefly from the long-standing prejudice of its publisher, James Gordon Bennett, against the operations of speculators in Wall Street. As early as 1854, when the speculative boom in railroad stocks was halted by a sharp decline of prices, the *Herald* had predicted the imminent approach of a crisis, one that would mark the end of the current "Fitful Spasmodic System" of American business. During the winter of 1854-1855 business stagnated, unemployment increased greatly, and there was considerable distress and popular unrest, especially in New York City. Here was an advance view, as it were, of the pattern of depression which was to develop in 1857.[2]

Although the anticipated crisis of 1854 did not completely materialize, the financial situation remained feverish between 1854 and 1857; indeed, according to William Graham Sumner, "there is no real interval between the two."[3] Railroad stock prices failed to recover, and speculation was

---

[1] *New York Herald*, August 26, 27, September 4, 1857; *see also* G. F. Train, *Young America in Wall Street* (New York, 1857), viii.

[2] *New York Herald*, January 4, 6, February 25, 1855; *New York Tribune*, October 25, December 6, 18, 1854; *see* the *Twelfth Annual Report* of the New York Association for Improving the Condition of the Poor (New York, 1855), 20 ff.

[3] W. G. Sumner, *A History of Banking in the United States* (New York, 1896), 424.

"bearish." Wholesale commodity prices, on the other hand, were but little affected in 1854 and resumed their upward course, partly under the stimulus of the special demand created by the Crimean War (1854-1856). They reached a peak in the early summer of 1857; then the decline began, and it was greatly accelerated as the financial crisis developed between August and October.[4]

The crisis proper, according to the contemporary reviewer, passed through three stages. First "scouted as a panic, senseless and causeless," it was then discussed "under the name of a pressure," and "at length arrived at the dignity and importance of a crisis."[5] The initial panic was precipitated by the failure of the Ohio Life Insurance Company to meet its New York obligations, which "struck on the public mind like a cannon shot." Panic spread as the banks called their loans, and depositors withdrew their funds. The crisis culminated on October 13, when the New York City banks decided to suspend specie payments. Their example was quickly followed by virtually all the other banks of the country.[6]

The crisis not only demonstrated the dominant place which New York had acquired in the nation's business; it also exposed the essential weaknesses of the imperfectly coördinated financial system which had grown up around the New York City banks. Much of the blame for the panic was somewhat superficially placed upon the use made of the still novel instrument of the electric telegraph, particularly upon the

---

[4] The contrasting trends of commodity and stock prices between 1854 and 1857 are illustrated statistically in W. B. Smith and A. H. Cole, *Fluctuations in American Business, 1790-1860* (Cambridge, Mass., 1935), 93 ff., 108 ff. The Index Table of Railroad Stock Prices on page 184 reveals, for example, that by the end of 1854 the index was down to 67 from the base of 100 for 1853. It hovered at that level until July 1857, when it declined further, and was down to 39 by October. The index remained in the neighborhood of 50 for more than two years thereafter. Wholesale commodity prices, however, continued to rise after 1854, reaching a high peak of 133 in the summer of 1857 (the index being based on the average for the decade 1848-1858 as 100). This index did not decline sharply until October, and by the end of the year was down to 108. It was to hover at or below 100 until late in 1861 (table at page 167). *See,* however, W. T. Hutchinson, *Cyrus H. McCormick* (New York, 1935), II, 75, for the report that grain prices began to decline in 1856, after the conclusion of the Crimean War, and that poor crops and poor prices kept the West in a state of depression for several years thereafter.

[5] *Hunt's Merchants' Magazine* (January 1858), XXXVIII, 100.

[6] J. S. Gibbons, *The Banks of New York and the Panic of 1857* (New York, 1858), 344 ff. The banks of Philadelphia and Baltimore had already suspended specie payments on September 24 and 25; and, after October 16, the only exception to the general bank suspension were the banks of Kentucky and five of the nine banks of New Orleans (C. F. Dunbar, "The Crisis of 1857," in *Economic Essays,* New York, 1904, 280, 283). There was no real shortage of specie, however, and the premium was never higher than three per cent. The New York banks quickly accumulated a large supply of specie, so that they were able to resume payments in December. The Philadelphia and Baltimore banks did not resume until February, 1858, and resumption was general by midsummer of 1858 (Dunbar, 288; *The American Almanac,* Boston, 1859, 364 ff.).

[2]

facility with which sensational rumors and alarms were spread by means of the telegraph to newspapers greedy for increased circulation.[7] In the disturbed state of opinion which prevailed, the banks were also accused of aggravating the panic by their policy of calling in loans both precipitately and indiscriminately. They were further suspected of favoring speculative debtors and discriminating against legitimate merchants. Whatever the truth of these charges, the banks of New York paid the penalty when their depositors were frightened into a large-scale withdrawal of funds. Their meagre specie reserves of some twelve million dollars were rapidly reduced to less than six millions by October 13, when suspension was deemed unavoidable.[8]

In reality the much criticized bank policy was a symptom rather than the cause of the widespread loss of confidence. Unfortunately the crisis developed at a time of year when the New York City banks were normally in the habit of contracting their loans in order to meet the usual autumn demands for cash from the country banks. The additional pressure of financial stringency accelerated the process of call-loan contraction, but deposits declined even more rapidly as hoarding increased. Thus was produced what was then described as "the most extraordinary, violent, and destructive financial panic ever experienced in this country. . . ."[9]

The crisis was only the most acute phase of a broader pattern of depression, one so severe as to invite comparison with its unforgotten predecessor, the depression of 1837-1843. The familiar phenomena reappeared, as the prices of both commodities and stocks dropped, and as bankruptcies and business failures multiplied, providing abundant material for the publication of a "commercial necrology" in the newspapers. All of this, moreover, tended to foster a general sentiment of "universal bankruptcy" and "moral insolvency."[10] Industrial and commercial enterprise languished, unemployment increased, and immigration

---

[7] Gibbons, 345, 363, 373; *Hunt's Magazine* (December, 1857), XXXVII, 659.

[8] *Harper's New Monthly Magazine* (December, 1857), XVI, 114; Dunbar, 279; Sumner, 426.

[9] Gibbons, 344 ff.; Dunbar, 282; *see* Smith and Cole, 131-132, for an examination of the charges that the banks made the panic. This question will be considered more fully later on.

[10] Gibbons, 373; *'37 and '57: A Brief Popular Account of All the Financial Panics in the United States* (New York, 1857), 39 ff.; *see Hunt's Magazine* (February, 1858), XXXVIII, 195, for a summary of falling prices and property values; also A. C. Cole, *The Era of the Civil War* (vol. III of the Centennial History of Illinois, Springfield, 1919), 100; and D. Morier Evans, *The Crisis of 1857-58* (London, 1859), 135, for a tabular view of business failures reported by the American Commercial Agency.

declined, while recovery was slow during 1858 and 1859. Even in 1860, the *Bankers' Magazine* noted that the effects of depression were still being felt "in the shape of unemployed or unremunerated labor, an unhealthy accumulation of capital in some quarters, and a sad deficiency in others, . . . and general symptoms of poverty. . . ."[11]

II

No less remarkable than the depression itself were the opinions and the moods which were generated by depression among workers and business men, leading to a great deal of public discussion, social agitation, and some overt action. Evidence of this fermentation of opinion is to be found in the promises or evasions of politicians, in the preachments of business and labor leaders, and particularly in the records of the contemporary press, which served as a barometer of changing social pressures. The depression of 1857 was world-wide; its influence on American opinion, however, was closely related to the prevailing pattern of domestic political and social questions. The depression was thus fitted neatly into the great sectional controversy which was carrying the country to the verge of civil war. The South, for example, boasted of its relative immunity to the shock of depression, inasmuch as the depression was admittedly felt most severely in the East and in the West. At this juncture, Senator Hammond of South Carolina was able to make political capital by declaiming: "Cotton is King. Who can doubt it, that has looked upon recent events?" He told the North: "We have poured in upon you one million six hundred thousand bales of cotton just at the crisis to save you."[12]

In the North, the *New York Herald* took advantage of the crisis to dwell upon the blessings of slavery, alleging that, while 200,000 workers had lost employment in the North and a million persons were threatened with starvation, the South had no need of soup kitchens. The slaves would be fed. "In view of these . . . facts," the *Herald* asked, "how can

[11] *Bankers' Magazine* (Baltimore, May, 1860), XIV, 833; Dunbar, 289 ff.; *New York Tribune*, June 15, July 1, August 5, 1858; January 1, 1859: "The prospect of relief is distant . . . Immigration has almost ceased. Wages, rents, and profits have greatly fallen. Yet such is the power of the human mind to adjust itself to circumstances that, although nobody anticipates, as almost everybody did a year ago, a speedy issue out of these troubles, the general feeling, nevertheless, is much less gloomy than then."

[12] Quoted in T. C. Smith, *Parties and Slavery* (American Nation Series, Boston, 1907), 180; *The South in the Building of a Nation* (Richmond, 1909), V, 440. *See* Dunbar, 291, 294, for the opinion that the South withstood the depression better than the rest of the country.

any candid, common sense man profess the belief that slavery is a horrible, atrocious, accursed, God-defying sin?" Now, therefore, was the time, the *Herald* insisted, for the North to come to its senses and to abandon all its specious reforms. People must forget about "Bleeding Kansas" and the "Nigger Agitation." The solid business interests should rally to the Federal Government and look to it for relief.[13] From the dynamic though eccentric George Francis Train came a similar appeal that the slaves were provided for, but who would care for the poor white men? They also "demand a hearing!"[14]

The hoped-for realignment and healing of sectional interests did not, however, materialize. The *New Orleans Delta* was alarmed over the prospect and issued a warning to the South to be on guard against the Northern "Pocket Interests," which were now likely to resurrect the old issues of protection and bank monopoly.[15] In 1857 there was no such concentration upon the problems of relief and reform as there has been after 1837. This may have been because the depression of 1857 was shorter and less severe; but it should also be pointed out that by 1857 the larger issues of national union and sectional division had become acute, and these issues tended to eclipse those created by the depression. By 1860 discussion of the depression was submerged in the impending political crisis, even though the advent of civil war produced another temporary business crisis.[16]

While it lasted, however, the depression of 1857 did provide the occasion for a general public debate, centering around two questions: "What caused it? . . . What lessons did it teach?"[17] The answers given were varied and often more raucous than right. One ironic commentator asked his readers to look and listen: "How the Diogenidae tumble and thump their tubs! . . . each one rapping out his own tune; each one screaming to boot, to be heard above the din!"[18] The contemporary search for causes was more than an academic one; aside from the temptation to moralize, there was the need for a kind of collective catharsis. And there were, of course, special political and economic causes to plead, so that many of the explanations served merely as a convenient introduction for some pet program of reform or relief.

---

[13] *New York Herald,* September 29, October 7, 22, 25, 1857.
[14] Train, 345.
[15] Quoted in the *New York Herald,* November 2, 1857.
[16] Dunbar, 294 ff.
[17] Gibbons, 347.
[18] *Atlantic Monthly* (November, 1857), I, 115.

III

Peculiarly suitable as a theme for the penitential mood induced by depression was a condemnation of extravagant and wasteful living, a national habit nurtured by the preceding prosperity.[19] A writer in the *North American Review,* for example, deplored the fact that "all except the very poorest sacrifice large portions of their earnings to mere idle show." Anticipating Veblen's doctrine of conspicuous consumption, he insisted that the measure of "our standard is not healthful nourishment but cost," and concluded that the prevailing distress might prove to be a public benefit if it restored "more simple and frugal habits among those whose social position gives weight to their example."[20] With more practical pertinence, the *New York Journal of Commerce* criticized the Civic Board of Education for increasing its budget to nearly a million and a quarter dollars, when taxes already stood at the "staggering level of eight million dollars," and when a deficit of two millions was in prospect. In particular the writer challenged the extravagance of appropriating nine thousand dollars for pianos for the boys' grammar schools, "queer-looking items" in "these unmusically hard times."[21]

Another writer protested against the waste of one hundred million yards of goods on "ladies' voluminous costumes"; but, together with other such critics of extravagance, he immediately betrayed his real purpose, when he attributed the crisis to the extensive and excessive importation of foreign goods.[22] The theme of extravagance was also dealt with in fiction; in a story bearing the title "Hard Times," one of the characters, a woman, indignantly objects that this complaint "is in the columns of all the newspapers, and in the mouths of all men. One would think to hear your sex talk, that ours was the cause of all these hard times."[23]

The gospel of economy and frugal living became popular, and fashionable society responded with its "poverty parties." Part of a "calico movement" in New York society, these social affairs sought to combine simplicity and charity as an appropriate program for the relief of the poor.

---

[19] *See* the "Defence of Bubbles," which was reprinted from an English journal in the *Eclectic Magazine* in April, 1853 (XXVIII, 474 ff.), in which the author waxes eloquent on the benefits of the current "commercial excitement," and defies the panic to come, "as I believe it surely will. I have little hesitation in affirming that the good will have outbalanced the evil."

[20] *North American Review* (January, 1858), LXXXVI, 172 ff.

[21] *Journal of Commerce,* November 7, 1857.

[22] *'37 and '57,* 44, 47.

[23] *Peterson's Magazine* (January, 1858), XXXIII, 61; *see also* another "True Story of the Hard Times" in the February issue.

They supplemented the "concerts for the poor," which had been initiated in 1854, and were described as being "provocative of a great deal of fun. The ladies are obliged to dress in calico or some cheap stuffs, and the gentlemen are attired in similar manner. . . . The refreshments are confined to cold water, bread and butter." Such parties promised the further advantage of freedom "from the annoyance of snobs, who go only to guzzle champagne and to stuff themselves with oysters."[24]

IV

Depression directed opinion against another and allegedly a still greater evil of the age. In prosperity, it was charged, America, and particularly its youth, had lost the taste for manual labor, which was left to the slave or to the immigrant. Everybody else, so ran the complaint, "has been seized with the desire to acquire a fortune without bending the back or straining the sinews, and buying and selling have taken the place of planting and reaping."[25] To this indictment the conservative *North American Review* added other counts: commodities paid "blackmail to half a dozen intermediary holders"; there was a "wasteful glut of the professions of law and medicine, trade and commerce"; worst of all, "there is the horde of speculators, whose only function is to derange prices, unsettle markets, entrap purchasers, defraud sellers, and introduce into transactions intrinsically necessary and honest the hazards and chicanery of the gambling table."[26]

Speculation and speculators were thus made to bear the full brunt of responsibility for the depression. Here was an occasion for both public penitence and the sacrifice of a scapegoat. Wall Street became the symbol of rampant speculation, which now, more than ever before, was condemned as both false and immoral. Comfort was found in the hope (which fathered the belief) that the speculators were the chief victims of their own sins. The country as a whole was sound and should now return to the first principles of "sober and legitimate trade." Now that commodity prices were lower, it was also believed that the people would profit by cheaper living costs and by the dissolution of the speculative

---

[24] *New York Herald,* December 12, 1857; Hiram Fuller, *Belle Brittan on Tour* (New York, 1858), 238; Train, 222; E. Douglas Branch, *The Sentimental Years* (New York, 1934), 200.

[25] *Hunt's Magazine* (July, 1857), XXXVII, 70.

[26] *North American Review* (January, 1858), LXXXVI, 171; *'37 and '57,* 44; *The Knickerbocker Magazine* (September, 1858), LII, 298.

combinations which had previously forced them up.[27] The admission was nevertheless made that "in this gambling game the whole community has more or less participated," and one writer estimated that perhaps as many as 200,000 persons had been involved in it. People of all conditions, merchants and their clerks, lawyers, and even ministers, had dabbled in pools or engaged in "secretly buying and selling stocks." After all this intoxication, asked Henry Ward Beecher, "is it strange that the head is sick, the whole body faint, and the Commonwealth lies at length upon the ground, wallowing like one possessed, foaming and rending itself ?"[28]

All sections of the country contributed to the stream of invective and censure which was turned upon New York City in general and upon Wall Street in particular. The New York City banks were included in the indictment, since they had attracted the surplus funds of the country banks by offering interest on demand deposits as bait. In their greed for profits, they had loaned out these funds in the call-money market, and thereby had supported stock-market operations and fostered financial instability. Self-righteous Boston, for example, gloated over New York's misfortune and boasted that there everything was solid, except in so far as its capital had been lured away by the magnet of speculation. Nathan Appleton, Boston's leading business man, deplored the failure of New York to live up to its responsibility as the "great central banking power."[29] Rochester called upon its rich men to cease being "the football of Wall Street stock jobbers" and to devote their capital to the development of domestic manufactures for Western markets. The *Providence Journal* charged that Wall Street did "more mischief than is done by that gambling which seeks the shades of the night. . . ." Cincinnati, Chi-

---

[27] *New York Herald*, August 26, September 1, 2, 4, December 13, 1857; James K. Medbury, *Men and Mysteries of Wall Street* (Boston, 1870), 306, 313 ff.

[28] *'37 and '57*, 46; *New Englander* (November, 1857), XV, 705. *See* Max Wirth, *Geschichte der Handelskrisen* (first edition, Frankfurt, 1858), for an account of the special characteristics of the American depression in the setting of the world depression (334 ff. of the third edition of 1883) ; also Hans Rosenberg, *Die Weltwirtschaftskrisis von 1857-59* (Stuttgart, 1934), 36 ff.

[29] *Hunt's Magazine* (November, 1857), XXXVII, 594; XXXVIII, 723; *New York Herald*, August 30, 1857, quoting the *Boston Advertiser*. On the development of the call-money market, *see* Margaret S. Myers, *The New York Money Market* (New York, 1931), I, 122; Joseph E. Hedges, *Commercial Banking and the Stock Market before 1860* (Baltimore, 1938), 102, 116 ff.; Smith and Cole, 133. *See also* Evans, 114, for the view that after 1837 New York had won out over Philadelphia and Boston in the rivalry for financial leadership, and that the current crisis involved a struggle with London; in time New York "will become the financial centre, not only of the New World, but also, to a great extent, of the Old World."

cago, St. Louis, and St. Paul contributed to the general denunciation of "Wall Street and its harpies." The West disclaimed any responsibility for the crisis and offered its rich crops as an "antidote for the poison. Take it and recover from the stock-jobbing bite, or cast it aside, and allow the serpent to wind himself closer and closer around you. . . ." George Francis Train, that knight-errant of American business, reported that among many questions being asked was this one: "Don't you think it would be a good move to sink Wall Street; explode the Brokers' Board; and kill every 'Bull' and 'Bear' in the country?"[30]

A Wall Street broker subsequently recorded his vivid recollection of "the aroused morality of the United States." He remembered that "the summer visit of brokers in rural communities was an occasion of suspicion." Stock brokers, moreover, adopted a policy of protective coloration. They insisted that "they performed a purely commission business," and they proclaimed themselves "high-priests of the ideal in stock market transactions." In the wave of good resolutions which followed, new rules were adopted for the Stock Exchange, in general shortening the time allowed for the settlement of transactions.[31]

V

The mysteries of the current crisis were, of course, probed more deeply by those who were less concerned with the abuses of speculation than with the basic misdirection of capital which had characterized the preceding period of expansion. It was noted, for example, that approximately a billion dollars had been absorbed into the construction of railroads, and this investment had resulted not so much in dividends as in an enhancement of land values. The railroads, moreover, carried a large current floating debt, which was an important factor in the crisis. In the meantime, the scandals of railroad mismanagement, which had been exposed since 1854, had brought all corporations into public disfavor.[32]

---

[30] Train, 250; press quotations in the *New York Herald,* August 1, 27, 28, 30, September 2, 3, 13, 1857; *New York Tribune,* November 6, 1857.

[31] Medbury, 7 ff.; Myers, I, 38. Henry Clews recalled years later that the Board of Brokers underwent a shaking up in 1857, and that "a younger race of financiers," including himself, then arose and displaced "the old crew" in Wall Street (H. Clews, *Twenty-Eight Years in Wall Street,* New York, 1888, 5 ff.).

[32] Medbury, 317, 327; *Hunt's Magazine* (September, 1857), XXXVII, 325, 378, 665. Admitting that the railroads had not averaged one per cent a year in dividends, the argument, nevertheless, concluded that they were "a success." Under the heading "Advice

The whole system of credit invited critical examination at a time when defaulting borrowers and demanding creditors were engaged in mutual recrimination. The Mercantile Agency of New York, which collected the statistics of business failures, deplored the tendency toward the congestion of credit at the base of the business structure. Total rural debts to the cities were estimated at approximately two and a quarter billion dollars. Neither buying nor selling was done prudently enough, and little discrimination was shown in the granting of credit. Country merchants usually sold on twelve months' time, and neither they nor their customers were prompt in settling their debts. Since jobbers and city merchants bought on much shorter time, they had their capital tied up in long rural credits or were compelled to borrow from the banks at high interest rates. Critics pointed out that the telegraph and the railroad were expediting business, and an average credit of four months should, therefore, be enough for most purposes. European exporters, furthermore, were held partly responsible, since they took advantage of American manufacturers and contributed to the bloated system of credit by means of their liberal credit policy. During the depression cash buying increased, and it was hoped that the crisis would bring a permanent reform of credit.[33] The West was, however, criticized for its reluctance to pay its debts: "That paradise of usurers," charged Greeley's *Tribune*, was ready "for any preposterous scheme of assumption." Instead of meeting their creditors, "too many have tried to stave off, and fight executions, and invoke the aid of stay laws, and put their property into the hands of relatives or confederates, . . . to the advantage of sheriffs and sharking lawyers, and the disadvantage of everybody else."[34]

VI

Inevitably any investigation of the causes of the crisis was bound to return to the long-standing controversy over banking and bank cur-

---

to the Wise," people were urged "to buy now that the prices of the stocks were low" (p. 646). On "the extensive absorption of capital from the floating to the fixed state," *see* H. E. Miller, *Banking Theories in the United States Before 1860* (Cambridge, Mass., 1927), 206; also *New Englander* (November, 1857), XV, 705.

[33] Evans, 122; *'37 and '57*, 54; *New York Tribune*, October 19, 1857, January 4, 1859; *New York Journal of Commerce*, November 7, 1857; Fuller, 232; Edward Everett, *The Mount Vernon Papers* (New York, 1860), 179; *see also* Gibbons, 375, for a criticism of the current confusion between personal and true commercial credit.

[34] *New York Tribune*, October 14, 1857, December 25, 1858; *Hunt's Magazine* (October, 1857), XXXVII, 444; Hutchinson, II, 70 (McCormick found the farmers eager to buy reapers but unable to pay for them).

rency. Of one great gain, as compared with 1837, the Buchanan Administration made boast in 1857. Through the Independent Treasury System
the Federal Government had preserved its funds intact despite bank suspensions; it was able to continue specie payments, and it thereby helped
relieve the stringency created by bank suspensions, albeit its separate
specie reserves, amounting to twenty million dollars, may have contributed to the stringency itself.[35] As Federal revenues declined, however,
and as surplus turned into deficit, the Treasury was compelled to apply
to Congress for authority to issue twenty million dollars of Treasury
Notes; and subsequently the permanent public debt was increased by as
much more.[36] Officially, President Buchanan gave his sanction to the
view that a vicious paper-money system was chiefly responsible for both
the boom and the collapse. He recommended the withdrawal of all notes
under twenty dollars; furthermore, he advised the States to break away
from the banks, urging them to follow the example of the Federal
Government. The conservative *North American Review* agreed, suggesting, moreover, that eventually all notes under fifty dollars might be with-
drawn, thereby forcing more specie into active circulation. Amasa
Walker objected that the gold of California had gone to England, while
our channels of business became clogged with a paper currency, which
he alleged was to the advantage only of the banks and the swarm of
speculators "who spread over the land like locusts."[37] The supporters of
the hard money policy admitted that this would mean deflation and lower
prices, but it was argued that the "low prices of labor, provisions, and
home-grown materials would at once give our manufacturers such protection as a precarious tariff could never afford. . . ." Low costs would
even help open foreign markets to American goods and enable them to
compete with those of England.[38]

While an inflated bank-note currency was again being made the scapegoat for an American depression, those more familiar with banking
practices recognized that bank notes were no longer the only, or even the
principal, instrument of credit inflation. For the banks of New York
City the volume of notes in circulation had become a relatively static and

---

[35] *Hunt's Magazine* (November, 1857), XXXVII, 533; Miller, 216; *Harper's Monthly Magazine* (December, 1857), XVI, 115.
[36] *The American Almanac* (1859), 138, 148. Between the fiscal years ending on June 30, 1857 and 1858, respectively, the Federal revenues fell from nearly sixty-nine million to forty-five million dollars, while expenses rose to more than seventy-one million dollars.
[37] *Hunt's Magazine* (December, 1857), XXXVII, 674, XXXVIII, 532 ff.; *North American Review* (January, 1858), LXXXVI, 174 ff.
[38] *North American Review*, LXXXVI, 179.

minor part of their total liabilities. While New York City bank deposits more than doubled between 1853 and 1860 (reaching eighty million dollars by the latter date), the volume of notes in circulation flattened out at an average level of eight million dollars. For the country as a whole, the bank notes were, of course, much more important, nearly equaling in volume the total deposits.[39] The New York City banks, furthermore, held some fifteen million dollars of country-bank deposits, amounting to nearly a fifth of their total deposits. Coupled with the development of a call-loan market, these demand deposits had become by 1857 a serious source of financial instability, and a factor contributing to potential panic. If the country banks suddenly withdrew their deposits, the city banks were compelled to contract their loans immediately. Borrowers were thereby liable to be reduced to the condition described in a Wall Street doggerel of 1857:

> Rushing around the corners,
> Chasing every friend
> Plunging into bank—
> Nothing there to lend—
> Piteously begging
> Of every man you meet.[40]

Banks were thus exposed to the charge that they had made the panic. Their chief defense was that they were merely barometers of approaching disasters. It was urged in their behalf that "banks managed by conscientious and prudent directors are the great conservatives which arrest the proclivity of financial profligacy to national destruction."[41] But this in turn provoked the criticism that the managers, particularly of the key banks of New York City, had displayed a lack of leadership in 1857. Many of the banks had been founded since 1850, and their managers were often retired merchants and former bill brokers, novices in banking. The banks, moreover, lacked the necessary facilities for coöperation, although the establishment of the New York Clearing House in 1853 had marked a beginning step in that direction.[42] Recom-

---

[39] *New York Tribune,* January 8, 1858; A. H. Cole, "The New York Money Market, 1843-1862," in *Review of Economic Statistics* (August, 1929), XI, 167; Dunbar, 287; *Hunt's Magazine,* XXXVIII, 533. (Early in 1857, all the bank deposits totaled 230 million, and the notes in circulation 214 million dollars.)

[40] *Hunt's Magazine,* XXXVII, 641; Gibbons, 356 ff.; Cole, 168; *Bankers' Magazine* (February, 1858), XII, 601.

[41] Quoted in Miller, 199.

[42] Gibbons, 365, 369 ff., 387.

mendation was, therefore, made for the establishment of a more effective "College of Finance," which should include merchants as well as
bankers. Its function would be to collect statistics, which were now left
to the fancy of the press, and to keep the goal of a stable money market
constantly in view. Such a body, it was argued, might have prevented the
crisis in 1857.[43]

VII

That specific remedies for particular abuses of banking and currency
were needed was generally recognized. Many proposals were made, and a
few of them were adopted. The Boston Board of Trade, after analyzing
the causes of the depression, recommended that banks should not be
allowed to pay interest on demand deposits or to make loans on call.
Total bank loans should be limited to one and a half times bank capital,
while note circulation should be restricted to half the capital. Massachusetts adopted a law in 1858 requiring a minimum specie reserve of
fifteen per cent of all bank liabilities, a legal reserve which Samuel
Hooper, a leading Boston merchant, thought inadequate. The governor
of New York recommended the enactment of a twenty-five per cent
specie reserve requirement for all banks, but action was left to the banks
themselves. In New York City, the Clearing House Committee proposed
new rules, to which most of the member banks agreed. Under them the
payment of interest on demand deposits was prohibited, while specie
reserves were to be kept at twenty per cent of net deposits.[44]

On the special subject of the currency there was a wide variety of
reform proposals, reflecting in the main two types of opinion. One of
these held to the feasibility of imposing some limit upon the quantity of
the bank-note currency; the other favored a different kind of currency
issue altogether. The proposals for limiting the currency ranged from a
five-dollar note minimum to a twenty- and even a fifty-dollar minimum
note issue. Some people advocated fixing a maximum note issue in terms
of twenty-five or fifty per cent of the total bank capital.[45] Others, however, used the recent bank suspensions to point to the need for a more

---

[43] Gibbons, 388 ff.; *see* Train, 333, for the proposal of "a congress of merchants,
bankers, manufacturers, and farmers," to discuss practical needs, but no "isms."

[44] Gibbons, 368; *New York Tribune,* January 6, 1858; for the report and recommendations of the Boston Board of Trade, *see Hunt's Magazine* (June, 1858), XXXVIII,
722 ff.; also *Bankers' Magazine* (May, 1860), XIV, 834.

[45] *North American Review* (January, 1858), LXXXVI, 178; *Hunt's Magazine*
(December, 1857), XXXVII, 677; *New Englander* (November, 1857), XV, 713; *New
York Tribune,* January 8, 1858; Hedges, 127, 131.

thorough reform of the currency. Some form of national currency was thought desirable, to be issued either by the Treasury or by a special bank. This proposal, of course, revived the old Bank of United States controversy; but there was also a modified version, which would have given national scope to the New York system of a bond-secured note issue. Under this plan, the issuing banks were to acquire low-interest-bearing Government bonds as security for their notes. These notes were to be made receivable at the Treasury; and, on the failure of any bank to redeeem them, a corresponding amount of the bonds would be canceled. The *New York Journal of Commerce* was scornful of this as well as of all the other nostrums; very soon, however, the urgency of Civil War finance was to lead to the enactment of a national bank-note currency.[46] For the moment, however, the opinion prevailed that the politicians should leave the subject of credit and currency alone altogether, allowing it to adjust itself naturally on the basis of "Mutual Responsibility and Guaranty."[47]

At the other extreme were those persons who proposed drastic changes in the currency, offering reforms that were related to more general social and political programs. George Francis Train, for example, advocated the relief of unemployment by means of public works, urging the issue of 150 million dollars in national scrip with which to pay for the construction of a railroad to the Pacific. He proposed another issue for the purchase or conquest of Cuba; in time he thought such scrip, amounting to perhaps 350 million dollars, might entirely replace all other currency. This plan for national notes, however implausible it seemed in 1857, was shortly to be realized in the guise of the greenbacks, issued for the purpose of financing the Civil War.[48] In the meantime, another monetary reformer, William Dealtry, self-styled Mechanic of Schenectady, went to a still greater extreme in his proposal to free the country from the "paper money makers." Since bank notes were merely "an invention to get other people's wealth and labor," Dealtry proposed to have the "states, counties, and cities issue scrip notes as a circulation medium to pay for internal improvements." Each public authority might be assigned its share of the existing volume of currency, so that excessive inflation could be avoided. Disregarding completely the dubious

[46] *Journal of Commerce,* November 4, 1857; Train, 324; Fuller, 263.

[47] *New York Tribune,* January 8, 1858; *Atlantic Monthly* (February, 1858), I, 392.

[48] Train, 330 ff. This, together with other similar theories, bears resemblance to the better known ideas of Edward Kellogg, whose speculations about some kind of national currency dated back to the panic of 1837 and first appeared in published form in 1843 (*Currency, The Evil and the Remedy*).

constitutionality of the plan, and harking back to the colonial public loan offices as precedents, Dealtry also advocated the lending of these notes to private borrowers at interest. Thus, in so simple a fashion, he believed would be achieved the multiple benefits of ample public credit, interest saved, and public revenue earned, while taxes could also be largely dispensed with. According to Dealtry's facile conclusion, society would have both the improvements and the money which paid for them. Dealtry was, however, not very hopeful of success, since his scheme depended upon "honest men . . . chosen to legislate." Striking a note of class conflict, he concluded that "the extremely wealthy cannot make good laws, they have to oppress men to gain wealth. He who has learned to labor, and has a moderate amount of money, will make a good law-maker."[49]

In a similar vein, but with a greater parade of abstruse economic theorizing, John Mason advocated a kind of managed state currency. He rejected the "stunted financial theories" of Europe which would tie money to gold and thus enslave men. The gold of California and Australia had afforded only temporary relief, and a permanently convertible bank-note money was in any case an illusion. Our currency could readily be expanded to a billion dollars, he wrote, if it were freed from dependence upon "a mineral product—the least adequate of all in the list of supply, . . . and the least necessary of any commodity to the absolute wants of civilization." In order to achieve an adequate currency, Mason recommended two policies. One was to require the issuing banks to deposit State bonds or other good assets as security for the notes. The second was to maintain a definite relation between the prevailing interest rate and current prices. It was to be mandatory to raise or lower the discount rate as prices rose or fell; such a variable rate, adjusted periodically, would thus serve as a guide to the enterprise of the business community. The ultimate objective, Mason concluded, was to be a stable average level of prices, and money would truly become "the aid and agent of industry," and not "its enslaver."[50]

VIII

A question which inevitably arose in the course of the crisis was what the Federal Government might do to relieve it. In his messages to Congress, both in 1857 and 1858, President Buchanan gave the official

[49] William Dealtry, *Money, Its History, Evils, and Remedy* (Albany, 1858), 26 ff.

[50] John Mason, *An Inquiry into the Laws Which Regulate the Circulation and Distribution of Wealth* (New York, 1858), 1 ff.

answer that government "can do but little" to alleviate depression, since it could have done nothing to avert the crisis. No useful public works were to be stopped, but economy was necessary in order to keep government borrowing at a minimum. Only two recommendations of positive action were made: a national bankruptcy law to facilitate the liquidation of insolvent debtors, and a moderate increase of customs duties to improve government revenues. The incidental protection thus offered to manufacturers might at this time help restore confidence and give an impetus to business recovery.[51]

The Administration achieved even less than its modest program called for. Congress failed to pass the bankruptcy bill; while the recommended tariff revision was long blocked in the Senate and was not finally enacted until early in 1861.[52] There was some impatience with the Federal "picayune policy," and there arose a disturbing new doctrine that the government "must employ, not discharge workmen. The people must be taken care of." It was agreed that the California railroad could now be built cheaply; moreover, States, cities, and towns could use surplus labor on public buildings and roads.[53] From another quarter, however, came a call urging resistance to the nostrums of quacks who would regulate "everything . . . in trade or morals which is liable to go wrong." Even if it were feasible, "such an infringement of the liberty of private action would far outweigh any consequent public advantage."[54]

IX

One favorite remedy was not to be disposed of so easily. The cause of protectionism, in eclipse since 1846, was revived in the hour of distress; and its most zealous advocates, Horace Greeley and Henry C. Carey, became eloquent and tireless on the theme that free trade always begot depression, and that only a return to protection could restore prosperity. Even a moderate tariff, they insisted, besides relieving a "Treasury completely out at the elbows," would free the country from excessive imports. It was argued that the unfavorable balance of trade had produced a chronic and dangerous dependence upon the London money

---

[51] James D. Richardson, *A Compilation of the Messages and Papers of the Presidents* (1907), V, 437, 440, 520 ff.

[52] *Hunt's Magazine*, XXXVIII, 71; *Harper's Weekly*, March 13, May 15, 1858; *New York Tribune*, April 21, 1858; *Harper's New Monthly Magazine* (April, 1859), XVIII, 687; J. F. Rhodes, *History of the United States* (New York, 1895), III, 56.

[53] Train, 328 ff.

[54] *Journal of Commerce*, November 4, 1857.

market, so that American business was once more, as in 1839, exposed to the jibes of foreign creditors that "simple, confiding, straightforward John Bull has again been swindled." With a new tariff, however, "the erection of new factories, furnaces, etc. will give employment to thousands of mechanics, artisans, laborers, who have for months languished in unwilling idleness."[55] Most persistent of all the protectionists was Henry C. Carey, who admittedly had once been a free trader. During 1857 and 1858, he addressed a series of open letters to President Buchanan and engaged in public controversy with William Cullen Bryant. He gave warning that protection had become the major issue; in Pennsylvania and New Jersey it was the "only question." The West, too, was anxious to be freed from British domination; moreover, starvation under the free-trade system was driving American labor into abolitionism. A return to protection for domestic industry might help avert the impending struggle between North and South. Do this, Carey addressed the President, and relieve "us of all further necessity for perusing the shocking accounts of poverty, despair, crime, and death, with which our journals are now filled."[56]

X

It was perhaps the chief merit of the protectionists that they directed attention to the plight of the working class, thousands of whom were unemployed as a result of the crisis. The wage earners were, therefore, drawn into the debate over the problems of the depression; moreover, they became a direct source of unrest and alarm in the country. The statistics of unemployment for this depression were, of course, very inadequate, and only rough estimates of the number of unemployed were given, but these were widely publicized. During the winter of 1857,

---

[55] *New York Tribune,* December 24, 1858, January 20, 1859, March 11, 1859; *Harper's Weekly,* October 10, 1857; Gibbons, 364; *Bankers' Magazine* (May, 1858), XII, 849; *Fourth Annual Report of the Boston Board of Trade* (Boston, 1858, 11, which cautioned, however, against the overexpansion of domestic industry and recommended that manufacturing corporations be required to keep adequate working capital as a safeguard against excessive borrowing for commodity speculation. A similar plea, coupled with the recommendation of "moderation in business, in private and public expenditure, in legislation and in everything else," appeared also in the *New Englander* (XV, 715).

[56] Henry C. Carey, *Letters to the President on the Foreign and Domestic Policy of the Union* (Philadelphia, 1858), *passim;* also *Financial Crises, Their Causes and Effects* (Philadelphia, 1864), 4, 18 ff.; *see* Allan Nevins, *Abram S. Hewitt* (New York, 1935), 190, for the suggestion that the crisis thus became a factor in the election of Lincoln in 1860; also Hutchinson, *McCormick,* II, 69 (depression and "the hope of relief sent many into the ranks of the Republican Party between 1856 and 1860").

for example, two hundred thousand persons were reported as unemployed, and perhaps a million as directly affected by the crisis. In New York City alone more than twenty-five thousand were said to be without work, and one hundred thousand persons were faced with want. The situation in New York and New England was described as "absolutely sickening."[57]

Already in 1854 the Association for Improving the Condition of the Poor had become greatly alarmed over the growth of unemployment in New York City, as a result of a sharp business crisis followed by a winter of unusual distress. The Association had come into existence in 1843 as an outgrowth of a prolonged period of depression which had created new problems of relief. Its annual reports traced the secular trends of urban poverty and the normal demands upon its philanthropy; but in 1855, and again in 1858 and 1859, these reports revealed the heavy impact of depression in the greatly increased costs of poor relief. These reports, moreover, conveyed the sentiments and fears of the Association as distress and discontent among the unemployed became alarmingly manifest. Pauperism and crime were found to be on the increase in both city and State. During 1858 it was reported that some 130,000 persons, or approximately one seventh of the city's population, had received relief of some kind, while in the State as a whole one out of every thirteen persons had been assisted. Commitments for crime in New York City also showed an increase of twenty-five per cent for 1858 over 1857.[58]

The Association for Improving the Condition of the Poor was particularly disturbed by the mushroom growth of pauperizing agencies. It reaffirmed its faith in its own kind of preventive charity, and was severely critical of those well-meaning persons who organized rival systems of indiscriminate relief, by the soup-kitchen method, during the hard winters of 1855 and 1857. It, furthermore, denounced all those "misleaders," who were trying to corrupt the masses with "shallow and degrading theories." For whosoever dared to challenge charity, "the divine method of treating indigence," could but offer alternatives which must lead to "anarchy and lawlessness." Included among the "mislead-

---

[57] *Hunt's Magazine*, XXXVII, 582; *New York Herald*, October 22, 1857; Train, 319; Dunbar, 290; *Fifteenth Annual Report* of the New York Association for Improving the Condition of the Poor (1858), 29, 57.
[58] *See* the Annual Reports of the Association, *passim*, but especially the Twelfth (1855), Fifteenth (1858), Sixteenth (1859), 47. For the controversy over the relief of unemployment in this period, *see* L. H. Feder, *Unemployment Relief in Periods of Depression* (New York, 1936), 18 ff.

ers," according to the Association, were political demagogues who
offered promises in return for votes, "pseudo-reformers" who asserted
a universal right to subsistence, as well as "the ultra-communistic radicals who openly advocated pillage and plunder, . . . and other foreigners, who, though they have changed their soil and allegiance, still
keep their nature intact, and insist upon having food put into their
mouths, and labor into their hands. . . ." As a result, the report of the
Association for 1857 concluded, "our city . . . presented a more appalling
picture of social wretchedness than was probably ever witnessed on this
side of the Atlantic."[59]

XI

The condition to which this gloomy review referred had been created
by an epidemic of mass meetings, in Tompkins Square and City Hall
Park, during November of 1857. Such "hunger meetings" had had
earlier precedents during the hard winter of 1854-1855, and there were
similar manifestations in other cities.[60] In New York City, however,
"hunger meetings" were almost daily occurrences, and the brawls which
sometimes accompanied them were magnified into bread riots by the
lurid reports in the newspapers. Police and fire companies were sometimes used to disperse the crowds, while on one occasion even a detach-
ment of Federal troops was posted at the Customs House and at the Sub-
treasury to protect the public funds.[61] At these meetings the clamor of
"the dangerous classes" was crystallized into a demand for public works
as the proper means of relieving unemployment. The press reaction was
twofold; it combined the denunciation of such unsound doctrines with
the cautious advice that perhaps something had to be done. This was
not Europe, *Harper's Weekly* warned, and we were not to be frightened
by foreign agitators or by riots. But since costs were now lower, public
works offered a practical solution for unemployment. The *Journal of
Commerce* accused Madam Rank and her "Teutonic Socialists" of
trying to ruin the city with their demands for public works, city-built
houses, and municipal refectories. The *New York Herald* blamed the
"Fourierite" agitators for inciting the people and condemned the public-
works program as a French invention. It advised, however, that a par-

---

[59] *Fifteenth Annual Report,* 22, 28, 32.
[60] *Fifteenth Report,* 20; *New York Tribune,* November 3, 10, 12, 1857; *New York
Herald,* November 13, 16, 1857; *Journal of Commerce,* November 6, 10, 11, 12, and 20,
1857; Carey, *Crises,* 22; A. E. Hutcheson, "Philadelphia and the Panic of 1857" in
Pennsylvania History (July, 1936), III, 193.
[61] *Fifteenth Report,* 20; Fuller, 238.

tial acceptance of the plan might be desirable. There was no reason, said the New York papers, to fear these meetings, since they were, on the whole, harmless; and the Southern press was cautioned against the premature proclamation that "the workingmen of the North are making the welkin ring with the wild and vociferous cry of blood and bread."[62]

"Work or bread" meetings were not limited to New York, but in that city they were linked with municipal politics. The immediate impulse to the Tompkins Square gatherings during November, 1857, came from the fact that the Council had failed to act promptly upon a proposal of Mayor Fernando Wood to appropriate funds for the development of the new Central Park. Mayor Wood was engaged in a campaign for reëlection as the "friend of the people," and his plan, among other things, was to have the city buy fifty thousand barrels of flour and other supplies. These were to be used to pay the wages of the Central Park workers at cost. In these "communistic notions" the Association for Improving the Condition of the Poor saw "a darker omen for all the classes of the community than had frowned upon it from the suspension of banks and the closing of factories."[63] The City Council eventually yielded to the pressure and appropriated a quarter of a million dollars for Central Park. Ten thousand persons were registered for the work, but the slow progress of the project occasioned further meetings in protest. The immediate sequel to these disturbances was the defeat of Mayor Wood for reëlection by a rival reputedly representing Wall Street.[64]

In the general clamor for work relief and the antiphonal charges of communism and pauperism, none could, however, lose sight of the fact that unemployment and distress were real. Opposition to relief measures was based on the argument that it "corrupts a people, even in starvation, to be fed by a government." Workers were advised to accept lower wages, even half the former rates, inasmuch as work at any price was better than charity. Both workers and capitalists were rebuked for their extravagant living in past prosperity and for their previously exorbitant demands.[65] But the depression also brought the suggestion that the hours of work might be reduced. The use of machin-

---

[62] *New York Herald,* November 12, 1857; *Journal of Commerce,* November 13, 1857; *Harper's Weekly,* November 14, 1857; Fuller, 236.

[63] *Fifteenth Annual Report* (1858), 19; *New York Herald,* October 23, November 25, 1857.

[64] *Journal of Commerce,* November 16, 18, 20, 21, 1857; *New York Herald,* December 2, 1857.

[65] *'37 and '57,* 53; *Journal of Commerce,* November 10, 1857.

ery, it was alleged, tended to result in overproduction, and the resulting problem was not local but national. The remedy, must, therefore, be on a national scale, and a national convention was proposed for the purpose of recommending changes.[66] There was the further advice that workers should not despair, but avoid all waste, and stay away from the grogshop. While waiting for work, they could use their time profitably by studying all the writings upon trade and currency, banks and corporations.[67]

XII

Ever since the depression of 1837, perhaps no American had been more acutely conscious of the problems of urban unemployment and poverty than Horace Greeley; nor had any contemporary been more concerned with broad theories of social reform. Somewhat pathetically, Greeley now admitted that he no longer entertained any such theories as had in the past exposed him to the loose charges of atheism and Fourierism. He realized that something should be done in the present crisis, but he had little to offer save the remedy of a tariff. Greeley further remarked that the workers also showed little real desire to free themselves from industrial serfdom. And so, in 1857, Greeley's proposed remedies extended little beyond a public employment office and a charitable pawnshop for the poor. He repeated his familiar convictions that the cities were already too crowded and that the unemployed should scatter to the hamlets and farms away from the main highways. If these city people would shun "liquor and ruffianism," the farmers would be glad to share with them.[68]

During 1857 an effort was actually made to arrange for a systematic exodus of surplus workers from New York City to the countryside. An American Industrial Association was organized; it appealed for funds and issued an "Address to Workers," urging them to apply for removal to the country.[69] The New York Association for Improving the Condi-

---

[66] *New York Tribune*, November 26, 1857.

[67] *'37 and '57*, 56. During the hard winter of 1854-1855, unemployment and distress among the workers had also brought forward a similar harvest of "Plain Words to Mechanics," advising them, for example, to "boggle at nothing which will save a few pennies," or "No American has ever fairly tried what he can live upon, if driven to a stress." (*See The New York Times*, December 26, 1854; *New York Tribune*, December 28, 1854.)

[68] *New York Tribune*, October 22, November 7, 10, 1857, January 1, December 3, 1859.

[69] *Journal of Commerce*, November 4, 10, 1857; *New York Tribune*, November 11, 1857.

tion of the Poor also circularized the farmers of the State, asking them to take on city workers. Few, however, responded, and not one of the more than 50,000 persons on the Association's relief rolls applied for removal. In 1858, the Woman's Protective Emigrant Society engaged in a similar effort, but it "came up in a night and perished in a night." In 1859, the Association again investigated more than 9,000 families on relief; but few were found eligible for emigration to the country and fewer still willing to leave the city. The Catholics opposed such a policy;[70] by 1859, moreover, an outbreak of strikes for the restoration of wage levels was noted as a major symptom of improving business conditions. Even the Central Park workers were involved in strikes, and the 3,000 employed there were granted an increase from one dollar to one dollar and ten cents a day. The pressure of unemployment appeared to have been relieved. The *Tribune* deplored these "industrial wars," but reminded employers that good wages "received by the journeyman today are apt to come back over the counter tomorrow."[71]

XIII

Amid all the prevailing distress comfort was found in the conclusion that, as contrasted with prosperity, depression had the merit of disabusing the mind of all illusions. It was reported that depression taught men a new political economy; namely, "that Property, resting . . . on a deceitful basis of fluctuating values, is among the least solid and permanent of all the things in which a man can invest himself. . . . Material possessions lack the permanency of the spiritual. . . ."[72] If proof was needed, it could be found in the fact that in December, 1857, the *Journal of Commerce* was calling upon its readers to "steal awhile away from Wall Street and every worldly care, and spend an hour about mid-day in humble, hopeful prayer." This appeal was one note in a religious revival which had begun in November in New York City and which had quickly been hailed as the best antidote to the Tompkins Square disturbances.[73] The revival expressed itself through the medium of informal noonday prayer meetings, which spread all over the country and which were attended by all classes and conditions of people.[74] The cycle of religious

---

[70] *Thirty-Second Annual Report* (1875), 70 ff.

[71] *New York Tribune,* April 6, May 3, 1859.

[72] *Harper's Monthly Magazine* (April, 1858), XVI, 695.

[73] *Journal of Commerce,* November 26, December 2, 1857; Branch, 32.

[74] *New York Tribune,* March 1, April 3, 5, 1858. In April the *Tribune* issued a Special Revival Edition.

decline and revival was expounded and shown to have an inverse relation to the cycle of business prosperity and depression.[75] One contemporary historian interpreted the revival as a "reaction from an over-stimulated state, . . . whose waters covered the flats left bare by retreating prosperity." Here was an example of a law which "is constant in every age and race. . . . Every race has oscillated between its shop and its temple. . . . When the characteristic activity languishes or suffers foreign interference, they resound with threats, Misereres, and confessions."[76]

---

[75] On the supposed connection between the depression and the revival, *see Harper's Monthly Magazine* (May, 1858), XVI, 839 ff.; *New Englander* (August, 1858), XVI, 656; Rhodes, III, 102; A. C. Cole, *The Irrepressible Conflict* (New York, 1934), 252.

[76] John Weiss, *Life and Correspondence of Theodore Parker* (New York, 1864), II, 248-249. Only Garrison, the abolitionist, protested that "the whole thing is an emotional contagion without principle. . ." (*W. L. Garrison, The Story of His Life* [New York, 1899], III, 463).

CHAPTER VI

Distress, Relief, and Discontent in the United States During the Depression of 1873-1878

The following essay originally appeared in *The Journal of Political Economy*, Volume LVIII, Number 6 (December 1950), pp. 494-512. It is reprinted here, in its entirety, with the permission of The University of Chicago Press and the author. The original pagination appears in brackets at the bottom of each page.

DISTRESS, RELIEF, AND DISCONTENT IN THE UNITED STATES DURING THE DEPRESSION OF 1873–78

DURING the week of September 13, 1873, the financial market of New York City suffered a series of shocks through the suspension of payments by several banking firms, chief among which was Jay Cooke and Company. By Saturday, September 20, a full-fledged panic had developed, and the New York Stock Exchange was closed for ten days. The New York City banks, serving as the central reserve depositaries of the national banking system, also came under the heavy pressure of cash withdrawals by country banks. Through their clearing-house, established in 1853, the city banks promptly resorted to the issue of clearing-house certificates for the settlement of balances among themselves, and they agreed to pool their reserves of legal-tender greenbacks in order to meet essential cash payments. Extraordinary evidence of the seriousness of the crisis was supplied by the hurried visit of President Grant and his Secretary of the Treasury, W. A. Richardson, to New York City, where they spent Sunday, September 21, in conference with bankers and merchants. Although refusing, for lack of legal authority, to release the Treasury greenback reserve of forty-four million dollars, they undertook to help relieve the stringency by the limited purchase of federal bonds.[1]

The immediate circumstances and the initial manifestations of the crisis were thus chiefly financial, and they resulted in the revival of controversial issues and remedies, affecting both contemporary banking practices and national monetary policy. The great concentration of funds in New York City, attracted by the lure of lucrative interest rates, became a particular object of criticism, since it had fostered an unhealthy and unstable diversion of capital into speculative channels. "Is it surprising," so ran the warning in the *Bankers' Magazine* already in May, 1873, "that capital concentrates here from the wilds of Maine, the recesses of Connecticut, the prairies of the West, or the tobacco fields of the South, to be used at one or two per cent per month, instead of six per cent at home? . . . We caution our country bankers to keep a healthy reserve at home, and not to trust too large a fund in Wall Street on 'call.' "[2]

Such commentary merely pointed up the intimate and sensitive interrelation-

[1] For a contemporary account and criticism of the role of the New York banks see *Bankers' Magazine*, XXVIII (October, 1873), 308 ff. For more circumstantial and comprehensive treatments of the financial panic see Max Wirth, *Geschichte der Handelskrisen* (3d ed.; Frankfurt-am-Main, 1883), pp. 450 ff., 540 ff., especially in its world-wide scope and perspective; and O. M. W. Sprague, *History of Crises under the National Banking System* (61st Cong., 2d sess.; Senate Doc. 538 [Washington, D.C., 1910]), pp. 29 ff.

[2] Quoted in Sprague, *op. cit.*, p. 30; for a contemporary critique of banking and monetary policy see "Why the New York Panic Happened at This Particular Moment," *Economist* (London), XXXI (September 27 and October 4, 1873), 1174 and 1201; for a more general coverage of the issues see J. Dorfman, *The Economic Mind in American Civilization* (New York: Viking Press, 1949), III, 15 ff.

ships through which the financial shocks were quickly communicated from New York City to other sections of the country, to be accompanied by similar suspensions and resort to emergency measures of monetary relief. Premonitions and tremors of financial pressure had been felt intermittently during preceding years, despite apparently continued prosperity. The first phase of what was to become, according to Max Wirth, a universal crisis occurred in Austria as early as May, 1873, thence extending to Germany, where it brought the speculative boom, fed by the great Franco-Prussian War Indemnity, to an abrupt end. The tightened European market for American securities was a major factor in producing panic in the United States, and the swelling tide of pressure spread virtually around the world.

What had, however, begun as a financial panic, currently minimized in familiar language as "excessive alarm from causes theorized to be but temporary and of exaggerated importance," rapidly developed into a prolonged period of industrial and business depression, lasting until 1879; according to D. A. Wells, the noted economist, it even extended into the 1880's, after a brief interlude of revival between 1879 and 1881.[3] Thus was precipitated a major example of what Max Wirth aptly labeled "die soziale Krankheit," whose symptoms and consequences were manifold and widespread, affecting all classes. Apart from its worldwide character, the Great Depression of the 1870's was especially significant in the United States, still recovering from

the effects of civil war and in the process of building a great industrial and urban superstructure upon an agrarian foundation. Both foundation and superstructure were shaken by a depression which at once revealed the stresses of an expanding economy and intensified the uneven effects of wartime and postwar changes upon the balance of agrarian and industrial interests. The circumstances of rapid urban industrial development combined with the distress of prolonged depression to produce mass discontent and to foster the fermentation of radical economic and social doctrines, in which indigenous elements were blended with newly imported European theories and influences. Out of these emerged a complex pattern of political and social movements, some of which were even magnified by the sharpened fears flourishing in depression into the vague shape of a Communist scare, one of the earliest in American experience.

Inadequate statistical data hamper any attempt at precise measurement of the scope of the depression of the 1870's and its accompanying distress. The most comprehensive estimate available, calculated on the basis of six major series, including pig-iron and coal production, cotton consumption, railroad revenues, merchandise imports, and bank clearings, indicates a decline of 32 per cent between 1873 and 1878, second only in size to a comparable decline of 55 per cent between 1929 and 1932.[4] Clearing-house figures of the New York City banks dropped approximately 40 per cent between 1872 and 1878.[5] The index of railroad stock prices fell nearly 60 per cent, while wholesale commodity prices de-

[3] David A. Wells, "The Economic Disturbances since 1873," a series of articles appearing in the *Popular Science Monthly*, Vols. XXXI–XXXIII (1887–89), *passim;* also by the same author, *Recent Economic Changes* (New York, 1890), pp. 1 ff.; F. W. Smith, *Hard Times, Agricultural Development the True Remedy* (Boston, 1877), p. 6.

[4] A. R. Eckler, "A Measure of the Severity of Depressions, 1873–1932," *Review of Economic Statistics*, XV (May, 1933), 77.

[5] Wirth, *op. cit.*, p. 542.

clined about 30 per cent in the same period.[6] A contemporary series covering some sixty articles in common use, intended to measure the cycle of inflation and deflation since the Civil War, indicated that retail prices, already down in 1873 from their wartime peak, were further reduced by about 20 per cent by 1877.[7]

In the search for causes to account for the prolonged process of deflation, Wells, the contemporary economic analyst, gave particular emphasis to the influence of technological advances and concluded that the "change is more like a revolution in prices than anything which usually happens in an ordinary cycle of prosperity and depression of trade." Quoting Major J. W. Powell, government geologist and noted authority on the Far West, that "all the good public lands fit for settlement are sold," and citing, furthermore, an estimated 10 per cent current surplus of labor, Wells posed the crucial question: "What disposition is it proposed to make of the labor of the country which labor-saving machinery and new methods of business have now . . . made manifestly surplus?" This was but one of various theories that pointed either to overproduction or to underconsumption as a plausible explanation of the existing depression. Wells himself supplied a ready remedy for this dilemma in the expansion of foreign trade: "In shutting out others, we have at the same

time shut ourselves in. . . . The house is too small, measured by the power of producing, for those that live in it."[8] In an even more critical vein, that relentless champion of laissez faire and free trade, W. G. Sumner, observed that under the influence of commercial crises people "lose their heads and begin to doubt the economic doctrines which have been most thoroughly established." He decried the notion gaining ground that "the key to successful production consists in knowing how to limit it" and the resulting trend toward combinations which "live in fear and anxiety lest they create too much wealth." It was not strange, therefore, that labor too was adopting similar notions of reducing hours and production.[9]

The impact of depression upon the propertied classes was made manifest through declining values and a rising toll of failures. The reports of Dun and Company, conveniently issued in quarterly form after 1875, indicated a doubling of the number of bankruptcies, from 5,183

---

[6] E. Frickey, in *Review of Economic Statistics*, X (August, 1928), 118; W. M. Persons, P. M. Tuttle, and E. Frickey, "Business and Financial Conditions Following the Civil War," in *Review of Economic Statistics and Supplements*, II (Cambridge: Harvard University Press, 1920), 16 ff., 39.

[7] Smith, *op. cit.*, p. 12; O. V. Wells, in *Agricultural History*, XI (July, 1937), 237 ff., notes that, while the decline of farm prices paralleled that of industrial prices, expanding production tended to lessen the shock of depression upon agriculture during the 1870's.

[8] D. A. Wells, "How Shall the Nation Regain Prosperity?" *North American Review*, CXXV (July–October, 1877), 126 ff., 287. Significantly, Wells advocated the benefits of closer trade relations particularly with Canada and South America, arguing that a *Zollverein* would in time make Canada "applicants of their own accord for incorporation as States in the American Union, or would enable the United States, if it was deemed expedient, to force them to become such, by the threat not of armed compulsion, but by simply clouding the sun." For theories of overproduction and underconsumption cf. also Wells, "The Economic Disturbances since 1873," *op. cit.*, XXXI, 768; cf. C. D. Wright's first report as United States Commissioner of Labor, *Industrial Depressions* (Washington, D.C.: Government Printing Office, 1886), p. 257; Dorfman, *op. cit.*, pp. 123 ff.

[9] M. R. Davie (ed.), *Sumner Today*, for address on "The Influence of Commercial Crises on Opinions about Economic Doctrines," before the Free Trade Club in 1879, p. 42; also "Errors of the Time," in *Journal of Social Science*, No. 6 (1874), p. 187. Cf. Thorstein Veblen, *The Engineers and the Price System* (New York: Viking Press, 1923), pp. 1-26.

in 1873 to 10,478 in 1878, although the liabilities involved spurted to 228 million dollars as early as 1873 and stood only slightly higher at 234 million dollars by 1878; but they dropped off sharply to less than 100 million dollars in 1879.[10] Contemporary appraisals of the intensity of depression tended to be the more alarming by their very vagueness and contributed to the prevailing pessimism. From various sources, both official and unofficial, came plaintive accounts of distress. Governor Rice, for example, reported that assessed property valuations in Massachusetts had declined by 1877 to the level of 1871, thereby emphasizing the supposed need for public economy, which was repeatedly echoed in the messages of federal and state executives. The treasurer of Iowa testified before a congressional committee investigating the depression in 1879 that between one-third and one-half of the farms in the state were mortgaged and that many were still in danger of foreclosure. From Chicago came the complaint, presented by the secretary of the Board of Trade, that tax arrears were large, despite many forced sales, and that the city was over its debt limit, with three million dollars outstanding in scrip, issued in order to pay creditors and employees. The governor of Rhode Island announced that more savings banks had been placed in receivership in 1878 than in the whole past history of the state, while, in Boston, Archbishop Williams prepared an address to be read in all churches urging people to end the run on the savings banks. In New York and Pennsylvania also savings banks passed through a severe ordeal, resulting in losses and bank closures; Governor Hartranft of Pennsylvania censured savings bank prac-

tices and abuses and gave support in 1878 to the current agitation in Congress for a National Postal Savings Fund, which promised "enduring benefits to the people individually and to the nation."[11]

In the pervasive pessimism characteristic of depression, the end seemed out of sight, despite occasional reports of incipient recovery. The *Bankers' Magazine* discussed the prevailing notion of "Capital on Strike," while the *New York Nation* inquired caustically how one would ever know "the bottom" had been reached; on another occasion it called for the formulation of a law of panics and for indexes by which their coming and going could be determined. Even in 1879 the governor of Pennsylvania opened his message in a mood of uncertain hope: "We are still in the gray of hard times, and the giant industries of coal and iron are yet slumbering restlessly; but, everywhere, the stir of awakening confidence betokens the beginning of a more prosperous day." Only as the year progressed was R. P. Porter able to announce "The Dawn of Better Times," in the shape of expanding exports, diminishing failures, a sound currency, and the lesson of "economy" learned in five years of depression.[12]

[10] Wright, *op. cit.*, p. 67; *Economist* (London), XXXV (February 3, 1877), 126.

[11] *Annual Message of Governor J. F. Hartranft of Pennsylvania* (Harrisburg, 1878), p. 7; *Nation*, XXVI (April 4, 1878), 223; *Acts & Resolves of the General Court of Massachusetts* (Boston, 1877), p. 694; *Acts and Resolves of Rhode Island* (Providence, 1879), p. 32; *Causes of General Depression in Labor and Business* (46th Cong., 2d sess. [House Misc. Doc. 5 (Washington, D.C., 1879)]), pp. 41, 366. For an unusual note of economy see the *Message of Governor L. Robinson of New York* (Albany, 1878), p. 21, deploring the high costs of public education and particularly the support of high schools: "We educate them [the children of the poor] in such a way as to make them discontented with their condition. . . ."

[12] *International Review*, VII (November, 1879), 531 ff.; *Message of Governor Hartranft*, p. 2; *Fort-*

Among the many consequences of depression, unemployment was the most disturbing in its contribution to distress and unrest. Its immediate effects embraced an intensified pressure upon existing charitable institutions and newly created *ad hoc* relief agencies, as well as great concern over the most suitable methods of relief. The exact nature and volume of unemployment due to depression became the subject of speculation but remained undetermined and essentially indistinguishable from recognized chronic and seasonal types of unemployment. During the first winter of depression, 1873–74, the New York Society for Improving the Condition of the Poor reported unemployment in the city, on the basis of reports from its four hundred visitors, at 93,750, or approximately one-fourth of all available workers; for the following winter it gave estimates of between 75,000 and 100,000 and quoted press totals amounting to one-third of the city's workers. The Society's rolls reflected this condition by soaring from some 5,000 families on relief in 1873 to 24,000 in 1874, and to an average of more than 20,000 families during the later 1870's.[13]

Similar estimates of unemployment were made for other cities and for the industrial East generally. By 1878 the *New York Nation* expressed impatience with the current wild surmises of unemployment which tended to retard con-

fidence and recovery. Somewhat querulously it inquired what was meant by "lack of employment," and it recommended that the newly appointed congressional committee for investigation into the causes of depression, under the chairmanship of the public-spirited ironmaster, Abram Hewitt, actually determine the extent of unemployment in such industrial cities as Fall River, Scranton, and Pittsburgh. One official and rather belated attempt was made, in 1878, to measure unemployment. This was the accomplishment of Carroll D. Wright, as chief of the Massachusetts Bureau of Labor, the first of its kind in the country. In May, 1878, Wright gave a total for Massachusetts of less than 29,000 unemployed, further declining to 23,000 as "wanting work" by November. On this basis he estimated less than half a million unemployed in the entire country, as compared with current estimates of three million.[14]

Wright's methods and findings on labor conditions did not, however, pass without criticism. Charles Litchman, a shoeworker and labor leader, appeared before the congressional committee of investigation in Boston in 1879 and indicted the Massachusetts Bureau of Labor under Wright as "a political machine which can furnish an argument on any question affecting capital and labor . . . which argument is always in the interest of capital." He advocated the establishment of a national labor bureau that would enjoy the confidence of labor and possess "principles and ability" rather than serve as "a shelf on which to place political favorites."[15]

nightly Review, XXV (June, 1876), 810; *Nation,* October 28, 1875, and October, 25 1877; *Bankers' Magazine,* XXXI (June, 1877), 914. For an early attempt to advance "the science of price cycles" by relating it to a Jupiter cycle of magnetic storms, mixed with a naïve venture in forecasting, see Samuel Benner, *Benner's Prophecies of Future Ups and Downs in Prices* (Cincinnati, 1876), pp. 128 ff.

13 *Thirty-first Report of the New York Society for Improving the Condition of the Poor* (New York, 1874), p. 29; *Thirty-second Report . . .* (1875), p. 30; *Thirty-third Report . . .* (1876), p. 31.

14 *Tenth Annual Report of the Massachusetts Labor Bureau* (Boston, 1879), pp. 80 ff.; Wright, *op. cit.,* p. 64; *Nation,* March 11, 1875, and February 14 and August 15, 1878; Wirth, *op. cit.,* p. 558.

15 *Causes of General Depression in Labor and Business,* p. 425.

A more pointed and comprehensive criticism of Wright's report on unemployment in Massachusetts came from William Godwin Moody, a former Boston printer and labor reformer, who appeared before the congressional committee in 1878, and who subsequently enlarged his analysis of the depression in a volume entitled *Land and Labor*, proposing a comprehensive program of relief and reform. Moody disputed Wright's figures as tortuous and ridiculously low, and he offered instead the rather startling thesis that only war had provided full employment, while peace had "disemployed" millions, amounting during the depression to perhaps half the working population either wholly or partially unemployed. Moody advocated the drastic remedy of a national six-hour working day, moved up or down in accordance with the findings of a National Bureau of Labor that enough were employed and enough was produced to provide all "with a sufficiency of necessaries and comforts of life." With the addition of agrarian and tax reforms, Moody emphasized that his program was neither "socialism nor communism"; it was simply action rather than "non-action" for the promotion of the "general welfare of the United States."[16]

However controversial its extent, unemployment was real enough to generate an immediate problem of relief and to precipitate serious social unrest and agitation. In a typical industrial city like Troy, New York, as depression made itself felt during the winter of 1873–74, the press combined pleas for help with warnings that the soup houses were attracting the lazy and the pauper; and it urged a wise organization of charity: "In the name of God feed, in the interest of humanity devise some means to reform." The expanding activities of soup distribution were reported daily as a major item of news and even with an occasional note of levity: "Business at the soup house continues lively, and every day proves more and more the necessity of the institution." Notice was given that "the ladies plan to furnish either salt fish, oyster soup, or fish chowder for Fridays hereafter."[17] In other cities the problem of relief was met in a similar manner; in the larger cities, however, it was complicated by organized demonstrations of the unemployed, accompanied by extravagant demands. In Boston, for example, the idle workers petitioned the city to provide work by building larger public markets, more adequate reservoirs, and other needed improvements, to be paid for with scrip; but Mayor Cobb rejected the program as injurious to the city's credit.[18] Chicago witnessed a struggle between the Chicago Relief and Aid Society and a Socio-political Association, described as an "anarchist" group, over the distribution of a $700,000 relief fund left over from the fire of 1871; a kind of run was organized on the Aid Society by applicants for relief. In addition, a demonstration by some twenty thousand persons demanded public works from the Common Council.[19]

---

[16] W. G. Moody, *Land and Labor* (New York, 1883), pp. 130, 253, 307; *Depression in Labor and Business* (45th Cong., 3d sess. [House Misc. Doc. 29 (Washington, D.C., 1878)]), pp. 164 ff. Moody also quoted approvingly Herbert Spencer's lecture on "The Gospel of Relaxation," advising Americans against "Intemperance in Work."

[17] *Troy Morning Whig*, January 1, 3, and 5 and March 20, 24, and 25, 1874, *et passim; Troy Daily Press*, November 24 and December 23, 1874, *et passim.*

[18] Reported in *Troy Morning Whig*, January 13, 14, and 15, 1874.

[19] L. H. Feder, *Unemployment Relief in Periods of Depression, 1857 to 1922* (New York: Russell Sage Foundation, 1936), pp. 52–53, 62 ff.

Similar mass meetings of the unemployed were held in New York City during the winter of 1873-74; one of these precipitated a collision with the police in what became known as the Tompkins Square Riot, which was denounced as a denial of freedom of assembly. The New York Society for the Improvement of the Condition of the Poor reported the incident with great alarm as the mischievous product of "well-known Communists, Internationalists, and Free-thinkers, with a sprinkling of sympathizing natives." As a result cries had been raised for "a complete overthrow of the social and political system" and to "hang the thieves and robbers in Wall and Broad Streets." An ominously named Committee of Public Safety, claiming to represent the unemployed, scattered handbills proposing, "as a measure of safety to the city, that work and pay for the same be immediately furnished . . . that salaries be limited to $5,000 a year, and that a tax be laid on surplus wealth, so as to limit its accumulation at a definite point." The New York Society for Improving the Condition of the Poor used the occasion to deplore the "outgush of morbid sympathy," in the form of free lunches and free dormitories, as offering an invitation to tramps and encouragement to workers to stay out on strike against the reduction of wages and as contributing to the demoralization of the poor.[20] A year later the Society was able to report that wiser counsels had prevailed among the unemployed, despite a renewed threat of revolt. The *New York Nation* was disturbed by the developing struggle between the "Short-hairs" and the "Swallow-tails" in municipal politics over the issue of relief, and it approved the strict enforcement of poll-tax and literacy requirements for

[20] *Thirty-first Report* . . . (1874), pp. 33, 52 ff.

voting, as in the case of Boston, in order to stay the trend toward perpetual municipal workshops. The *Nation*, indeed, denounced the universal spread of the "free soup" appetite; and it warned that "free soup must be prohibited, and all classes must learn that soup of any kind, beef or turtle, can be had only by being paid for."[21]

The unhappy experiences with relief during the first winter of depression prompted the summoning of a conference on charities in New York City in May, 1874, under the auspices of the American Association of Social Science. Similar meetings followed in succeeding years at Detroit, Saratoga Springs, Cleveland, and Chicago; by 1878 these had evolved into a permanent association to be known as the National Conference of Charities and Correction. The first gathering of 1874 heard reports on the demoralizing effects promoted by indiscriminate relief. It was estimated that twenty thousand imposter paupers throve on charity in New York City alone; the "relief-houses" were ruining the cheaper eating places in the city; petty crime and street begging by a horde of tramps had increased; and, worst of all, "charity assisted labor in the combat to keep up wages." Moreover, the first attempt to co-ordinate all relief in the city by means of a Bureau of Charities had failed for want of co-operation.[22]

This last was in allusion to the rise and growth of a movement for a more effective organization of charity in a number of American cities. Modeled upon the London and Elberfeld plans,

[21] *Nation*, April 1 and December 23, 1875, and March 9, 1876; *Thirty-second Report* . . . (1875), pp. 51, 60.

[22] *Journal of Social Science*, No. 6 (1874), pp. 74 ff.; No. 8 (1876); No. 9 (1878), *passim*.

its chief recommended features were the employment of district visitors to investigate deserving cases and a central registration bureau for the elimination of duplication and fraud. As early as 1873 such charity organization agencies were initiated in Germantown and Indianapolis as an outgrowth of public relief meetings; in 1875 the Co-operative Society of Volunteer Visitors among the Poor was founded in Boston, followed by a Registration Bureau in 1876. Between 1877 and 1879, charity organization societies were established in Buffalo and Brooklyn, where one-tenth of the population was reported to be on relief, as well as in cities as widely separated as New Haven, Newport, Philadelphia, Detroit, and Cincinnati. In 1882 New York City also achieved a Charity Organization Society on the approved plan, and by 1883 there were twenty-five such societies in the country, amounting to "an uprising of the people in the field of charity," in the somewhat exaggerated language of its historian.[23]

Such measures were, however, merely palliative and scarcely adequate to cope with the discontent stemming from prolonged depression. Broader implications and even exaggerated pessimistic deductions were derived from the situation, as in the case of the *Nation*, which concluded that "the times will probably never be as good again as they have been." The difficulty was that "people are less shrewd and self-reliant, more apt to lean on others and on the government." The poor man was now in politics, and "the more he is coddled in this way the more oppressed he will feel." The issue was thus drawn beween laissez

faire and state intervention, and responsibility was laid in part upon the influence of the "New German Political Economy," with its doctrine that the state can work miracles.[24] How to counter this collectivist trend became the theme of many contemporary observers. In the *Atlantic Monthly* an anonymous analyst of "Certain Dangerous Tendencies in American Life" advanced a program of positive "propagandism," which would profit men of property to spend a million dollars in the next three years for the preparation and circulation of broadsides among country newspapers, repeating the simple truths on such topics as debt, paper money, economy, and thrift. A cheap popular newspaper and talks by sound men would be helpful, "not to perplex the brains of the workingmen, but to drive straight at the mark and stop."[25]

A ringing call to return to "the old foundations of American self-government" was sounded in the annual message of Governor Samuel J. Tilden of New York in 1876, which addressed itself to the national scene; in the manner of an available candidate in the approaching presidential election, Tilden deplored the rise of a class of "Tax Con-

[23] F. D. Watson, *The Charity Organization Movement in the United States* (New York: Macmillan Co., 1922), pp. 173 ff.; Feder, *op. cit.*, pp. 44 ff.

[24] *Nation*, September 9 and 23, 1875; September 19, 1878. Note, however, the expression of admiration elsewhere (March 4, 1875) for the German method of consulting "statisticians, lawyers, and professors" in preparing a law: "Barbarians and blatherskites are not allowed to take hold of the legislation of a civilized people, and 'go it blind,' to 'help the party,' or 'ease the market,' or 'move the crops.'" In 1879 E. L. Godkin, editor of the *Nation*, warned that government was already overexpanded and that there was not enough administrative ability available for the needs of either business or government (*International Review*, VI [June, 1879], 687 ff.).

[25] *Atlantic Monthly*, XLII (October, 1878), 385 ff.; see *New Englander*, XXXVIII (January, 1879), 85 ff., for a characteristic jeremiad on "the National decay," the "general stagnation," and "the dislike of stern recuperative theories."

sumers" and protested that "by its ascendancy over opinion acquired in a period of public danger, during which the people formed the habit of following its leadership ... the federal government has, therefore, practically dominated over all business and all industries." He proceeded to plead for "government institutions, simple, frugal, meddling little with the private concerns of individuals —aiming at fraternity among ourselves and peace abroad—and trusting to the people to work out their own prosperity and happiness."[26]

Academic support for the doctrine of total freedom came principally from William Graham Sumner, who was warmly welcomed as a witness by Abram S. Hewitt, chairman of the congressional committee investigating the depression in 1878: "Having got you, we propose to make the most of you." Sumner expounded his theory of depression, arguing that there was no alternative to natural freedom and no escape from the pains inflicted by depression upon individuals and classes. Society owed no man a living except "in the State prison"; and it was false doctrine that "like cures like" or that more inflation will correct the evils of past inflation. Sumner, however, admitted that "we have got to have a struggle with the great corporations before we get through.... We have not yet learned to charter corporations and still exercise the necessary control over them in the public interest." Sumner further advocated the substitution of an income tax for the tariff as relief for the "non-capitalists," provided that the exemption were as low as $1,000 and that no graduated rates be allowed to restrain the energy and the self-denial of the enterprising.[27]

[26] *Annual Message of Governor S. J. Tilden* (Albany, 1876), pp. 48, 58.

Abram S. Hewitt himself also held to the belief that "government interference is the last resort and a poor substitute for other courses, which, in the atmosphere of freedom and intelligence, ought to be effective." In 1876, in his presidential address before the American Institute of Mining Engineers, Hewitt had outlined such a course of voluntary action by proposing the creation of an annual fund of one million dollars in the anthracite coal industry by the levy of five cents on each ton produced. This money was to be spent for benevolent purposes, including schoolhouses, Sunday and night schools, hospitals, and reading-rooms, which might serve to stabilize a "growing and restless population," and help convert "a hell upon earth" into a "terrestrial and a Christian paradise." Such an example, Hewitt believed, would spread to other industries; he warned, however, that "the effort must be as serious and as earnest as is the business of producing the coal" and that the workers "must themselves be associated in the administration of the fund created and expended for their benefit."[28]

In contrast to the welcome and warm champions of "laissez faire" were the spokesmen of the "unprosperous" who strained the patience of two successive congressional committees in 1878 and 1879 with their "extreme views." The common theme characterizing their testimony was insistence on the propriety and necessity of positive government action. To Hewitt's question whether "society is improved by having the poorer

[27] *Depression in Labor and Business* (1878), pp. 183 ff., 206 ff.

[28] A. S. Hewitt, "A Century of Mining and Metallurgy in the United States," *Transactions of the American Institute of Mining Engineers* (Easton, Pa.), V (1877), 183 ff.; see also Allan Nevins, *Abram S. Hewitt* (New York: Harper & Bros., 1935), pp. 410 ff.

members aided," William A. Carsey, self-described bricklayer, editor, and spokesman for the Greenback Labor party, replied that it was "always improved. It is the best government that takes the best care of its people." Disclaiming socialism, Carsey argued that "the Working Classes are not opposed to the centralization of power in the hands of their own servants at Washington." Charles Sotheran, chronicler of early American socialists, protested against the scoffing attitude of the committee. The government must do these things, by amending the Constitution if necessary, or "the people will take it into their own hands." The Committee chairman, Hewitt, spurned this "foreign idea" and argued that the present Constitution was sufficient.[29]

A wealth of proposals for relief by governmental action was presented both inside and outside the congressional committees. Many of them related specifically to unemployment and the problem of surplus labor. Andrew Van Tuyl, superintendent of the New York Plaster Works, who also disclaimed radicalism, offered a typical program. Two million workers were without steady employment, and many were "tramping" the country looking for work and bread. They had been long patient but might not remain so. Hence the remedy lay in a compulsory eight-hour working day; in addition, there should be public works for the idle at lower wages and an asylum for the hungry and homeless in every county. Funds for these purposes should be raised by means of an income tax rising to as high as one-third on incomes of over $50,000. Charles B. Litchman, shoeworker and labor leader in Boston, waxed eloquent over the prospect that "the

time will come when mankind will have two Sundays in the week . . . one of them to devote to himself, the other to devote to his God. . . . That may appear radical and theoretical . . . but I think it is perfectly logical." A. R. Parsons, who described himself as "an active member of nearly every industrial or trade organization" in Chicago, and who became the central tragic figure in the trials growing out of the Haymarket Square Explosion in 1886, also demanded that Congress establish the eight-hour day or "the workers in world union will do it." This was only the start, according to Parsons; he envisaged an ultimate four-hour day; in the meantime, reduction of hours must continue until "the ingenuity of man will no longer be able to supply his wants by machinery to which the motive power of steam or electricity can be applied."[30]

With the eight-hour day were associated other proposals, some of which harked back to earlier crises; and they were to acquire familiarity through repetition and eventual acceptance. Among them were demands for a federal Bureau of Labor Statistics and for the financing of public works by means of government credit. Adolph Douai, representing the young Socialist Labor party, founded in 1876, offered the congressional committee his pamphlet entitled *Better Times*, containing a sixteen-point program.[31] It included, among others, legalization of the rights of labor to form unions and to strike, industrial accident compensation, government banking and insurance, as well as federal aid for education, woman

[30] *Ibid.*, pp. 111 ff., 124; *Causes of General Depression in Labor and Business* (1879), pp. 47, 192, 432.

[31] *Depression in Labor and Business* (1878), pp. 30 ff.; Adolph Douai, *Better Times* (Chicago, 1877), p. 31.

[29] *Depression in Labor and Business* (1878), pp. 54 ff., 151.

suffrage, the recall, referendum, and minority representation.

The paper-money issue was the subject of bitter controversy during these years of depression, even after it was apparently disposed of in 1875 by the provision for resumption, effective in 1879. It was linked with a policy of price stabilization by David J. King, a manufacturer of straw hats in Boston, in a manner reminiscent of proposals in earlier depressions. Arguing that constant purchasing power was the criterion of honest money rather than the fluctuations which favored shrewd manipulators, King advocated the establishment of a commission to follow the price changes of a number of staple products, as well as the trends of bank loans and discounts. An initial Treasury currency of 750 million dollars might then be varied as needed, in order to prevent deflation and to preserve a stable relationship between money and property values. A similar plan for honest money by tying it to a stable price level was offered to the committee by H. H. Bryant, a wholesale clothier of Boston, who charged that English bankers had spent half a million dollars to influence resumption legislation. Only a domestic national currency, freed from foreign domination, could provide protection for the American system and indeed serve in place of a tariff.[32]

Peter Cooper, the Greenback party candidate for the presidency in 1876, also appeared as a witness before the congressional committee in 1879 to plead

the cause of a people's money, as against the selfish interests of the English bankers and their American allies, who wanted to be paid in gold. He outlined a program by which the federal government would issue paper money to the states at 1 per cent interest; these in turn would issue it to the counties at 2 per cent, and the last would lend it to the people at 3 per cent.[33] This was only one example illustrating the persistent popularity of public credit schemes, represented best by Edward Kellogg's *A New Monetary System*, first published under a different title in the 1840's, in the wake of the depression following 1837, and reissued in the fifth to eighth editions between 1874 and 1883 alone.[34] The *Nation* thundered in 1875 that "the seizure of the Government by the inflationists would in fact mean that, for the first time since the Fall of the Roman Empire, the affairs of a vast society had passed into the hands of its most ignorant and unscrupulous class." It commented caustically upon the proposal in the *Cincinnati Enquirer* that the government pay its expenses with paper money for a few months: "Why should we all toil and moil when the Treasury could,

[33] *Causes of General Depression in Labor and Business* (1879), pp. 373 ff.; cf. the intense antiforeign note in the charge that "all the European bankers want is to bind you with a gold chain . . ." (*Depression in Labor and Business* [1878], p. 86).

[34] For the evolution of Kellogg's monetary theories since their inception in the 1840's see the biographical sketch prepared by his daughter in the fifth edition in 1874, and C. McA. Destler, *American Radicalism* (New London: Connecticut College, 1946), pp. 50 ff.; cf. the revival of old land-bank ideas in the mutual banking scheme advocated by Colonel W. B. Greene and sponsored by Wendell Phillips and B. F. Butler in 1875 (W. B. Greene, *Socialistic, Communistic, Mutualistic, and Financial Fragments* [Boston, 1875], pp. 51 ff.); also, for the newer co-operative credit banking scheme on the German plan, see *Bankers' Magazine*, XXX (September, 1875), 210.

[32] *Causes of General Depression in Labor and Business* (1879), pp. 395 ff. For similar proposals in earlier versions see S. Rezneck, "The Social History of an American Depression, 1837-43," *American Historical Review*, XL (July, 1935), 673; and "The Influence of Depression upon American Opinion, 1857-59," *Journal of Economic History*, II (May, 1942), 14.

if it pleased, foot our bills without loss to anybody?" By 1877, moreover, the *Nation*, ever sensitive to the shifting currents of opinion, deplored the rise of "The Silver Movement." Noting that silver bullion was falling below par, it challenged the constitutionality of recent acts of the Ohio and Illinois legislatures which made silver coins full legal tender for debts. In the same year, moreover, a congressional commission recommended the restoration of silver to full monetary standing, and the struggle for silver was on, replacing the lost battle for greenbacks.[35]

Popular sentiment against the scarcity of money and prevailing high interest rates was reflected in the agitation to retain the usury laws in the face of renewed efforts to repeal them in various states. With it was revived the traditional debate embracing arguments for and against regulation which reached back to Jeremy Bentham. In 1873 the *Albany Argus* hailed the failure of a bill to repeal the usury laws: "Wall Street, aided by 3700 of the most influential names of the State, has been defeated; and the Shylocks who would seize the small profits of struggling enterprise by demanding high rates of interest are thoroughly discomfited. New York has narrowly escaped the fate of Eastern States." In other states, among them New Hampshire, Connecticut, and New Jersey, usury laws were retained or reenacted. In 1876 Senator Morton C. Hunter of Indiana moved to fix a national interest rate of 6 per cent, arguing that the principal cause of depression, "and the one that lies at the bottom of all . . . is the enormous rates of interest

that our people have been compelled to pay, and are still paying." To the question why other prices should not be fixed as well, Senator Hunter replied that money was a yardstick for all other prices. Make money cheap, and "all articles of clothing and food will be correspondingly cheap."[36]

With the impact of depression upon creditor-debtor relations, the problem of a bankruptcy law also forged to the front as a political issue after 1873. President Grant recommended the repeal of the Bankruptcy Act of 1867 on the ground that its provision for involuntary bankruptcy on the initiative of a single creditor promoted panic and favored the sacrifice of assets by means of forced sales. Congress, however, merely amended the law in 1874, permitting the composition of debts with the assent of one-fourth of the creditors representing half the claims. This mild prodebtor legislation provoked the opposition of creditors, who complained that it encouraged delay, fraud, and waste of assets, thereby undermining the confidence of capitalists. The Bankruptcy Act thus became a football of politics; and repeal was finally voted in 1878, leaving the country without national bankruptcy legislation until 1898.[37]

In a number of states there was resort to the familiar stay laws for the protection of debtors' assets; and in 1878 the Supreme Court declared such laws an

---

[35] *Nation*, August 19, 1875; May 10 and 24 and June 21, 1877; *Bankers' Magazine*, XXXII (October, 1877), 287; *Economist* (London), XXXV (March 31, 1877), 352.

[36] For a collection of materials relating to this subject, both historical and contemporary, see *Stringent Laws against Usury the Best Defence of the People against Hard Times* (New York, 1878), esp. pp. 35 ff., compiled by Dr. Nahum Capen, self-designated adviser to state legislatures on usury laws.

[37] C. Warren, *Bankruptcy in United States History* (Cambridge: Harvard University Press, 1935), pp. 114 ff., 184; *Nation*, February 24, 1876, and March 8, 1877; *Depression in Labor and Business* (1878), p. 270.

unconstitutional impairment of contracts. The so-called "Granger laws" for the regulation of railroads were also under fire as an attack on property. In 1875 the *Nation*, for example, challenged the clause in the Illinois constitution requiring that a majority of the directors of a railroad company holding a state charter be citizens of that state. It warned that eastern stockholders wanted protection for their property; if the West wanted easy money, "the best thing it can do is to call off its legislatures and attorney-generals, as Minnesota has so sensibly done, and let the Eastern monopolists alone."[38] From an opposite viewpoint, however, Willard L. Flagg, president of the Illinois State Farmers' Association, expressed the intense sectional antagonism of interests in an address before the New York meeting of the Social Science Association in 1874. Quoting the famous passage from La Bruyère on the oppressed peasants of France, which supplied the theme of Millet's famous painting and through it the inspiration for Edwin Markham's poem, "The Man with the Hoe," at a later date, Flagg defended the current uprising of the western farmers as "an effort to reverse the unwise legislation that has, in the guise of corporate and other monopolies, created, fostered, and perpetuated a Shylock aristocracy, whose nobility compels no nobility, but, insatiate, plunders rich and poor with a cruel impartiality." It was part of an irrepressible conflict, and "as inevitable

as the progress of Democracy on the Earth."[39]

In the same period the myth of the free West was also being criticized, and the issue of land monopoly came under debate. The prospect of removing surplus labor to the land provoked sharply opposed views. On the one hand, the New York Society for Improving the Condition of the Poor insisted that, while cities must not make relief too easy, or recognize in any way the foreign idea of a right to work or to subsistence, the West, too, had its unemployed and certainly did not want the chaff from the East. The *Denver News* spurned "the refuse of the great city" and warned that " 'Be it ever so humble, there is no place like home' to starve in with comfort." On the other hand, a writer in the *Boston Advertiser* in 1877 argued that it was "the duty of government, philanthropic associations, and individuals to awaken attention . . . and to devise measures to help people to land ownership." He proposed the establishment of "Boards of Aid to Land-Ownership" in large cities, which would organize colonization companies for "associated migration, not communism, which is repulsive to American habits."[40] George Marshall Sloane, a former lawyer in Chicago but at the time a farmer in Wisconsin, complained to the congressional committee investigating the depression in 1879 that newspaper agitation had stirred the farmers'

[38] *Nation*, April 1, 1875, and May 2, 1878; Warren, *op. cit.*, p. 150; *Popular Science Monthly*, XXXII (December, 1887), 202 ff., quoting from the first program of the Grange adopted in 1874: "We shall endeavor . . . to discountenance the credit system, the mortgage system, . . . and every other system tending to prodigality and bankruptcy. . . . We are not enemies of railroads. In our noble order there is no Communism, no agrarianism. . . ."

[39] *Nation*, January 28, 1875; *Journal of Social Science*, No. 6 (1874), p. 112.

[40] Smith, *op. cit.*, pp. 64 ff.; cf. also R. S. Wright, *Cause and Cure of Hard Times* (Philadelphia, 1878), p. 18, urging that "peace armies be enlisted, instead of war armies. Let the national government enroll men as settlers, regularly, . . . who are to advance in proper order." For the opposite views see *Troy Daily Press*, December 1, 1874, quoting the *Denver News; Thirty-second Report of the New York Society for Improving the Condition of the Poor* (1875), pp. 65, 83.

prejudices against all strangers seeking work, and he cited the severe tramp laws which made it a crime for any man to ask for food at a dwelling. Other witnesses advocated a more effective Homestead Act to provide financial assistance as well as land for the settlement of poor men, and such bills were proposed in Congress.[41]

The fact of the matter was, however, that the rising issue of monopoly in land was stirring popular resentment. In 1877 a writer in the *Radical Review* protested that, while "between labor the parent and property its child there is no conflict, ... the gravest and most fraudulent usurpation of capital is property in land, which begets rent ... , ground rent, an inexorable, perpetual claim for the use of land, which, like air and light, is the gift of Nature." In its hearings at San Francisco the congressional committee of 1879 heard complaints against the concentration of landownership and received demands for the equal taxation of all land, in order to make large unutilized holdings unprofitable. This sentiment was echoed in Godwin Moody's account of bonanza farming in the West, with its accompanying class of wandering, landless laborers. It received definitive and passionate expression through Henry George, who wrote his *Progress and Poverty* between 1877 and 1879, as an "Inquiry into the Cause of Industrial Depressions, and of Increase of Want with Increase of Wealth," which proposed the liberation of both capital and labor from

the incubus of rent by the single remedy of taxation of land values.[42]

Another critic of monopoly in business also emerged during the depression of the 1870's. As a financial writer for the *Chicago Tribune*, Henry Demarest Lloyd became interested in the collusive relations between the railroads and the Standard Oil Company; and his article, "The Story of a Great Monopoly," was first delivered before the Chicago Literary Club. Rejected by the *North American Review*, it was finally published in the *Atlantic Monthly* in 1881, and the demand reportedly exhausted seven editions. Amplified by subsequent articles, written in the new manner of historical and realistic rather than abstract economics, Lloyd's study of the Standard Oil monopoly was eventually enlarged into the epoch-making *Wealth against Commonwealth* in 1894.[43]

The influence of depression was not confined to verbal grievance and vocal remedy, for which the two congressional investigating committees in 1878 and 1879 provided a sounding board. It made itself felt also in the shattered ranks of labor organizations, as illustrated by the fact that the number of national trade-unions was reduced from more than thirty to nine between 1873 and 1877 and that total union membership by 1878 was estimated at only 50,000. The drastic suppression of the terroristic Molly Maguires in the Pennsylvania anthracite coal area by the methods of espionage and legal prosecution revealed

---

[41] *Depression in Labor and Business* (1878), pp. 75, 148, 202, 407; C. Danhof, "Economic Validity of the Safety-Valve Doctrine," *The Tasks of Economic History*, December, 1941, p. 102. See *Troy Morning Whig*, January 8, 1874, for a communication from the International Workmen's Association, addressed to the Honorable B. F. Butler, and recommending a bill for assisted colonization, under the heading: "They Want To Go West"; also *Atlantic Monthly*, XLIII (May, 1879), 554, for other similar proposals.

[42] G. E. McNeill, *The Labor Movement* (Boston, 1887), p. 608; R. T. Ely, *Recent American Socialism* (Baltimore: Johns Hopkins University Press, 1885), p. 16; Moody, *op. cit.*, pp. 64, 134; *Causes of General Depression in Labor and Business* (1879), p. 310; *Radical Review*, I (November, 1877), 556.

[43] C. Lloyd, *Henry D. Lloyd* (New York: G. P. Putnam Co., 1912), I, 59; H. D. Lloyd, *The Lords of Industry* (New York: G. P. Putnam Co., 1910), pp. 1 ff., 52; Destler, *op. cit.*, pp. 134 ff.

the violent nature of the conflict between employers and labor in one industrial region.[44] In response, however, to the pressure of distress and opportunity, the scattered remnants of labor were temporarily rallied into various channels of political action and even became subject to the agitation of an incipient socialistic movement. There was, among other trends, the formation of a National party, which offered a program of industrial and agricultural reforms, including a labor bureau, public works, and the eventual regulation of "the agricultural production of the country—to determine for instance how many sweet potatoes would probably be needed each year, so that the market might not be oversupplied." It even visualized an international union with an international money, which will "lead to the gradual disuse or comparative abolition of nationalities, and the association of the people of the whole world for the government of the whole world." By the fusion of labor with the contemporary agrarian and greenback movements, there was founded after 1876 a kind of popular front in the shape of the National Greenback Labor party, which showed its greatest strength in 1878, with over one million votes cast and fourteen seats won in Congress. The Indiana platform of the party denounced equally "the red flag communism imported from Europe ... and the communism of the national banks, of the bond syndicates, and of the consolidated railroad companies."[45]

Another manifestation of renewed labor activity was the spread of the hitherto local and dormant Knights of Labor by the formation of district assemblies outside Philadelphia and by the adoption of a "Declaration of Principles" at its first General Assembly in 1878 at Reading, Pennsylvania. Its initial secrecy, viewed with alarm against the background of the troubled times, prompted Allan Pinkerton, the founder of the labor-spy system, to describe the Knights of Labor in his vitriolic compilation entitled *Strikers, Communists, Tramps, and Detectives* "as probably an amalgamation of the Molly Maguires and the Commune." Pinkerton further noted the outgrowth "during the past few years, under the leadership of agents of the Commune, ... of numerous organizations which have the same object in view, ... namely, the destruction of all government by the ballot, and if that shall fail, by force when the proper opportunity arrives."[46]

Pinkerton's allusion was to the increased activity of a relatively small number of socialistic agitators and advocates, many of them recent arrivals from Europe, who were exploiting the opportunity offered by depression to convert the remnants of the International Workingmen's Association into an American movement. Their efforts materialized in 1876 at a Philadelphia Congress in the guise of a Workingmen's party, which was in turn renamed the Socialist Labor party in 1877, the first appearance of an avowedly socialistic party on the American political scene.[47] The congressional

[44] J. R. Commons et al., *History of Labor in the United States* (New York: Macmillan Co., 1921), II, 175 ff., 195; N. J. Ware, *The Labor Movement in the United States, 1860–95* (New York: D. Appleton & Co., 1929), pp. 51 ff.

[45] "The National Party and Their Program," *Atlantic Monthly*, XLII (November, 1878), 521 ff.; N. Fine, *Labor and Farmer Parties in the United States* (New York: Rand School of Social Science, 1928), p. 67; Commons et al., op. cit., p. 240.

[46] McNeill, op. cit., p. 404; Allan Pinkerton, *Strikers, Communists, Tramps, and Detectives* (New York, 1878), p. 88.

[47] Fine, op. cit., pp. 88 ff.; Commons et al., op. cit., pp. 219 ff., 290; T. H. Greer, *American Social Reform Movements* (New York: Prentice-Hall, Inc., 1949), pp. 38 ff.

committee of 1879 heard several of its leaders or so-called "gate-money men," including one Benjamin Sibley, who testified that the Chicago membership was about six hundred, of which only 10 per cent was American, and the rest predominantly German, Scandinavian, Slavic, and Irish; but that the party had received nearly 12,000 votes in the recent municipal elections.[48] Chicago, moreover, early witnessed the split of the movement into moderate and militant branches, and the latter came under the influence of anarchist syndicalism during the 1880's, culminating in the Haymarket affair of 1886. Already in 1875 Chicago had become the seat of the first Lehr und Wehr Verein, whose object was announced in a German-language newspaper: "Inasmuch as the bourgeoisie of this place are building up a servile militia with its power directed against the workingman, the workingmen ... should join this organization and willingly give the few dollars necessary to arm and uniform themselves. When the workingmen are on their guard, their just demands will not be answered with bullets."[49]

In New York City evidence of similar agitation was revealed in the manifesto issued in 1877 by the Bread-Winners' League: "Citizens, organize. Unite with us and we will redeem the nation from bond, bank, and railroad monopolists by converting every city in this vast, rich, idle country into an active workshop."[50] In a more practical way, Samuel Gompers, as a rising young labor leader, was disturbed by the infiltration of "so-called Communists, ... perfectly willing to use human necessity as propaganda mate-

rial," and he concluded that the resulting sensationalism turned all organized society against the labor movement "and nullified in advance normal, necessary activity." With Adolph Strasser, who argued the case for pure and simple unionism before the congressional committee in 1878, Gompers then became confirmed in his belief that the trade-union "had to acquire a new meaning before it became an industrial agency." Both industry and unionism were in their "fledgling period" and must cease to be planless and uncouth.[51]

Uriah S. Stephens, first master-workman of the expanding Knights of Labor, was also alarmed by the infiltrating tactics of the socialists, and he warned a correspondent in 1879: "You must not allow the Socialists to get control of your assembly. They are simply disturbers, and only gain entrance to labor societies that they may be in better position to break them up. You cannot fathom them, for they are crafty, cunning, unscrupulous. . . . They rush to every gathering and attempt to man or officer it. Having done that, and having driven all decent men away, they are supremely happy in the delusion that they have spread their ideas still further."[52]

The combination of depression, labor unrest, and socialistic agitation provided a lurid setting for the great railroad strike in July, 1877, which stirred up passions and created an unprece-

---

[48] *Causes of General Depression in Labor and Business* (1879), p. 159.

[49] Fine, *op. cit.*, p. 106; Ely, *op. cit.*, p. 21.

[50] *Appleton's Annual Cyclopaedia* (New York, 1877), p. 750.

[51] Samuel Gompers, *Seventy Years of Life and Labor* (New York: E. P. Dutton & Co., 1925), I, 93 ff. Note that already in July, 1877, at the time of the great railroad strikes, a mass meeting held under the auspices of the New York Amalgamated Trades and Labor Union, under the leadership of Strasser and Gompers, adopted a resolution calling upon "all workingmen to organize in trade unions and to aid in the establishment of a national federation of trades, so that combined capital can be successfully resisted and overcome" (*ibid.*, p. 141).

[52] Fine, *op. cit.*, p. 47.

dented panic of public opinion. The provocation for the strike was a series of wage cuts, coupled with other money-saving and labor-cutting retrenchments in the operation of trains. Three of the four trunk lines in the East were tied up by the strikes, and for more than a week violent clashes occurred at a number of junction points in Pennsylvania, New York, Maryland, and West Virginia, which required the use of state militias and even federal troops. The bloodiest conflict took place at Pittsburgh, where the state military forces were besieged in a railroad roundhouse; and deaths totaled fifty civilians and five soldiers, in addition to a hundred or more wounded. In Chicago and St. Louis, moreover, something like general strikes developed, affecting factories as well; and socialists called mass meetings and arranged for the election of factory delegates to a general strike committee.[53]

The labor disturbances of 1877 thus constituted the climactic event of the depression and precipitated a violent outburst of alarm and threat that reflected a growing fear of class conflict and the "red spectre of communism." The anarchist, Peter Kropotkin, commended the railroad strikers, despite their failure, as an example "to the proletariat of Europe.... The blood of our brothers of America shall not have flowed in vain." Richard Ely, in his pioneer study *Recent American Socialism*, noted that "Get ready for another 1877" and "Buy dynamite for a second 1877" had become the slogans of violence and that an article

in *Truth, a Journal for the Poor*, offered advice on "Street Fighting ... Military Tactics for the Lower Classes." Ely explained the division between the "Blues" and the "Reds" as constituting the moderate and radical branches of socialism and cautioned the public that Bismarck's repressive measures had failed and that "Ameliorative Measures" might be a better remedy.[54] Henry James, another contemporary historian of American socialism, also observed that the riots of 1877 had "fitted exactly into the popular notion of communism," and one of their major consequences had been the creation of sections in more than fifty cities as "nurseries of socialism."[55]

The prevailing alarm communicated itself through both official and unofficial channels. The *New York Times* outdid even Pinkerton in describing the strikers as "hoodlums, rabble, bummers, looters, blacklegs, thieves, tramps, incendiaries, enemies of society, brigands, rapscallions, riff-raff, felons and idiots." The governors of New York, Rhode Island, and Pennsylvania deplored the frequent and costly resort to the militia for the restoration of order; but they recommended, nevertheless, reorganization and increased expenditures for this purpose.[56] Cyrus McCormick wrote to his son at Princeton about "the muttering of the coming storm" and warned him that his generation would have to deal

---

[53] *Message of Governor Hartranft*, pp. 9 ff.; *Message of Governor L. Robinson*, p. 16; *Nation*, August 2, 1877; *Economist* (London), XXXV (July 28, August 4, and December 29, 1877), 879, 912, and 1547; Fine, *op. cit.*, p. 34; Commons *et al.*, *op. cit.*, p. 185; Allan Nevins, *Emergence of Modern America* (New York: Macmillan Co., 1927), pp. 390 ff.

[54] Ely, *op. cit.*, pp. 21 ff., 61; R. Hunter, *Violence and the Labor Movement* (New York: Macmillan Co., 1914), p. 63; Fine, *op. cit.*, p. 108; S. Logan, *A City's Danger and Defence* (Scranton, Pa., 1887), pp. 9 ff.

[55] H. A. James, *Communism in America* (New York, 1879), pp. 28 ff.

[56] *Acts and Resolves of the General Assembly of Rhode Island* (Providence, 1877), p. 7; *Message of Governor Hartranft*, pp. 21 ff.; H. Harris, *American Labor* (New Haven: Yale University Press, 1939), p. 225; Pinkerton, *op. cit.*, p. 215; *Message of Governor L. Robinson*, p. 21.

with the problem. In 1877 McCormick bought equipment for the Second Regiment of the Illinois militia, which had "won great credit for its action during ... disturbances and can be equally relied on in the future." In 1878 Chicago businessmen formed a Citizens' Association for their mutual protection and raised a secret fund for the equipment of the Sixth Regiment with a battery; and Cyrus McCormick was urged to contribute liberally, since it was of "vital importance for our preservation."[57] In Cleveland, John Hay was shocked by the strikes of 1877 into an awareness that "a profound misfortune and disgrace had fallen upon the country." He was moved to write: "We are not Mexicans yet—but that is about the only advantage we have over Mexico." His sentiments eventually germinated into a novel, published anonymously as *The Breadwinners*, which indicted the alarming new phenomenon of labor politics and politicians catering to "the dangerous classes."[58]

Fear spread to religious circles as well, and Joseph Cook, a popular minister whose *Boston Monday Lectures* had wide circulation, condemned the "secret socialistic societies," composed mainly of foreigners and infidels; he gave notice to "the lawless classes at the bottom of our cities that, if they thoroughly alarm capital in this country, it will treat them with as much severity ... as the public peace may require. We shall keep order roughly here, if necessary; for all Ameri-

cans are capitalists, or expect to be." Professor Hitchcock of Union Theological Seminary concluded that "today there is not in our language, nor in any language, a more hateful word than Communism. The instant duty of society is to smite it with the swiftness and fury of lightning."[59] On the other hand, the Reverend R. Heber Newton, who was, with Washington Gladden, among the contemporary founders of the new social gospel of liberal Christianity, protested that "communism is a word wildly flung about in our social discussions. It is the stock bogy of our dry nurses of the pulpit, the press, and the platform, whereby they scare children of a larger growth from peeping into the darker places of our social system. ... It is even mixed up with the late 'complex marriages' of Oneida, and turned into a social diabolus, a name utterly shocking to polite ears."[60] The lofty humanitarian spirit of the new gospel was ably exemplified by President Chadbourne of Williams College, who argued that the alleged elevation of the masses had thus far been "the result of the chance conditions of our new fertile country rather than of the superiority of any system of labor or social order that prevails among us." But now there was "a cry for bread in a land of plenty. ... Men are without employment and look with jealous eyes upon capital as the oppressor, while capital is paralyzed by a sense of inse-

---

[57] W. T. Hutchinson, *Cyrus Hall McCormick* (New York: Appleton-Century Co., 1935), II, 615 ff. Colonel Thomas Scott, president of the Pennsylvania Railroad, urged the need of adequate federal forces for future use in such cases (*North American Review*, CXXV [September, 1877], 357).

[58] Introduction by C. L. Hay, son of John Hay, to *The Breadwinners: A Social Study* (New York: Harper & Bros., 1916).

[59] J. Dombrowski, *The Early Days of Christian Socialism in America* (New York: Columbia University Press, 1936), p. 6; Joseph Cook, "Secret Socialistic Societies," in *Boston Monday Lectures* (Boston, 1881), p. 47.

[60] R. H. Newton, "Communism," in *Social Studies* (New York, 1887), p. 299; C. H. Hopkins, *The Rise of the Social Gospel in American Protestantism, 1865–1915* (New Haven: Yale University Press, 1940), pp. 24 ff.; H. F. May, *Protestant Churches and Industrial America* (New York: Harper & Bros., 1949), pp. 79 ff.

curity." To the prevailing opinion that "things will in the end mend themselves," President Chadbourne rejoined that "the principle of action, in the end, must be that men must be cared for, and business must be subservient to this great work." Specifically he urged that "no city tolerate within its borders those who are not fairly housed, clothed, and fed, or that cannot show honest means of living."[61]

As if in reply to this plea, E. L. Godkin, the editor of the *Nation*, cautioned that "the didactic method" of Christianity would not work with socialism, which "is a revolt against all authority," and that to discuss it was to encourage it. In his own editorial column, Godkin criticized even more vigorously the "vague preaching about the wrongs of the poor" as a dangerous trend: "In our time and country both social speculation as well as the power to embody it in practice have ceased to be confined to parlors and dining rooms; it has got into the cabins and shanties, and has a look of possibility and reality there it has never had before."[62]

The alarmed state of mind, stirred by the labor disturbances of 1877, received violent and vehement expression in an article entitled "The Communist and the Railway," by W. M. Grosvenor, finan-

cial editor and publicist. Detecting the shadow of communism in such varied manifestations as the Granger laws, the greenback agitation, and the trade-union and labor demands, Grosvenor saw approaching, "by the light of flames at Pittsburgh, a terrible trial for free institutions in this country. The Communist is here . . . and already intelligent men are heard crying for a large standing army." Ominously he warned that "our free institutions will be destroyed by that spirit of communism, if unchecked, but not less surely by a centralization of power to prevent Communistic laws and suppress Communistic societies. . . . It would be simpler to elect Colonel Scott Perpetual President of the United States with the powers of a dictator. . . . We shall surely escape Communism, in that case, because we shall surely take Despotism as better."[63] With the confidence growing out of improved business conditions by 1881, the first report of the Illinois Bureau of Labor Statistics was, however, more reassuring that communism did not belong in this country, since it was based on the idea of retrogression rather than progress. Warning workers that socialism wanted more than high wages, the report reviewed its recent rumbling, concluding that better business would destroy it and that "it will be remembered only as a mad dream of the past."[64]

[61] "The Cry of Labor—What Answer?" *International Review*, V (September, 1878), 577 ff.; see also G. W. Julian, "The Pending Ordeals of Democracy," *International Review*, V (November, 1878), 734 ff.

[62] "Some of the Remedies for Socialism," *International Review*, VI (June, 1879), 676 ff.; *Nation*, July 18, 1878.

[63] *International Review*, IV (September, 1877), 585 ff.

[64] *First Biennial Report of the Illinois Bureau of Labor Statistics* (Springfield, 1881), pp. 163 ff.

CHAPTER VII

Patterns of Thought and Action in an American Depression, 1882-1886

The following essay originally appeared in the *American Historical Review*, Volume LXI, Number 2 (January 1956), pp. 284-307. It is reprinted here, in its entirety, with the permission of the American Historical Association and the author. The original pagination appears in brackets at the bottom of each page.

Patterns of Thought and Action in an American Depression, 1882-1886

IN the annals of American depressions, certain years have acquired both actual and symbolic significance as the customary and convenient means of dating them. Years of panic like 1837, 1873, 1893, and most recently 1929, have ushered in such cataclysmic runs on banks, breaks in the stock exchange, dramatic business failures, and particularly that so abrupt transformation of the public mood from optimism to pessimism as to obscure the more prolonged scope and evolutionary nature of the business cycle. In this respect, the period of depression falling between 1882 and 1886 appears to be uniquely different and scarcely typical. It was a depression without an initial or introductory panic, although one of modest and limited proportions gave promise of developing during 1884. The undramatic aspect of this period of depression became a matter for contemporary comment, as evidenced by the observations of Horace White on the "State of Trade" that here were all the marks of a "commercial crisis except one. It was not introduced by a money panic." Instead, since 1881 "the decline in stocks has been gradual, and there has been no collapse of credit, yet we are having all the other effects of a crisis in full measure. Manufacturing industry is depressed to a degree hardly surpassed in our history. . . . It is a common remark amongst those who do not look below the surface of things, that this is a 'rich man's panic'."[1] Carroll D. Wright, who pioneered in the new professional role of official economist, first as chief of the Massachusetts Bureau of the Statistics of Labor, and then in a similar capacity in the federal government after 1885, made this depression the subject of his first investigation and report. He also noted that it had developed without an accompanying financial panic and used it, indeed, as a basis for distinguishing between financial panics and industrial depressions. His conclusion was that "the present industrial depression is the first of its kind as an entirety. . . ."[2]

David A. Wells, on the other hand, interpreted the depression of the 1880's as only one stage in a sequence of "Economic Disturbances since 1873,"

[1] New York *Nation*, XXXVIII (Feb. 7, 1884), 112; George H. Hull, *Industrial Depressions* (New York, 1911), p. 155; Wesley C. Mitchell, *What Happens during Business Cycles* (New York, 1951), p. 12.

[2] Carroll D. Wright, *Industrial Depressions* (Washington, D. C., 1886), pp. 11, 65, 256.

constituting a relapse from the brief recovery of 1879–1881. It was fitted into the pattern of a "Great Depression," extending from the 1870's into the 1890's, whose deeper, underlying causes became a matter of concern and investigation by a Royal Commission on the Depression of Trade and Industry in Britain, and whose world-wide concatenation of cause, circumstance, and recurring crisis was traced by Max Wirth, the historian of commercial crises, to its culmination in 1893, when "The whole human race seemed to be in collapse: revolution and financial bankruptcy in Portugal and Brazil, the *coup d'état* in Chile, war in Central America, a financial and commercial crisis in Argentina, a building crisis in Italy."[3] In the United States too, the troubled 1880's provided a link of continuity between the stormy seventies and the rebellious nineties. If this was the gilded age of business expansion and laissez-faire dominance, it also became literally a silver age of populist agitation and radical upheaval. Frequent and prolonged depression provided a crucible in which were fired and tested ambivalent philosophies and programs, whether for the preservation of the status quo or the introduction of utopian innovations.

The symptoms and manifestations of depression during the 1880's were small and cumulative, rather than intensive and acute. They took shape in a steady decline of prices, both of commodities and stocks, a persistent dullness of business, and a continuing and rather plaintive cry: "When Will Business Improve?" With a steady stream of business failures, rising from 6,738 in 1883 to nearly 10,000 for both 1884 and 1885, there developed the threat of panic and the reported exposure of business scandals, as in the cases of Grant and Ward, involving the ex-President himself, as well as several national banks. It was noted that such "painful disclosures . . . have produced a natural insecurity which extends quite beyond the speculators in Wall Street to the great community of staid people who have more or less money to invest. Such events . . . are public disasters, because they shake faith in the personal honor upon which all business proceeds. It is that loss of confidence which produces panics."[4]

---

[3] D. A. Wells, "Economic Disturbances since 1873," *Popular Science Monthly*, XXXI–XXXIII (1887–89), *passim;* also by the same author, *Recent Economic Changes* (New York, 1890), pp. 1 ff.; H. L. Beales, "The Great Depression," *Economic History Review*, V (October, 1934), 65 ff.; Max Wirth, "The Crisis of 1890," *Journal of Political Economy*, I (March, 1893), 214 f., 234; H. C. Ager, in *American Journal of Politics*, IV (March, 1894), 246; J. W. Jenks, "The Causes of the Fall in Prices since 1872," *Journal of Social Science*, no. 35 (December, 1897), pp. 34 ff.

[4] *Harper's Weekly*, XXVIII (May 24, 31, 1884), 326, 342; *Bankers' Magazine* (New York), XXXVIII (September, 1883; June, 1884), 161, 901 ff.; XXXIX (July, 1884), 420, 460; Oliver M. W. Sprague, *History of Crises under the National Banking System* (Washington, 1910), pp. 108 ff.; A. G. Auble, "The Depressions of 1873 and 1882" (Ph.D. thesis in economics, 1949, in Harvard University Library), pp. 144 ff.

To the question, "Are We a Nation of Rascals?" was given the sober warning that "a young borrowing nation . . . with a character to establish cannot afford to be dishonest." L. J. Gage, president of the American Bankers' Association, cautioned his colleagues against the rising specter of silver but also reminded them that "Lending cures panics, while non-lending or niggardly lending aggravates them."[5] While the New York Clearing House Association arranged for the issue of clearinghouse loan certificates to relieve the pressure, as in previous crises, there was also a renewed demand for the reform of national bank abuses and practices, particularly in the payment of interest on country bank deposits. Wall Street bore the brunt of accusation as "an evil in the land, a danger to private wealth, a disturbing force in general business, and a foe to public morals." Somewhat prematurely the critic predicted that "The Exchange has seen its palmiest days. . . . The hand of decay is on it. The not very distant future will probably see it relegated to the limbo of departed things."[6] The equally censorious *Nation* complained that "stocks have been 'dull' ever since Garfield's death [1881] and have been growing duller. . . . We have been told for about a dozen times within the last two years that 'the liquidation', whatever that is, is over. . . ." The effect of all this "has been to produce general blueness or despondency," while the important influence of Wall Street was reflected widely:

It restricts consumption in all but the necessaries. It makes capitalists timid and doubtful, and by keeping a good deal of money idle, lowers the interest on all investments, and makes people of fixed incomes feel poor and economical. Altogether it may fairly be pronounced one of the strangest phenomena of modern times.[7]

The impact of depression upon production, wages, and employment became a subject for complaint and speculation, corresponding often to a predetermined purpose and prejudice. In October, 1884, *Bradstreet's* conducted a field survey of "the Industrial Situation" in the northeast of the United States, comprising twenty-two states, and arrived at a figure of some 350,000 unemployed persons, an average of about thirteen per cent of total employment, but varying widely by section, city, and industry. It estimated the wage reductions at from twenty to thirty per cent and saw little hope for improvement in the new year.[8] The Michigan Bureau of Labor Statistics reported factories closed and wages reduced from ten to twenty-five per cent and posed the familiar paradox: "At no other time in the history of this coun-

[5] *Bankers' Magazine*, XXXIX (September, December, 1884), 172, 425 ff.
[6] J. F. Hume, "The Heart of Speculation," *Forum*, II (October, 1886), 130 ff.
[7] *Nation*, XXXVII (Aug. 16, 1883), 132; Wright, p. 290.
[8] *Bradstreet's*, X (Dec. 20, 1884), 386 ff.

try have we had so much wheat, corn, wool, clothing, or so many boots and shoes. Yet destitution was never more prevalent." In Massachusetts, the Bureau of Labor Statistics, under Carroll D. Wright, carried out the first comprehensive state census of employment "in a depressed state" during 1884–1885 and noted that some 241,000 persons, or nearly thirty per cent of all employed persons, had been unemployed an average of about four months during the preceding year. Unemployment had been particularly heavy in such industrial cities as Fall River, Lynn, and Brockton, with percentages of nearly half or more of total employment.[9]

In 1885, the newly established federal Bureau of Labor made a sample survey of employment through the medium of fifteen agents in the field and reported that one million persons were unemployed, equaling approximately seven and a half per cent of all those employed in industry, agriculture, and trade.[10] At the same time, however, Terence Powderly, master workman of the Knights of Labor, estimated unemployment at two million persons, which was the real reason why "a deep rooted feeling of discontent pervades the masses. . . . the army of the discontented is gathering fresh recruits day by day. . . ."[11] The New York *Times* commented sharply upon the midwinter half-time employment policy adopted by the coal operators in order to keep wages down, the coal supply short, and coal prices up, that it "sent a cold chill through this region and is received with great dissatisfaction by the workmen."[12] The trend toward short-time employment and wage reductions, which provoked an outburst of almost hopeless strikes, prompted the New York state commissioner of labor to remind

Employers . . . that a reduction of ten per cent, which is below the average, entails a great deal of pinching and dumb and insensible suffering on the part of the working people. . . . It is a pity that those whose wages are low enough at any time, the very lowness of which should give them the right to at least look forward to steadiness of work, should have to bear the brunt of the suffering which periods of depression entail.[13]

For the strike-ridden year, 1886, the labor commissioner scouted the "almost universal opinion that there is work for all." Describing "the strife for work," and the "almost impossible task to arrive at the true number of unemployed

[9] *Eighteenth Annual Report of the Bureau of Statistics of Labor* (Boston, 1887), pp. 261 ff.; *Second Annual Report of the Bureau of Labor and Industrial Statistics* (Lansing, Mich., 1885), p. 116.
[10] Wright, p. 65.
[11] *North American Review*, CXL (April, 1885), 369; Henry David, *History of the Haymarket Affair* (New York, 1936), pp. 17 ff.
[12] New York *Times*, Jan. 5, 1884; *Seventh Annual Report of the Ohio Bureau of Labor Statistics* (Columbus, Ohio, 1884), pp. 5 ff.
[13] *Third Annual Report of the New York State Bureau of Statistics of Labor for 1885* (Albany, 1886), p. 298.

... in a large city like New York," he raised the rather unorthodox question whether it was "to be wondered at that the unions have felt constrained to throw up barriers and place restrictions around their trades in attempts to prevent those out of work from competing with those at work. ... It almost seems to be enlightened selfishness, an extension of the ideas upon which business is generally conducted."[14]

The *Nation,* however, deplored the current wave of labor unrest and pointed out that the declining prices had actually favored the workers and that the burden of losses due to the great deflation had fallen upon the corporations, "all without one cent of direct loss to the laborers themselves, and without any suspension of employment. They kept on at full work and fair wages for the 'black year' (1885). Doubtless in some quarters such a year would naturally be followed by efforts at retrenchment on the part of managers." This had not been, therefore, "a period of social distress, of which there is very little indeed, but ... a period of mental craze," which was "the salient feature of the striking epidemic."[15]

The reality of the business decline between 1882 and 1886 was, however, not to be denied, although its magnitude was not easily determined. Measured by an index comprising six series, which included railway revenues, pig iron and coal production, domestic cotton consumption, bank clearings, and merchandise imports, business activity fell by almost a fourth. The decline in the production of durable goods alone was approximately the same. New York City Bank Clearings dropped from more than forty-six billion dollars in 1882 to approximately twenty-five billion dollars in 1885. Similarly, immigration declined from nearly three fourths of a million in 1882 to less than 400,000 in 1885. But, what was equally serious, depression generated what Wright described as "a mental and moral malady which seizes the public mind after the first influences of the depression are materially or physically felt. Falling prices ... create apprehensiveness on the part of all classes, and the result is that the depression is aggravated in all its features."[16] This was not confined to wage earners but affected all levels and classes of society, from ministers, economists, and philosophers to farmers, businessmen, and poli-

---

[14] *Fourth Annual Report ... for 1886* (Albany, 1887), pp. 24 ff., 36; John R. Commons, *History of Labor in the United States* (New York, 1921), II, 357 ff.

[15] *Nation,* XLIII (Sept. 2, 1886), 191.

[16] Wright, pp. 66 ff., 245, 290; Alvin H. Hansen, *Business Cycles and National Income* (New York, 1951), p. 40; Edwin Frickey, *Production in the United States, 1860–1914* (Cambridge, Mass., 1947), pp. 64, 128–29; A. R. Eckler, "A Measure of the Severity of Depressions, 1873–1932," *Review of Economic Statistics,* XV (May 15, 1933), 75 ff.; Joseph Schumpeter, *Business Cycles* (New York, 1939) I, 340; Henry Clews, "The Late Financial Crisis," *North American Review,* CLII (January, 1891), 105; *Fourth Annual Report of the New York State Bureau of Labor Statistics,* p. 62; Auble, "Depressions of 1873 and 1882," pp. 142, 154 ff.

ticians. Familiarity with the experience of depression past and present stimulated a renewed concern with its causes and a quest for its cure that made up
in earnestness of effort what it lacked in sophistication or thoroughness of
analysis. The very absence of the more modern statistical approach to the
business cycle tended to accentuate the moral and even religious, as well as
the social and political aspects and applications of the depression complex of
thought and action. The carry-over from one crisis to another during the
generation following 1873 contributed to a secular trend and intensified the
cyclical pattern of discomfort and discontent, particularly in the two major
areas of agricultural and labor problems and relations.

Dr. Robert Giffen, a British statistician, remarked in 1885 that the pessimism of depression echoed and re-echoed in a rather "unintelligent manner,
with more than the usual emphasis laid on the assumption . . . that depression
is itself an uncommon and bewildering phenomenon . . . and that the present
depression is the worst on record." With equal relevance Carroll Wright
made the shrewd observation that each group judges depression according to
its interest; thus for bankers and merchants the trouble appears to lie in
"some financial or commercial reasons," while

Clergymen and moralists largely incline to assert that social and moral influences
. . . produce the industrial difficulties, . . . manufacturers incline to give industrial
conditions, labor legislation, labor agitation, . . . overproduction . . . ; while the
workingmen attribute industrial diseases to combinations of capital, long hours,
low wages, machinery, and kindred causes.

Under Wright's direction, the field agents of the labor bureau collected a long
list of suggested causes, linked, of course, with favored remedies covering
both the trivial and the important, and classified under commercial and
financial, industrial, political, social, and moral headings.[17]

In much simpler fashion, the *Nation* resolved the discussion of the causes
of depression conveniently under two heads. One was the monetary explanation, placing the blame for declining prices on the contracted supply of
money. The second explanation paradoxically discovered the ultimate causes
of low prices and curtailment of industry in the very progress of industrial
mechanization and the accompanying increase of production and productivity. This actually carried the long-run promise of a rising standard of living
for the workers, and the *Nation* ironically concluded that, despite their
recently enlarged activities, "the future is increasingly dark for socialistic
agitators."[18] In spite of this cheering note, however, there was considerable

17 Wright, pp. 76, 79, 269 f.
18 *Nation*, XXXVIII (May 8, 1884), 401; XXXIX (Sept. 25, 1884), 259; C. D. Wright,
"Cheaper Living and the Rise of Wages," *Forum*, XVI (October, 1893), 226 f.

contemporary alarm over the many manifestations of radical activity, as exemplified by the labor disturbances and the almost hysterical public reaction to them during 1885 and 1886. Significantly, Friedrich Engels, the colleague of Karl Marx, saw the proletarian promise of these activities and advised his American correspondent in 1886 that "the great thing is to get the working class to move as a class; that once obtained, they will soon find the right direction." He, furthermore, encouraged Florence Kelley in the translation of his *Condition of the English Working Class in 1844,* for publication in the United States at this opportune moment, and he predicted that "what the downbreak of Russian czarism would be for the great monarchies of Europe —the snapping of their mainstay—that is for the bourgeois of the whole world the breaking out of class war in America. . . . I only wish Marx could have lived to see it."[19]

The explanation of depression in terms of a production theory took various forms and offered many shadings, from overproduction to under-consumption and oversaving, as illustrated by Uriel H. Crocker of Boston, who advanced the theme of "Excessive Saving a Cause of Commercial Distress" persistently and repeatedly in each depression between 1873 and 1895.[20] But it was given most effective and persuasive, if rather premature, formulation by both Wright and Wells in a kind of crude version of the mature or saturated economy, anticipating Keynes and his doctrine in some respects. While reviewing enthusiastically the remarkable technological progress of half a century, and by no means denying the prospect of future growth, Wells, nevertheless, argued that the "world has within recent years, and for the first time, become saturated, as it were, under existing conditions for use and consumption, with the results of these modern improvements." This, rather than any scarcity of gold or money, was the chief cause of the prevailing and prolonged period of economic disturbances.[21] A more optimistic commentator, Edward Atkinson, however, foresaw in 1884 the end of the "present commercial paralysis" in the future growth of population and capital needs. New housing needs alone would require investment at an annual rate of two hundred million dollars, and an equal amount for new railroad and

[19] Karl Marx and Friedrich Engels, *Letters to Americans 1848–1895* (New York, 1953), pp. 157, 165, 285 ff.

[20] Uriel H. Crocker, "Saving vs. Spending," *Atlantic Monthly,* December, 1878; *Excessive Saving a Cause of Commercial Distress* (Boston, 1884); *Overproduction and Commercial Distress* (Boston, 1887); *The Cause of Hard Times* (Boston, 1895); for a survey of opinions, see *Ninth Annual Report of the Ohio Bureau of Labor Statistics* (Columbus, 1886), pp. 140 ff., 191 ff.; Joseph Dorfman, *The Economic Mind in America* (New York, 1949), III, 123 ff.; Paul Barnett, *Business Cycle Theory in the United States, 1860–1920* (Chicago, 1941), pp. 25 ff.

[21] Wells, *Recent Economic Changes,* p. 63; also *Popular Science Monthly,* XXXI (October, 1887), 772; W. G. Moody, "Workingmen's Grievances," *North American Review,* CXXXVIII (May, 1884), 502 ff.

manufacturing equipment, and Atkinson concluded that "this is a mental and not a material question—a question of confidence and not of capital." Henry George also rejected overproduction as "preposterous . . . when there is actual want among large classes."[22]

The most telling statement of the saturation theory emanated from Carroll Wright as an integral part of his analysis of the current depression in 1885. Noting its universal occurrence and similarity in all the manufacturing nations, Wright deduced that common conditions must stem from common causes, namely:

What is strictly necessary has been done oftentimes to superfluity. This full supply of economic tools to meet the wants of nearly all branches of commerce and industry is the most important factor in the present industrial depression. It is true that the discovery of new processes of manufacture will undoubtedly continue, and this will act as an ameliorating influence, but it will not leave room for a market extension, such as has been witnessed during the last fifty years, or afford a remunerative employment of the vast amount of capital which has been created during that period.

Announcing somewhat forebodingly that "the market price of products will continue low. . . . The day of large profits is probably past," Wright anticipated, but tended to discount, the growing role of future investment and development

outside the area of a high state of civilization, in China, Japan, India, Australia . . . , but this of necessity will be accomplished slowly, as these countries, not having the capital to make speculative movements, must depend upon the money-lending countries. Supplying themselves with full facilities for industries and commerce will give to each of the great nations of Europe and America something to do, but the part of each will be small and far from enough to insure more than temporary activity.[23]

Wright was critical of most of the remedies proposed at this time, including those which proposed the reduction of tariffs for the encouragement of freer trade and foreign markets for American goods. While Wells called for "more liberty—liberty for labor and capital alike to buy where and what they want, and sell where and when they please, without the interference of the Legislature," Wright made the logical but embarrassing point, "If all the producing nations of the world succeed in supplying themselves with manufactured products, and then all seek the relief which comes from selling their surplus products at low rates to their neighbors, the world has indeed reached an industrial epoch, and governmental policies and the rules of political

[22] *Nation*, XXXIX (Aug. 21, 1884), 152; *North American Review*, CXXXVII (December, 1883), 585.
[23] Wright, *Industrial Depressions*, pp. 80, 254–57; Hansen, *Business Cycles*, p. 64.

economy must be changed to meet the new conditions. . . ."[24] Significantly, at this very time, a British Royal Commission on the Depression of Trade and Industry was considering the same problem; and while the majority urged a more intensive search for new markets, a minority report recommended a policy of higher tariffs and preferential duties to offer protection for British goods and colonial markets, particularly against the threatened American competition.[25]

Whether it was merely the characteristic and familiar consequence of depression and distress, or what Wright described as "the arrival at a novel industrial period," certainly there was a proliferation of new attitudes, new principles, and particularly new policies, demanding or defining a more active role for the state and government in business. This trend gathered momentum despite the persistent preachments and protests, among others, by the caustic E. L. Godkin of the New York *Nation* and by that arch-apostle of laissez-faire and of Spencerian and Darwinian doctrines of survival and selection, William Graham Sumner. Eloquent essays by the latter on the "Forgotten Man," and "What Social Classes Owe to Each Other," emphasized the contrast between the self-sufficing and the self-supporting and the indolent and the incompetent, for whose sins and failures the former were taxed in the name of "the coming duty and the coming love." Sumner scorned "the passion for dealing with social questions. . . . The amateurs in social science always ask: 'What shall we do?' "[26] More realistically, however, Carroll Wright directed attention to "many influences like the great expense of standing armies, or war and revolutions, . . . but the brief review of the present industrial situation of the great communities involved indicates that statesmanship is required to establish such guards and checks in human affairs as shall lead to a safer and surer progress than that which has attended the past decade."[27]

A writer in the *Bankers' Magazine* was more specific in proposing that the troubles of the times called for a reassessment of needs and objectives. Propounding a rather nationalistic concept of economic policy, he discounted the doctrine of free trade and its corollary of cheaper goods for world markets, and he asked the rhetorical question: "In other words, is the world too small for all that are in it?" Rejecting an affirmative answer, he advised instead: "Let us think less of driving down the price of labor than of readjusting it to

---

[24] Wright, *Industrial Depressions*, pp. 261 ff.; D. A. Wells, *Free Trade Essential to Future National Prosperity and Development* (New York, 1882), p. 29.

[25] *Fifth Report* (London, 1886), xx ff., xliii ff.

[26] William G. Sumner, *What Social Classes Owe to Each Other* (New York, 1883), pp. 7 ff., 112, 127 ff.; "What Is Sociology?" New York *Herald*, Mar. 7, 1883; Moses L. Scudder, *Congested Prices* (Chicago, 1883), pp. 37 ff.; *Nation*, XXXVIII (Jan. 3, 1883), 6.

[27] Wright, *Industrial Depressions*, p. 258.

fit existing conditions. Let us think less of competition than of providing work for all. Let us believe that every energy, every thought and imagination may be put to some wise purpose, if we only will." The remedies lay "in shortening, to some extent at least, the hours of labor; in readjusting the remuneration of it on a reasonable and equitable basis, enlarging our wants through better municipal government, and in other ways that we might mention. . . ."[28] In another context, the *Bankers' Magazine* regretted the state of mind in the country which looked hopefully to possible war between Russia and Britain as a means of restoring prosperity. "Of course we should desire prosperity, but ought we at such a cost, and is there no easier or better way for bringing about this blissful condition than with fire and sword?" More appropriately, relief lay in the "unsatisfied wants of a public nature," among them "the want for better water, better gas, better sewerage, better streets, and a large number of things of that nature. . . . We may note right here, that as society advances, more of these wants are shared by the people in common, and their satisfaction must come by uniting with other persons. . . . Our wants are indefinite. The public could supply many of them." In more orthodox protectionist fashion, however, George Dean proposed an automatic increase of duties whenever imports exceeded five sixths of the value of exports, in order to maintain an essential favorable balance of trade.[29]

Such a pronounced drift of opinion away from laissez-faire in the direction of social and political responsibility for public well-being, particularly in a time of depression, permeated the many groups comprising American society, ranging from the religious leaders of the Social Gospel to the more concrete and deliberate programs of labor and farm organizations and the political parties of protest. It penetrated the thinking of academic economists and was reflected in the motivation and the avowed purposes of the American Economic Association, founded in 1886, whose platform was largely the work of Richard Ely, its first secretary and early advocate of the new social economics. Already in 1884, Ely discussed "The Past and the Present of Political Economy," contrasting the abstract doctrines of the English school and the German or historical school of economics to the advantage of the latter. A sympathetic student of the newly emerging forces such as the idealism of the Social Gospel and the agitation both of labor and socialistic organizations, Ely argued that

[28] "The Industrial War," *Bankers' Magazine*, XL (June, 1886), 881 ff.
[29] "War and Good Times," *ibid.*, XXXIX (May, 1885), 801 ff.; George W. Dean, *The True Cause of Every American Panic and Depression of Labor and Business* (New York, 1884), pp. 13 ff.

This younger political economy no longer permits the science to be used as a tool in the hands of the greedy and the avaricious for keeping down and oppressing the laboring class. It does not acknowledge laissez-faire as an excuse for doing nothing while people starve. . . . It denotes a return to the grand principle of common sense and Christian precept. . . . They recognize the Golden Rule.[30]

In more formal language, the platform of the American Economic Association in 1886 advanced as its objectives:

We regard the state as an educational and ethical agency whose positive aid is an indispensable condition of human progress. While we recognize the necessity of individual initiative in industrial life, we hold that the doctrine of laissez-faire is unsafe in politics and unsound in morals. . . . We hold that the conflict of labor and capital has brought to the front a vast number of social problems whose solution is impossible without the united efforts of church, state, and science.[31]

Similar conceptions of the responsibilities and relations of business and government, coupled with the pressures of discontented farm and business groups, found expression in the Interstate Commerce Act of 1887, ushering in the federal regulation of railroads, in its provision for an Interstate Commerce Commission, and in the establishment of the Bureau of Labor in the Department of Interior. The effective functioning of such agencies called for the zealous and dedicated services of a new type of public servant, as exemplified in Carroll D. Wright, the first commissioner of labor, appointed in 1885, in Edward Moseley, the first secretary of the Interstate Commerce Commission, and in Henry C. Adams, academic economist and chief statistician of that commission.[32]

A leading protagonist of the new economics, Adams discussed before the Constitution Club of New York City in 1886 "The Principles That Should Control the Interference of the States in Industries." Like Ely, he acknowledged the cleavage between the English and German theories of the role of the state, and he offered as a compromise solution that "society is the organic entity about which all our reasoning should center, and both State action and the industrial activity of individuals are but functions of the complete social organism. . . . The true principle must recognize society as a unity subject only to the laws of its own development." True conservatism fell, according to Adams, between "Anarchy on the one hand, which is individualism gone

[30] Richard T. Ely, *The Past and the Present of Political Economy,* Johns Hopkins University Studies (Baltimore, 1884), p. 64.

[31] *Publications of the American Economic Association,* I (Baltimore, 1887), 6–7.

[32] William Z. Ripley, *Railroads, Rates and Regulation* (New York, 1924), pp. 441 ff.; Thomas C. Cochran, *Railroad Leaders* (Cambridge, Mass., 1953), p. 197; James Morgan, *The Life Work of Edward A. Moseley in the Service of Humanity* (New York, 1913).

to seed, and socialism on the other, which, both historically and logically, is a revolt against . . . laissez-faire." [33]

Such a modest, middle-of-the-road, and, in the language of Ely, "ameliorative" modification of laissez-faire received reinforcement and encouragement from the moral and religious emphasis of the new Christian social philosophy, as represented by liberal ministers like Washington Gladden, R. Heber Newton, Lyman Abbott, Bishop Potter, and their considerable following in many church circles. Their education in the problems of an industrial society had begun during the depression of the 1870's and was continued during the 1880's; as one of the historians of this movement put it:

In 1876 Protestantism presented a massive almost unbroken front in its defense of the social *status quo*. Two decades later social criticism had penetrated deeply into each major church. Some of the most prominent Protestant leaders were calling for social reform; Christian radicals, not unheard, were demanding complete reorganization of society. The immediate cause of this important change lay . . . in the resistless intrusion of social crises, and particularly in a series of large-scale, violent labor conflicts. . . . The events of 1877, of 1886, and of 1892–94 were, however, impossible to ignore and difficult to explain away. [34]

By 1886, during the great upheaval generated by the labor disturbances, and particularly by the Haymarket Square bomb episode in Chicago, there was a general apprehension of the spread of anarchism and socialism, but Reverend Washington Gladden was equally concerned over the alienation of the workers from the churches and called for an "applied Christianity." In 1886 Gladden addressed the strikers in Cleveland on "Is It Peace or War?" and demanded the recognition of the rights of labor. Reverend R. Heber Newton cautioned that it would not take "many panics for property to cry aloud for some strong man to come forth as the savior of society." [35] Richard Ely, both as an economist and still more as a liberal Christian layman, warned of the threatened division of America into two nations and of the need of Protestantism to assume a new role as mediator. He traced the rise of socialism in America and of the more alarming forms of anarchism under the leadership of A. R. Parsons and Johann Most, with their doctrines of force and "the propaganda of the deed." There was "no danger of overthrow in

[33] Henry C. Adams, *Principles That Should Control the Interference of the States in Industries* (New York, 1886), p. 6; also in *Publications of the American Economic Association*, I, no. 6, p. 76.

[34] Henry F. May, *Protestant Churches and Industrial America* (New York, 1949), p. 91; Howard H. Quint, *The Forging of American Socialism* (Columbia, S. C., 1953), pp. 103 ff., 111.

[35] May, pp. 97 ff., 170 ff.; Aaron I. Abell, *Urban Impact on American Protestantism, 1865–1900* (Cambridge, Mass., 1943), pp. 60 ff.; R. H. Newton, "Cooperative Distribution," *North American Review*, CXXXVII (October, 1883), 327 ff.; D. D. Field, "Industrial Cooperation," *ibid.*, CXL (May, 1885), 411 ff.

our lifetime," but repression was not enough. He urged the need for a "wider diffusion of sound ethics" and for progress through the co-operation of "Science, the State, and the Church." He approved the efforts at reform sponsored by such organs as the *Christian Union,* as well as the program of the Federation of Trades and Labor Unions, and he expressed "admiration for the Knights of Labor. I believe it is a grand society, but I dissent from some of its principles. . . ." His advice to workingmen was to avoid drink, demagoguery, and "political partyism," and to look to churchmen and Christ for guidance, for "Christ and all Christly people are with you for the right."[36]

In a strange mixture of nationalism, racialism, and religious reformism, Reverend Josiah Strong, secretary of the American Home Mission Society, analyzed the many perils of the nation in 1885, including among them both socialism and mammonism, and in a concluding chapter on "Money and the Kingdom," he called for the Christian use of money, since "money is power in the concrete. It commands learning, skill, experience, wisdom, talent, influence, numbers," and it was necessary, therefore, to "Christianize the money power."[37] Reverend J. H. Wayland addressed the New York Charity Organization Society in 1886 on "The Old Charity and the New" and developed the rather startling theme that the latter, "pursuing its quest for the causes of poverty outside the poor, . . . finds itself confronted with the relations of employer and employed. At the head of its alphabet come the letters that spell the word *Justice.* . . . This giving of what is just and equal would do away very largely with the need of what we call charity."[38]

In another, more practical sense, the "New Charity" was developing into a combination of science and sentiment, of "economic method and supra-economic impulse." The waxing problems of urban relief, accentuated in years of severe depression, had produced periodic waves of "soup-houses" and diverse "Societies for the Improvement of the Condition of the Poor," which "sank into the sea of almsgiving." Coupled with the growth of public grants for outdoor relief, the total cost of charity in New York City alone exceeded five million dollars by 1882, and nearly another million and a half in Brooklyn. This brought forth the complaint by Mrs. Josephine Lowell, a pioneer figure in the professional social welfare field, that "too diffuse and gratuitous charity works evil rather than good." Pressure became particularly strong

[36] Richard T. Ely, *Recent American Socialism* (New York, 1885), pp. 61 ff.; also Ely, *The Labor Movement in America* (New York, 1886), pp. vii ff.; and *Social Aspects of Christianity* (New York, 1889), *passim;* Sidney Fine, "R. T. Ely, Forerunner of Progressivism," *Mississippi Valley Historical Review,* XXXVII (March, 1951), 599 ff.

[37] Josiah Strong, *Our Country: Its Possible Future and Its Present Crisis* (New York, 1886), pp. 85 ff., 118, 181.

[38] Quoted in Frank D. Watson, *The Charity Organization Movement* (New York, 1922), p. 277.

for the curtailment or elimination of public outdoor relief, and the Philadelphia Society for Organizing Charity protested in 1885 that "Experience proves that the public money voted for such relief is often wasted and sometimes stolen. Even when dispensed by honest officials it aggravates the evil it is presumed to relieve. Outdoor relief is always a strong temptation to imposture. Its effect on taxpayers is misleading, for they suppose their duty to the needy is discharged when they have paid their tax bills." There was equal objection to the chaotic and indiscriminate forms of private charity, as represented by the advertised distribution of "Bread for the Hungry" on the steps of the New York City Hall, which brought out a milling crowd of women and children, or as in the case of the well-established Philadelphia soup-houses, which traditionally dispensed "free soup and bread daily during ten or twelve weeks each year," by which "the evils of pauperism are largely engendered or perpetuated." Above all there was the chaos of an "armed neutrality" prevailing among the numerous separate agencies in a city like Philadelphia.[39]

The chief corrective offered lay in the Charity Organization Societies, which had made their appearance during the depression of the 1870's. By 1883 there were twenty-five such societies, and the number more than doubled in the next decade, including the principal cities. In 1886 the movement acquired a national organ in the establishment of *Lend a Hand*, as a monthly "Journal of Organized Charity," under the editorship of Edward Everett Hale. At times derided as societies "for the suppression of benevolence," these organizations were, nevertheless, lauded for their systematic co-ordination of relief activities; and it was argued that all funds were used for the "benefit of the poor," even where half the money was admittedly spent for administration, in order to prevent pauperism. Among their major efforts they sponsored the work-test for relief and promoted the establishment of laundries, woodyards, workrooms, loan societies, as well as wayfarers' lodges for homeless men, to replace the more usual resort to the cells and cellars of police stations, especially in winters of severe unemployment.[40]

In 1883 the New York Charity Organization Society canvassed labor opportunities for the able-bodied unemployed by correspondence with other agencies throughout the country but found few openings except for those

---

[39] New York *Herald*, Dec. 30, 1883; Amos Warner, *American Charities* (New York, 1894), pp. 372 ff.; Watson, pp. 87 ff., 283; Leah H. Feder, *Unemployment Relief in Periods of Depression* (New York, 1936), p. 46; *Third Annual Report of the Philadelphia Society for Organizing Charity* (Philadelphia, 1881), pp. 15 ff.

[40] *Eighth Annual Report of the Philadelphia Society for Organizing Charity* (Philadelphia, 1886), *passim; Second Annual Report of the Charity Organization Society of New York City* (New York, 1884), pp. 10 ff.; *Lend a Hand* (1886), I, *passim;* Watson, p. 225.

"rough and ready hands willing to brave the toils and privations of frontier life" in the Far West and Southwest. It discovered few willing to leave the city, "especially if they have had a taste of the poison of unearned bread," but it stressed the need of a "society or bureau, designed to bring work and workers together." By 1886 both the Cleveland and the Minneapolis societies had established employment bureaus. In New York, however, the labor commissioner described the sad plight of the unemployed as the victims of private employment agency abuses and reported that "In many trades, particularly where there are no unions, the out-of-work members float quietly upon the surface, and but few know or care how they exist. They may get one day, or two days', or three days' work a week, or none at all. . . . Many, far too many are forced into the saloons, where they are expected to be found when wanted."[41]

The new "scientific" principles and policies of charity organization and restriction combined with the relatively moderate and modest scope of the depression during the 1880's to keep the relief activities within their limited and prescribed channels. Certainly there was no such pressure of unemployment and distress as was to burst the bounds of organized charity during the crucial winter of 1893-1894, and produce a new wave of relief agitation and activity. During the 1880's, both the New York and Boston Charity Organization Societies arrived at a similar figure of fifty-two per cent among their relief applications as needing work rather than relief; between a fifth and a fourth were "worthy of temporary relief," and some seventeen per cent were "unworthy of relief." In 1886, the long-established New York Association for Improving the Condition of the Poor congratulated itself that the demands upon it had been moderate, and summarized "the influences that had been at work. . . . Our machinery for sifting the wheat from the chaff has had a broad effect in deterring many . . . ; only those who have a strong case are privileged to become our clients. . . . Of course it is well known that the Association never knowingly aids persons refusing work."[42]

As if to compensate for the tightened theories and practices of relief, the reportedly materialistic and callous character of the gilded age was considerably leavened by a substantial volume of contemporary criticism and reformism, much of it frankly idealistic and utopian. This preoccupation with remedies and reforms in part stemmed from the deep roots of recurring

[41] *Fourth Annual Report of the New York State Bureau of Labor Statistics*, pp. 25 ff.; *Second Annual Report of the New York City Charity Organization*, pp. 21, 46; Watson, p. 226.
[42] *Forty-Third Annual Report of the New York Association for Improving the Condition of the Poor* (1886), p. 13; *Fourth Annual Report of the New York Charity Organization Society* (1886), p. 19; *Fifteenth Annual Report of the Philadelphia Society for Organizing Charity* (1894), p. 7.

depression since 1873; but the common denominator underlying much of it was the persistent quest for acceptable and practicable American solutions rather than an alien and socialistic program. The conservative John Hay and Henry Adams were, to be sure, reinforced in their pessimistic tendencies and turned to anonymous fiction during the 1880's, the former in *The Bread-winners* and the latter in *Democracy,* to depict the patterns of business, labor, and political corruption. Liberal opinion, however, was confirmed in its traditional optimism, despite depression, and intensified the purposeful if critical examination of the social scene. Even Andrew Carnegie, the articulate titan of industry, was eager to develop an apologetic rationale of the status quo, extolling the partnership of capital and labor and the achievements of "Triumphant Democracy," while also admitting the claims of unionism, collective bargaining, and arbitration. In 1884 it was reported that "hardly a novel is published without its little contribution to the literature of the social problem, hardly an issue of a newspaper but has its leader on some phase of what, as the world is coming to feel, is the greatest of all questions, or some lamentation over the threatening revolution."[43]

One special variety of this literature was the economic and utopian novel, of which numerous examples appeared in the two decades after 1880. Among them were businessmen's utopias, religious and humanitarian utopias, technocratic and theocratic utopias, and even a satiric utopia ridiculing the absurdities of these American dreams; only a few of the whole number could be described as strictly socialistic in intent.[44] Best known and most influential in this utopian flood was, of course, *Looking Backward,* first published in 1888, by Edward Bellamy, son of a New England minister and journalist by occupation. Already in 1879 he had serialized for the press the *Duke of Stockbridge,* a historical novel of class conflict in an earlier period of depression, dealing with Shays' Rebellion of 1786. In *Looking Backward,* he turned prophet and pictured the one "Great Trust" as the logical outgrowth of the current "Epoch of Trusts." This promise of a nationalist utopia struck an immediate popular response, and appealed particularly to middle-class reformers. It inspired moreover a nationalist movement throughout the country, and nationalist clubs sprang up after 1888 from Boston to the Pacific Coast.

[43] L. A. Rose, "A Bibliographical Survey of Economic and Political Writings, 1865–1900," *American Literature,* XV (January, 1944), 391, 407; Walter F. Taylor, *The Economic Novel in America* (Chapel Hill, 1942), p. 58; Boyd C. Shafer, "The American Heritage of Hope," *Mississippi Valley Historical Review,* XXXVII (December, 1950), 427 ff.; Edward C. Kirkland, *Business in the Gilded Age* (Madison, 1952), pp. 41 ff.; *Labor: Its Rights and Wrongs,* prepared under the auspices of the Knights of Labor (Washington, 1886), p. 104; *Forum,* I (April, August, 1886), 114, 538 ff.

[44] Vernon L. Parrington, *American Dreams* (Providence, 1947), pp. 176 ff.; A. Forbes, "Quest for Utopia," *Social Forces,* VI (December, 1927), 182.

Bellamy had become a household name and was indeed taking himself seriously as the source and sponsor of a program of reform which was hailed as "the American type of socialism, the new Nationalism."[45]

In contrast to Bellamy's acceptance of the nationalized trust, an equally popular but sharply antagonistic criticism was voiced by Henry Demarest Lloyd, whose views were also derived from a background of journalistic experience as a financial correspondent during the depression of the 1870's. In the following decade, Lloyd publicized the monopolistic trends and activities of the new "Lords of Industry," and particularly their abusive manipulations of the railroads and railroad rates. Lloyd too contributed to the shaping of the "new conscience," and eventually expounded the dilemma of "Wealth against Commonwealth"; he insisted that following an "era of material inventions, we now need a renaissance of moral inventions. . . . Morals and values rise and fall together. If our combinations have no morals, they can have no values."[46]

Still another proponent of protest and reform, distinctively American in inspiration and significantly appearing out of the West, became articulate in this period of rising agrarian depression and discontent. To the hazards and handicaps of climate and weather, tightened credit and depressed prices, and growing grievances against railroads, banks, and middlemen, was added the specter of land monopolization and the disappearing frontier. Henry George first published his epoch-making book, *Progress and Poverty,* in 1879, but the appeal of its program for the emancipation of both capital and labor from the burden of rent and land monopoly spread during the following decade, and by 1885, according to Ely, "tens of thousands of laborers have read *Progress and Poverty,* who never before looked between the two covers of an economic book, and its conclusions are widely accepted articles in the workingman's creed."[47] Even Karl Marx, who discounted Henry George as a bourgeois imitation of the early Ricardian radicals and land reformers, and

---

[45] Forbes, p. 183; F. L. Greene, "American Socialism," *American Journal of Politics,* IV (April, 1894), 414, 438; J. R. Bridge, "Nationalistic Socialism," *Arena,* I (January, 1890), 153 ff., 184 ff.; Arthur E. Morgan, *Edward Bellamy* (New York, 1944), pp. 73 ff., 204 ff.; Quint, chap. III, "Bellamy Makes Socialism Respectable"; Donald D. Egbert and Stow Persons, *Socialism and American Life* (Princeton, 1952), I, 269 f. Cf. the contemporary and popular *Caesar's Column,* by the eccentric Populist, Ignatius Donnelly, depicting the producers' utopia rising ultimately from the wreckage of repeated cycles of depression.

[46] H. D. Lloyd, "The Lords of Industry," *North American Review,* CXXXVIII (June, 1884), 552; Caro Lloyd, *H. D. Lloyd* (New York, 1912), I, 59 ff.; Chester McA. Destler, *American Radicalism* (New London, Conn., 1946), pp. 134 ff.

[47] Ely, *Recent American Socialism,* p. 17; Arthur N. Young, *The Single Tax Movement in the United States* (Princeton, 1916), pp. 66 ff.; John D. Hicks, *The Populist Revolt* (Minneapolis, 1931), pp. 1 ff.; Hallie Farmer, "The Economic Background of Frontier Populism," *Mississippi Valley Historical Review,* X (March, 1924), 406 ff.; Dorfman, *Economic Mind,* III, 141.

who scoffed at his suggestion that the evils of capitalism would vanish with the appropriation of rent, nevertheless wrote his American correspondent that George's book had created a "sensation . . . among you, because it is a first, though unsuccessful effort at emancipation from orthodox political economy."[48] In 1886, Henry George became the candidate of the United Labor party for mayor of New York City, and conducted an intensive campaign in which he ran second to the Democratic winner, Abram Hewitt, and ahead of Theodore Roosevelt, the rising young Republican politician. This temporary depression-inspired fusion of radical elements disintegrated with business recovery in 1887; and the single-tax movement was divorced from the more radical labor and socialist elements and from the anti-poverty agitation headed by Father McGlynn. The short-lived vogue of land and labor or Henry George clubs provided a precedent for the nationalist clubs inspired by Edward Bellamy's *Looking Backward;* and both illustrated the inclination of American opinion in this period to accept novel ideas and to grasp for their practical applications, however remote or utopian.[49]

The growth of landlordism and farm tenancy served as a favorite contemporary theme for doleful exposition and dire prediction. William Godwin Moody linked together the plight of the small farmer and the laborer and stressed their community of interest and policy in the breakup of large landholdings and railroad monopoly. He advised the formation of a "Central Council of representative men from leading labor organizations," to undertake a program of public education and political action, to be supported by the workers: "one dime each week, with their ballots to sustain the contributions, would be the beginning of a new era for the relief and comfort of labor."[50] In a more direct way, there was a nostalgic apprehension of the impending disappearance of free land as an outlet for discontented and depressed labor. Henry George voiced the Malthusian theme: "Our population is increasing. We have now practically reached the limit of our public domain. . . . The value of land is rising. . . . We are on the verge of an event which is, in some respects, the most important . . . since Columbus sighted land—the fencing in of the last available section of the American domain." As unemployment spread in the mills of Fall River during 1883, the Cotton Spinners' Union circularized "A Remedy for Surplus Labor" by suggesting the co-operative purchase and colonization of land by the unemployed, which

[48] Marx-Engels, *Letters to Americans*, pp. 128–29.
[49] Young, pp. 96 ff., 136; Egbert and Persons, I, 239 ff.
[50] William Godwin Moody, *Land and Labor in the United States* (New York, 1883), pp. 112 ff., 330 ff.; Roy M. Robbins, *Our Landed Heritage* (Princeton, 1942), pp. 268 ff.; *Bankers' Magazine*, LX (March, 1886), 646.

won approval as a better use of union funds than strikes. The Senate committee investigating the relations of labor and capital in 1883 received various proposals for the removal of surplus population to the interior, among others from T. A. Devyr, a veteran of the National Reform Association and the homestead agitation dating back to the 1840's. Picturing the unhappy plight of the unemployed, he repudiated Henry George's land nationalization doctrines and offered instead a modernized homestead program, under which the army engineers would lay out townships and the government would finance the settlement of workers on the land.[51]

The *Nation* derided the homestead "Cure for Discontent"; it pointed out that people preferred the town to the farm, and it summarized realistically the contemporary safety-valve theory:

There is doubtless always a reflex movement of population toward agriculture after a commercial or financial crisis, but the existing opportunities of getting farms are amply sufficient to create it. At best it works slowly. Men do not change their occupations by "rushes." They struggle, and hope and contrive, and wait for better times a good while before pulling up stakes and striking out for fresh woods and pastures new.

The *Nation* found occasion to comment upon a homestead bill in the Ohio legislature in 1885, "to provide against the evils resulting from periodical depression in manufacturing industries and to promote agriculture." It suggested that the lowering of duties and revival of industry would offer more immediate relief, and it argued that "briery, thistly land in Ohio is a bad place for the best farmer in existence. For a coal-and-iron man who never farmed in his life, it would be simply a sort of State poorhouse."[52]

The impact of depression reinforced the "need for a change," which took political as well as economic form. One major change concerned "the great issue" of tariff reform. In a year-end survey of growing unemployment for 1883, the New York *Herald* warned that workers were beginning to see "the deception and delusion practiced upon them by the policy of high protection." They were gradually learning that "under a high tariff the only way the manufacturers . . . have to reduce cost of production is to cut down their people's wages." The *Nation* too quoted approvingly the ironmaster, Abram Hewitt, that "extra-protective duties merely result in over-production, and in

---

[51] Senate Committee on Labor and Education, *Investigation of Labor and Capital* (Washington, 1885), II, 833 ff., 1337; New York *Herald*, Dec. 15, 1883; *North American Review*, CXLII (1886), 398; Lee Benson, "Background of Turner's Thesis," *Agricultural History*, XXV (1951), 62 ff.; Robbins, pp. 271 ff.; Henry N. Smith, *Virgin Land: Myth and Symbol* (Cambridge, Mass., 1950), p. 251.
[52] *Nation*, XL (June 25, 1885), 521; also XXXVII (Aug. 30, 1883), 178.

the general derangement of industry, and in consequent suffering to work-ingmen by the loss of employment and reduction of wages."[53]

Tariff revision, coupled with depression-inspired appeals to workers, thus figured prominently among the issues of the presidential campaign of 1884, which resulted in Cleveland's election. Henry Ward Beecher extolled the virtues of the workingmen and in a Wall Street mass meeting boasted of his own descent from them. The New York *Times* noted that "times have changed" since 1880. Then

> business was booming. . . . Both employers and workmen were contented, and were afraid of a change for the worse. . . . That is not the present situation. Busi-ness is dull. . . . Work is irregular. . . . Wages have been largely reduced. . . . Capital is timid. . . . The workingmen as well as their employers are asking them-selves why they should vote for a high-tax party when high taxes, uninterrupted for twenty years, have ended in general depression and distress.

The *Nation* rejected the Republican plea that change was dangerous and might bring on a crisis; the Republicans had no "saving grace . . . to ward off panics," since they have already had two since 1873. Paradoxically, the *Nation* argued that Cleveland was solid and safe, while Blaine was a specu-lator and corruptionist. It condemned, moreover, certain "Communistic fea-tures of the Republican platform, among them its opposition to "the importa-tion of contract labor," and "the acquisition of large tracts of land by corporations or individuals"; all of this was a "catering to the tastes and dogmas of the Communists."[54] Four years later, in 1888, President Cleveland, newly defeated for re-election, was still calling upon Congress for tariff revision; and he too invoked the charge of communism but in a quite dif-ferent connotation. He condemned "the communism of combined wealth and capital, the outgrowth of overweening cupidity and selfishness, . . . not less dangerous than the communism of oppressed poverty and toil, which, exasperated by injustice and discontent, attacks with wild disorder the citadel of rule."[55]

In the general sense of economic contraction and social conflict arising during the 1880's, the sentiment and agitation for the regulation and restric-tion of immigration gained headway. The Senate committee on labor and capital in 1883 heard protests against "imported labor," and a proposal from John E. Morrissey of New York for "a duty attached to every imported

---

[53] *Ibid.*, XXXVIII (Jan. 3, 1883), 6; New York *Herald*, Dec. 14, 17, 24, 1883.
[54] *Nation* XXXVIII (June 26, 1884), 540; XXXIX (Oct. 16, 1884), 324; New York *Times*, Oct. 28, Nov. 1, Dec. 4, 1884.
[55] James D. Richardson, ed., *A Compilation of the Messages and Papers of the Presidents* (20 vols., New York, 1911–16), XII, 5361.

laborer," since "the foreign element which has no real interest in the national welfare of this country has been and still is the greatest weapon in the hands of capital for crushing labor." Carroll D. Wright believed that the country could use beneficially an annual immigration of from two hundred to two hundred and fifty thousand, whereas even during the low year 1885 immigration totaled nearly four hundred thousand persons. The more optimistic Edward Atkinson, however, challenged the developing antagonism to immigration, as "almost pusillanimous to refuse a refuge to the oppressed and to the industrious and capable, for fear that the institutions of this country may suffer."[56]

Even such a liberal political and business leader as Abram Hewitt, mayor of New York City, became concerned over the problem of the many millions of immigrants received but not yet assimilated into the United States in the quarter century since the outbreak of the Civil War. Hugh McCulloch, formerly a Republican Secretary of the Treasury, reviewed the "Public Questions Still Pending" in 1887, against a background of strikes and violence which made the year 1886 one of the most turbulent in American labor and social history. He condemned the contemporary pressures for relief, the confiscation of land, the attack on property, for which he held universal suffrage responsible, particularly when conferred upon the foreigners: "With the workingmen have come men who are revolutionists by nature, or who have been made such by real or fancied injustice in their lands. . . . If the Republic is to be short-lived, unrestricted manhood suffrage will be the cause." That the foreigners "with their Old World passions" were primarily accountable for the economic and social disturbances also received the sanction of that noted observer of the American scene, James Bryce, who denied that any "of the questions which now agitate the nation is a question between the rich and poor. . . . Everything that government, as the Americans understand the term, can give them, the poorer class have already. . . . Hence the poorer have had little to fight for, no grounds for disliking the well-to-do, few complaints to make against them."[57] The *Bankers' Magazine* was, however, more realistic in reporting that, even more terrible and destructive than the March gales of 1886, "have been the labor troubles which have assumed such vast and serious proportions as have never been experienced in this or any other country." This was deplorable, but "when times are bad and there

[56] E. Atkinson, "Incalculable Room for Immigrants," *Forum*, XIII (May, 1892), 370; Wright, p. 245; Senate Committee on Labor and Education, II, 1338; M. Heald, "Business Attitudes toward Immigration," *Journal of Economic History*, XIII (Summer, 1953), 291; Harry Jerome, *Migration and Business Cycles* (New York, 1926), pp. 34 f.

[57] James Bryce, *The American Commonwealth* (London, 1888), II, 466; David, p. 24; Thomas H. Greer, *American Social Reform Movements* (New York, 1949), pp. 38 ff.; Hugh McCulloch, *Men and Measures of Half a Century* (New York, 1888), pp. 519, 529.

is not enough commerce to keep them employed, and they are compelled to fight each other for a share of that little, then wages are reduced. Strikes are the natural outcome of this state of things."[58]

The public reaction to the strikes and social disturbances of 1886 was, in any event, vehement, if not virulent. Samuel Gompers concluded that the Haymarket bomb not only killed the Chicago policemen but also the eight-hour movement for years, "notwithstanding we had absolutely no connection with these people." Henry Clews, English-born broker, reproachfully reminded labor that "strikes may be justifiable in other countries, but . . . not . . . in our country. The Almighty has made this country for the oppressed of other nations . . . and the hand of the laboring man should not be raised against it." Sumner was characteristically succinct: "If we want more wages, the only way to get them is by working, not by not working."[59] The *Nation* was at once sardonic and savage in approving the "cold lead" used by the Wisconsin militia ordered out by Governor Rusk when riots broke out in Milwaukee: "Unlike Illinois, Wisconsin has a governor to be proud of. . . . A single volley at long range showed the mob that the troops 'meant business', and broke the backbone of the insurrection against authority." The fact that a Polish-born alderman in Milwaukee had protested against the use of violence by the militia prompted the *Nation* to make the cruel jibe that such behavior was "producing a rapid change of opinion about the partition of Poland." Instead of regarding it "as a monstrous crime on the part of the three Powers which took part in it, . . . the events of the last few weeks are leading many to condemn the Powers for not having gone further and partitioned the individual Poles as well as Poland. . . ."[60]

From quite a different standpoint, and for a very different purpose, Friedrich Engels too was critical of the foreign and particularly the German element and its dogmatic attitude toward the American labor movement. Hailing the exciting events of 1886 as the birth of a real working-class consciousness, Engels advised his American correspondent on the proper tactics of infiltration by fostering a kind of popular front and fusion of all radical groups, and he warned that

the Germans have not understood how to use their theory as a lever which could set the American masses in motion. . . . What is more, they learn no English on principle. . . . But from all I hear, the Knights of Labor are a real power . . . and

[58] *Bankers' Magazine*, XL (April, 1886), 786; E. B. Mittelman, "Chicago Labor in Politics," *Journal of Political Economy*, XXVIII (May, 1920), 407 ff.

[59] David, pp. 39, 186 ff.; Commons, II, 386; Egbert and Persons, I, 238; *Harper's Weekly*, XXX (May 15, 1886), 315; *Public Opinion*, I (May 15, 1886), 83 ff.; cf. "The Chicago Anarchists of 1886," *Century Magazine*, XLV (April, 1893), 803 ff., for an apologetic by Judge J. E. Gary.

[60] *Nation*, XLII (May 13, 1886), 391.

I think it is necessary to work inside them, to form within this still quite plastic mass a core of people who understand the movement and its aims and will therefore take over the leadership . . . when the inevitably impending breakup of the present 'order' takes place.[61]

From this background of social unrest and violence, there emerged a number of problems and principles which called for calm and judicious consideration, if possible. In April, 1886, President Cleveland sent to Congress a special message on labor, the first of its kind in American history, recommending legislation "upon this serious and pressing subject." The principal proposal called for the creation of a three-member commission of labor that would investigate and report to Congress on labor disputes and would offer voluntary arbitration in cases of interstate commerce, and in all other cases at the request of the state government concerned. A number of states, including Kansas, New York, and Massachusetts, had already enacted similar provisions for arbitration, a currently popular cure-all for labor troubles. The *Nation,* however, protested against Cleveland's proposed measure, as uncalled-for intervention and centralization on the part of the government, and it complained that "state rights, regarded as a code of political principles, have long since disappeared."[62] The spreading practice of the labor boycott was reported by *Bradstreet's* in its enumeration of 237 cases during 1885 alone; and it was condemned as "a system of meddlesome tyranny. . . . But when it takes the attitude and spirit of a Malay running amuck through an innocent crowd, society must protect itself at any cost."[63]

Richard Ely, however, deplored the prevailing trends both toward labor violence and counter-repression by reminding the country that the boycott was an old American tradition, harking back to precedents in the Revolutionary and the antislavery movements; and, while "it is a movement in the wrong direction," legal and judicial methods of prohibition were not the best or only way to correct it. Ely pointed to Bismarck's failure in using force against the German socialists, and advised that "it is a time for those men to keep quiet, who, little in heart and mind, have no better remedy for social phenomena which do not please them, than physical force. They fail absolutely to understand the age in which they live, and will involve us all in ruin, if allowed to execute their savage plans. This applies equally to men of all social classes."[64]

[61] Marx-Engels, *Letters to Americans,* pp. 162–63; G. E. McNeill, ed., *The Labor Movement* (Boston, 1887), pp. 398 ff.; Quint, p. 25.
[62] *Nation,* XLII (April 29, 1886), 354; Richardson, *Messages and Papers of the Presidents,* XI, 4979 ff.; *Fifth Annual Report of the New York Bureau of the Statistics of Labor for 1887,* pp. 7, 703.
[63] *Nation,* XLI (Dec. 24, 1885), 526; Commons, II, 362.
[64] Ely, *Labor Movement in America.* pp. 295 ff., 324.

With equal relevance to the problems of the prevailing depression in 1885, Carroll Wright also appealed to the good sense of both capital and labor and recommended that proper attention be given to the reduction of working hours, arbitration, co-operation, and profit-sharing; above all, he pleaded for time and patience. He argued that

it is absurd to say that the interests of capital and labor are identical. They are no more identical than the interests of the buyer and seller. They are, however, reciprocal, and the intelligent comprehension of this reciprocal element can only be brought into the fullest play by the most complete organization, so that each party shall feel that he is an integral part of the whole establishment.

Wright elaborated upon the paradox that "none of these . . . suggested remedies can be experienced without organization, and yet organization at the present seems to constitute the chief bugbear in the public mind. The organization of capital or of the employing forces frightens the labor forces, and in return the rapid organization of the labor forces frightens capital." In this heyday of laissez-faire, Wright, nevertheless, proceeded to present the merits of organization sympathetically, admitting that "no such complete organization exists, but the wisdom of many men . . . indicates the tendency of things and these men have full faith that out of complete organization will come a better state of affairs than now exists. . . ." Such organization, he concluded, would achieve genuine freedom of contract for all, including labor.[65]

The temper of the times was, however, less reasonable, and indeed hailed the disintegration of the Knights of Labor, which had mushroomed so rapidly in 1885–1886 as evidence "that reason is resuming her sway among American workingmen. The only wonder is that the madness lasted so long . . . that men who called themselves free should have voluntarily become the slaves of masters whom they did not even know, and who for the most part were professional dead beats." The failure of the labor agitation in 1886 was, moreover, received as a welcome symptom and signal of improving business conditions and return to normality: "A failure, more or less general, of the eight-hour agitation, . . . a failure of over one-half of the strikes for higher wages, . . . a general resumption of work throughout the country; a returning confidence among capitalists and investors, and a reasonable hope for a continued improvement throughout the summer."[66]

---

[65] Wright, pp. 286 ff.
[66] *Public Opinion,* I (May 29, June 5, 1886), 136; *Nation,* XLIII (Aug. 19, Dec. 9, 1886), 147, 469.

CHAPTER VIII

Unemployment, Unrest, and Relief in the United States During the Depression of 1893-1897

The following essay originally appeared in *The Journal of Political Economy*, Volume LXI, Number 4 (August 1953), pp. 324-345. It is reprinted here, in its entirety, with the permission of The University of Chicago Press and the author. The original pagination appears in brackets at the bottom of each page.

UNEMPLOYMENT, UNREST, AND RELIEF IN THE UNITED STATES DURING THE DEPRESSION OF 1893–97

T HE Americans are a people of magnificent achievements and of equally magnificent fiascoes. At present they are in the throes of a fiasco unprecedented even in their broad experience." With this introduction, the American correspondent of *Bankers' Magazine* of London, for September, 1893, proceeded to describe "the ruin and disaster run riot over the land"; with a characteristic overtone of reproof and recrimination, he berated this country on its electricity and building booms, its trust bubbles, its faulty banking, tariff, and monetary policies.[1]

At home, too, the acute financial panic ushered in by the "Industrial Black Friday" of May 5, 1893, on the New York Stock Exchange provoked controversy as it spread to a nation-wide epidemic of some five hundred bank and nearly sixteen thousand business failures during the year.[2] On the one hand, there were those, like Henry Villard, the German-born railroad financier, and Henry Clews, the English-born broker, who saw virtually no excuse for the panic save lack of public confidence in government policy on either money or the tariff; they were impatient with the newly inaugurated President Cleveland over his failure to give quick and complete reassurance on this score.[3] There were those, on the other hand, Henry Adams

among them, who fostered the myth of the panic of 1893 as a Wall Street conspiracy, by that "dark, mysterious, crafty, wicked, rapacious, and tyrannical power . . . to rob and oppress and enslave the people."[4] J. W. Schuckers, onetime private secretary to Salmon Chase, secretary of the Treasury in Lincoln's cabinet, charged collusion and conspiracy between Cleveland and the New York City banks: "The South and West—the tributary sections—were being taught that they have a master in Wall Street."[5]

More judicious commentators, however, such as F. H. Cook, who, in turn, followed David A. Wells, viewed the crisis of 1893 as merely another stage in a long period of depression, dating from 1873, "unparalleled in the history of the world. It has been continuous during all

[1] *Bankers' Magazine* (London), LVI (September, 1893), 371 ff.

[2] O. M. W. Sprague, *History of Crises under the National Banking System* (61st Cong., 2d sess.; Senate Doc. No. 538 [Washington, D.C., 1910]), p. 413; *Bradstreet's*, XXII (December 29, 1894), 818.

[3] *Memoirs of Henry Villard* (Boston: Houghton Mifflin Co., 1904), pp. 360 ff.; Henry Clews, *The Wall Street Point of View* (New York, 1900), pp. 72 ff.; *Public Opinion*, XV (May 13, July 1, 1893), 133, 311; *North American Review*, CLVII (October, 1893), 386; *Bankers' Magazine* (New York), XLVIII (September, 1893), 180; *Harper's Weekly*, XXXVIII (August 25, 1894), 799.

[4] *Harper's Weekly*, XXXVII (September 2, 1893), 830; W. C. Ford (ed.), *Letters of Henry Adams* (Boston: Houghton Mifflin Co., 1938), II, 30 ff.

[5] J. W. Schuckers, *The New York National Bank Presidents' Conspiracy against Industry and Property* (Chicago, 1894), p. 42; *American Journal of Politics*, IV (June, 1894), 659.

these 20 years, though temporary and local causes have here and there tended to obscure the fact of continuity."[6] In 1897, J. W. Jenks, professor of political science at Cornell, also analyzed the "Causes of the Fall in Prices since 1872" in terms of "great waves covering a score or more of years and bearing the panic fluctuations on their surface like mere ripples."[7] Still others, including A. D. Noyes, historian of public finance, placed the major responsibility on the failure of the banks to perform their functions properly. Independently of the silver and other issues, there was renewed criticism of the chronic trend toward the concentration of the nation's bank reserves in the New York City banks and their dangerous absorption into the speculative but lucrative call-loan market.[8] Among the reforms advocated were tightened bank reserve requirements, some form of elastic "asset currency" better suited to the emergency than the clearing-house certificates already in use, and even a kind of bank deposit guaranty, recommended by Charles G. Dawes in 1894, then a rising young banker in Lincoln, Nebraska, and later comptroller of the currency under President McKinley.[9]

The financial panic of 1893 rapidly assumed the larger proportions of an industrial and business depression. As the

[6] *American Journal of Politics*, III (December, 1893), 597.

[7] *Journal of Social Science*, No. 35 (December, 1897), pp. 34 ff.

[8] Sprague, *op. cit.*, pp. 167 ff., 210; A. D. Noyes, "The Banks and the Panic of 1893," *Political Science Quarterly*, IX (March, 1894), 15 ff.

[9] C. G. Dawes, *A Journal of the McKinley Years* (LaGrange, Ill.: Towers, Inc., 1950), p. 7; also Dawes, *Essays and Speeches* (Boston: Houghton Mifflin Co., 1915), pp. 195 ff.; Sprague, *op. cit.*, p. 320; *Century Magazine*, XLIX (February, 1895), 636.

Commercial and Financial Chronicle put it:

The month of August will long remain memorable . . . in our industrial history. Never before has there been such a sudden and striking cessation of industrial activity. Nor was any section of the country exempt from the paralysis. Mills, factories, furnaces, mines nearly everywhere shut down in large numbers, and commerce and enterprise were arrested in an extraordinary degree . . . and hundreds of thousands of men thrown out of employment.[10]

There followed a winter of severe distress and suffering, which stimulated, in turn, an unprecedented amount of public and private relief. The accumulated social and economic pressures and tensions, nevertheless, precipitated during that terrible year 1894 a broad wave of discontent and unrest, manifested by such movements as Coxey's "Commonweal Army" and the Pullman strike. A long cycle of agrarian discontent, furthermore, simultaneously achieved its culmination in the Populist and silver agitation, with its sharp and almost shattering challenges to the prevailing political pattern of major party alignments in the elections of 1894 and 1896. Intellectually, also, the distress and discontent of depression were reflected, on the one hand, in the pessimistic prognostications offered by those twin prophets of gloom and doom, Henry and Brooks Adams, and, paradoxically, in the utopian and more optimistic speculations of the social reformers such as Flower, Bliss, Bellamy, and the numerous advocates of the "Social Gospel," on the other hand. By 1898, however, business revival and the return of confidence relaxed the tensions of depression and were, moreover, accelerated by the absorption of public interest and policy into the promising channels of territorial and trade expan-

[10] Quoted in Sprague, *op. cit.*, p. 202.

sion associated with the Spanish-American War, the annexation of Hawaii, and other manifestations of the new imperialism.

The magnitude of depression during the 1890's, as measured by an index combining six major activities, including railway-operating revenues, pig-iron and coal production, raw-cotton consumption, merchandise imports, and selected bank clearings, revealed a fluctuation of approximately one-fourth from high to low, as compared with a decline of one-third during the 1870's and of more than one-half between 1929 and 1932.[11] No such generalized index can, however, convey the contemporary sense of shrinkage of both prices and business as was revealed in the summary review of "a postpanic period . . . a time when, as one dealer put it, 'you have done business for nothing, and still there has been no business.' "[12] Recovery was slow, despite the recurring tendency, as during 1895, to grasp at "harbingers of widening prosperity," only to be warned that "the alleged era of prosperity is not in sight." British journals, such as the *Statist* and the *London Economist*, indeed, repeatedly punctured reports of revival and new American booms, and the *Economist* remarked as late as 1897: "It is wonderful how little it takes to lift up the spirits of our kinsmen in the United States." It further warned of unsettled tariff and financial issues, as well as of new problems abroad, and criticized the tendency of the American press "to ignore or minimize as far as possible the unfavorable side."[13]

At home, too, the *Commercial and Financial Chronicle* admitted in a year-end review of 1896 that "our depressed industries called for as seldom before favorable surroundings to give them the fresh impulse they needed." A subsequent summary of "what will bring prosperity" cited, among other requisites, confidence and a certain money standard, a new bankruptcy bill, a Department of Commerce and Manufactures, and an American merchant marine, since "the field is the world." It also urged a cessation of the provocative incitement of rivalries between capital and labor: "only what is fair and reasonable will bring permanent prosperity to either labor or capital."[14] On August 21, 1897, Charles Dawes recorded in his diary: "Wheat sold at one dollar per bushel today—the highest price since 1891. Prosperity seems to be dawning at last." Heavy wheat exports, moreover, combined with rising prices to support the cumulative "figures of prosperity." By the close of 1897, revival was admittedly on the way, "after three years of waiting and false starts," and it was hailed as "a supreme moment in the transition from depression to comparative prosperity."[15]

The burdens and stresses of depression fell on all classes and sections of the country. Henry Adams, himself summoned back to Boston from abroad, "because the community was bankrupt

[11] A. R. Eckler, "A Measure of the Severity of Depressions, 1873–1932," *Review of Economic Statistics*, XV (May 15, 1933), 75 ff.

[12] *Bankers' Magazine* (London), LX (August, 1895), 148; *Forum*, XVI (January, 1894), 527 ff.; *Bradstreet's*, XXII (January 6, 1894), 7 ff.

[13] *Economist*, LV (January 9, June 26, 1897), 46, 907; *American Journal of Civics*, VII (September, 1895), 324; *Bradstreet's*, XXIII (June 1, July 25, 1895), 338, 450.

[14] *North American Review*, CLXIV (April, 1897), 422 ff.; *Public Opinion*, XXI (December 31, 1896), 874.

[15] *Harper's Weekly*, XLI (December 25, 1897), 282; *Bradstreet's*, XXV (July 31, 1897), 482; Dawes, *A Journal of the McKinley Years*, p. 126; J. W. Pratt, *The Expansionists of 1898* (Baltimore: Johns Hopkins Press, 1936), p. 237.

and he probably a beggar," remarked upon "the unhealthy excitability and worry in society, high and low, rich and poor, industrial, financial, and political." Ironically, he noted that "we are now in the midst of a spasm of virtue, the outcome of hard times."[16] Governor Flower of New York directed attention to the "Army of the Unemployed" in an address at the State Fair on September 13, 1893:

Surrounded by the best products of the harvest season as we are today . . . it is hard to realize that in other parts of our state men and women, deprived of work, see destitution and misery confronting them. . . . This is one of the results of our recent panic. Its effects on the rich are bad enough. . . . But sad and startling as these effects are, they . . . are not to be compared . . . to the effects upon the thousands of persons who have been thrown out of employment. . . . How vast this army of unemployed is nobody can accurately estimate.[17]

Uncertainty regarding the scope and extent of unemployment, and the proper remedy for it, even in official quarters, was a characteristic manifestation of depression, and it colored both the controversy over and the fumbling experimentation with programs of relief and reform which formed a vital part of America's repeated, as well as cumulative, experience with depression. Estimates of unemployment were numerous and varied widely with the purpose and perspective of those who made them. In December, 1893, for example, Samuel Gompers, in his presidential address to the convention of the American Federation of Labor at Chicago, figured the unemployed at three million, in addition to reduced work and wages for many

more. He complained that, since 1879, "production, production, production, faster, greater, was the impulse, the thought, and motive of the capitalist class," while no heed was given to labor's long-standing warnings and demands for shorter working hours, as a result of which, "it is safe to say that the panic of 1893 would have been averted, deferred, and certainly less intense." The convention adopted resolutions proclaiming that "the right to work is the right to live" and calling for a legal eight-hour day and the issue of five hundred million dollars in paper money as a public works fund.[18]

In an early survey of "the effect on the manufacturing industries of the extreme liquidation in Wall Street," covering 800 establishments at 210 points in the country, *Bradstreet's* estimated in August, 1893, the unemployed at from eight to nine hundred thousand.[19] At approximately the same time, however, Richard T. Ely gave two million as a probable measure of current unemployment and warned that "unemployed" had become an ominous term both for workers and for employers. The workers were advised neither to strike nor to tramp, while employers should not add to the bitterness of the times by "selfish exploitation of the hard times." Similarly and simultaneously, Edward Thimme noted the world-wide implications of the prevailing depression, including, among others, Pope Leo XIII's Encyclical on Labor, the International Socialist Labor Congress at Zurich, the miners' strike in England, bread riots in Buffalo, and the rising threat of political labor activity in the West; and he inquired prophetically:

---

[16] *Letters of Henry Adams*, II, 47 ff.; *The Education of Henry Adams* (Boston: Houghton Mifflin Co., 1927), pp. 337 ff.

[17] *Public Papers of Governor Flower, 1893* (Albany, 1894), p. 345; also *Public Papers of Governor Flower, 1894* (Albany, 1895), p. 37.

[18] *Outlook*, XLVIII (December 30, 1893), 1222; *First Annual Report of the Labor Bureau of New Hampshire* (Concord, 1894), p. 268.

[19] *Bradstreet's*, XXI (August 12, 1893), 502.

"Are we perhaps on the eve of another political uprising similar to that of 1886, though on a grander, a more national scale?"[20]

More official, but equally tentative and temporary, appraisals of unemployment were made by various state bureaus of labor statistics, themselves largely the outgrowth of the previous period of depression in the 1870's; but none compared in scope with the pioneer survey made in 1885 under the auspices of Carroll D. Wright, first United States commissioner of labor, and published as his first report under the title *Industrial Depressions*. Thus Maine, Massachusetts, New Hampshire, Connecticut, Kansas, West Virginia, and New York used the sample questionnaire method to investigate the extent of unemployment caused by depression in 1893 and 1894. In Massachusetts, moreover, a special three-man board was authorized by the legislature in 1894 to "Investigate the Subject of the Unemployed"; and it prepared a five-part report, covering such topics as relief measures, public works, wayfarers and tramps, as well as "The Amount of Non-employment and Causes Thereof."[21]

The more poignant and personal aspects of unemployment were, however, conveyed less in such general statistical surveys, whatever their validity, than in the cumulative effects of reports from communities throughout the country.

These came from the large cities such as New York, where a police poll tabulated 67,280 resident unemployed, in addition to 20,000 homeless and vagrant, who overflowed police stations and other shelters. In Chicago more than 100,000 were reportedly out of work during the winter of 1893–94, including thousands attracted to the city by the glamour and promise of the World's Fair which had opened in May, on the very eve of the panic. These vagrants now overflowed even the corridors of the City Hall, and the police were guarding the railroad stations to cut off a further influx. There were also the smaller communities, such as Amsterdam, New York, where all industry was at one time reported shut down and the entire population "approaching beggary." The virtual suspension of all silver mining in Colorado produced a drift of the unemployed toward Denver and intensified the plight of that community. A relief camp under canvas was established there, and arrangements were made to ship whole trainloads of unemployed eastward, free or at nominal fares.[22] This was the prophetic background of and introduction to the organized march of the Commonweal Armies on Washington, under Coxey and other leaders in the spring of 1894.

In the East the police of Troy, New York, for example, raided a colony of tramps located on the Fitchburg Railroad, and the press reported that "although most of them were hale and hearty . . . there was some ground for pity. They told of enforced idleness, the closing of factories and workshops all over the country and the inability to

---

[20] *Social Economist*, V (September and October, 1893), 171 ff., 242 ff.; *Harper's Weekly*, XXXVII (September 2, 1893), 845.

[21] *Reports of the Massachusetts Board To Investigate the Subject of the Unemployed* (Boston, 1895), *passim; Twenty-fourth Report of the Massachusetts Bureau of Labor Statistics* (Boston, 1894), pp. 114 ff.; L. H. Feder, *Unemployment Relief in Periods of Depression* (New York: Russell Sage Foundation, 1936), pp. 78 ff.; cf. the survey of expert opinion, labeled "Sociology," in *Eleventh Annual Report of the Kansas Bureau of Labor* (Topeka, 1896), pp. 185 ff.

[22] *Social Economist*, VI (January, 1894), 11 ff.; *Harper's Weekly*, XXXVII (August 19, 1893), 787; XXXVIII (January 6, 1894), 38; *Proceedings of the Twenty-first National Conference of Charities and Correction* (Boston, 1894), pp. 21 ff.

obtain work. In nearly every case a wife and children had been left in some distant city"[23] More precise and even more telling was the testimony of T. H. Wickes, a vice-president of the Pullman Company, given to the Chicago Strike Commission in 1894, following the famous Pullman strike. Illustrating the plight of an industrial community like Pullman, Illinois, Wickes explained that employment there had fallen from a normal level of 4,500 to less than 1,100 by November, 1893, while a smaller plant at Detroit had been completely shut down. With special sales efforts made by the company, accompanied by sharp wage cuts, work had been found for three-fourths of the men on the eve of the strike in May, 1894; but even now, at the time of the hearings on the strike, in August, 1894, only about half the men had been re-employed in this model one-industry town.[24]

Related to such estimates of unemployment was, of course, the problem of relief, whether projected or actual. In this connection an extensive survey of "The Unemployed in American Cities" was made by C. C. Closson, and reported in the *Quarterly Journal of Economics* during the troubled year 1894. Embracing the returns to 1,200 circulars of inquiry sent to municipal officials, relief committees, and charity societies, this survey provided a remarkably comprehensive and systematic tabulation of the private and public relief efforts adopted for the emergency, many of them representing novel, controversial, and highly publicized experiments in social welfare.[25] The new fashion of the

sociological approach was even extended to the special problem of the tramp; and Professor J. G. McCook, of Trinity College at Hartford, Connecticut, made such a study in 1893, covering 1,349 replies and recommendations from the police and other city authorities, as well as an analysis of antitramp laws in all the states, concluding: "Nearly all the real tramp laws have a panicky look which suggests a pressing evil, real or imaginary." Josiah Flynt, himself a kind of amateur and literary tramp, contributed reports on such aspects of this peculiarly intriguing subject as "The Tramp at Home," "The City Tramp," "Tramping with Tramps," and "What To Do with Tramps."[26]

The novelty and variety of relief projects adopted particularly during 1893–94 were perhaps more remarkable than the actual amount of relief provided. As a spokesman for organized charity summed it up: "Some communities when the hard times came this winter, and the army of unemployed swept through the streets, were panic-stricken, the inhabitants fortified themselves behind soup-houses, threw loaves of bread out upon the besiegers; naturally the siege continued."[27] New York City, as usual, played a central role both in the proliferation of relief activities and in the debate over the respective merits of private and public, regular and emergency, forms of charity. Celebrating a half-century of existence since its foundation in an earlier period of depression, the New York Association for Improving the Condition of the Poor reviewed in

[23] *Troy Northern Budget* (July 23, 1893; January 7, 1894).

[24] United States Strike Commission, *Report on the Chicago Strike* (Washington, D.C.: Government Printing Office, 1895), pp. 572 ff.

[25] *Quarterly Journal of Economics*, VIII (January–July, 1894), *passim.*

[26] *Arena*, IX (April, 1894), 593; *Forum*, XV (August, 1893), 753 ff.; *Century Magazine*, XXV (1894), 99, 517, 706.

[27] Feder, *op. cit.*, p. 155.

1894 its own past efforts "in dealing with the great question of poverty from the moral and economic standpoints." In this it welcomed the co-operation of the Charity Organization Society, the outgrowth of a later period of depression and established in New York City by 1882. In 1893, this society issued a circular on "How To Relieve Emergent Distress," and it added a model wayfarers' lodge as well as a provident loan society to its other projects—a woodyard for men, and a laundry for women.[28]

Admittedly, however, even the record outlay of $100,000 by the New York association during 1893–94 was a small part of the total relief funds in New York City, estimated at from $2½ to $5 million. It was far below the million-dollar Work Fund of the Park Commissioners, and little, if any, greater than the sums spent by such agencies as the Tammany Fund, the *New York World* Bread Fund, the *Herald* Free Clothing Fund, the East Side Relief-Work Committee, or Nathan Straus's low-cost food centers, which were charged with hurting small competitive enterprises and with attracting the thrifty as well as the needy. Despite its critical tone toward such rival relief activities, the New York association was, nevertheless, moved to commend the "unruffled maintenance of peace and order" in the city, in contrast with the experience of past depressions: "it was anticipated that the turbulent elements of riot and discord would appear, but hardly a cloud rose above the social horizon."[29]

A more censorious commentary upon the unsystematic character and de-moralizing dangers of prevailing relief policies was presented by Mrs. Josephine Shaw Lowell, the noted social welfare pioneer. Stressing particularly the sensational newspaper activities in this field, she pointed out that

when, day after day, for weeks and months, the offers of food and clothing were reiterated, and it was made to appear that public opinion was in favor of getting something for nothing, it is not to be wondered at that the temptation was not always resisted. . . . The socialistic teaching that such gifts were not a favor received, but only a small part of what was due from the rich to the poor, was fostered by the tone of the newspapers. Moreover, the publicity forced on those who received the newspaper gifts, standing in line . . . all this was a further degradation, a moral stripping naked of the suffering of the poor, which was cruel in the extreme.

Equally critical of work relief programs as used in both Chicago and New York, Mrs. Lowell offered as a corrective that "relief work, to be a benefit and not an injury, must be continuous, hard, and underpaid," and not of a type to attract the lazy, the vagrant, and the pauper.[30]

Summarizing the similar experience of Boston during 1893–94, John G. Brooks admitted that only the urgency of the condition justified the waste of the public works program, which was, in fact, neither adequate nor productive. He admitted that the " 'Knights of the Panacea' will be impatient of the slow disciplinary influences" he was advocating; but he was resignedly philosophical about the fact that "all the phrases of 'our right to work' have literally been drilled into the heads of thousands of

[28] *Semi-centennial Report of the New York Association for Improving the Condition of the Poor* (New York, 1894), pp. 12 ff.; *History of the Charity Organization Society of the City of New York: Twenty-fifth Annual Report* (New York, 1907), pp. 15 ff.

[29] *Semi-centennial Report*, p. 52; *Proceedings of the National Conference of Charities and Correction*, pp. 24 ff.; *Journal of Social Science*, No. 32 (1894), pp. 7 ff.; *Harper's Weekly*, XXXVIII (March 17, 1894), 255.

[30] *Journal of Social Science*, No. 32 (1894), p. 20; *Forum*, XVI (February, 1894), 655 ff.

workingmen in Boston and several neighboring cities." In agreement with other contemporary advocates of sound relief programs, such as Mrs. Lowell, Jacob J. Riis, William T. Stead, and the Massachusetts Board on Unemployment, Brooks proposed strict tests of need and tight conditions and standards of work, as well as employment exchanges and schools to train the genuinely unemployed, as distinguished from the tramps, in new labor skills.[31] In the developing controversy over the relative merits of public and private relief, J. R. Commons, then a young professor of sociology at Syracuse University, made "A Comparison of Day Labor and Contract System on Municipal Works," and recommended the former on the ground that "the city must . . . support the unemployed in . . . a way economical to itself and honorable to them."[32]

The principal cities of the country, such as New York, Chicago, Philadelphia, and Boston, were not alone in their various citizens' committees or associations with their programs of work or other relief. Lesser cities also resorted to such organizations, and some of them became nationally noted because of some novel program or method of relief. There was, for example, the "Indianapolis Plan," which operated a market under the auspices of the Commercial Club for the supply of food in return for work. A weekly family ration worth eighty-two cents and consisting of cornmeal, potatoes, bread, molasses, salt, soap, and pork was made the equivalent

of a day's labor; on the complaint of the unemployed, it was later raised to one dollar with the addition of coffee, sugar, and lard. Similar programs were set up in Toledo, Ohio, and Paterson, New Jersey; in the latter case the adult's average daily ration was reduced to four cents' worth of bread, pork, beans, rice, tea, and sugar. Wood-cutting, stonebreaking, and sewing shops were common provisions for both private and public work relief. Most newsworthy among the diverse forms of relief proved to be the Detroit Garden Plot Plan, which was copied in many places, including Buffalo, Brooklyn, and New York City, as well as Cincinnati, Toledo, and Duluth. Sponsored first by Mayor Hazen S. Pingree, of Detroit, the so-called "Pingree Potato Scheme" was described by its originator, a Captain Cornelius Gardener, as "municipal farming for the poor," utilizing vacant land for the self-support of the idle and unemployed.[33]

Trade-unions, too, participated to some degree in the expanding relief activities of the time. The cigar-makers' union was reported to have increased its unemployment payments fivefold between 1892 and 1893, to a total of nearly $90,000 in the latter year. The shoe lasters of Lynn supplied meal tickets to their unemployed associates, and the five-cent meal ticket good at special low-cost restaurants became a common form of unemployment relief and almost synonymous with it.[34] Private charity, however uncertain in motive and effect, remained, nevertheless, a major source of

---

[31] *Annals of the American Academy of Political and Social Science*, V (July, 1894), 1 ff.; *Forum*, XVIII (September, 1894), 122.

[32] *American Federationist*, III (1897), 299 ff.; *Yale Review*, V (February, 1897), 428 ff.; Feder, *op. cit.*, pp. 126 ff.

[33] H. S. Pingree, *Facts and Opinions* (Détroit, 1895), pp. 161 ff.; *Report of the Massachusetts Board on the Unemployed*, pp. vi ff.; *Arena*, X (October, 1894), 701 ff.

[34] *Report of the Massachusetts Board on the Unemployed*, pp. xxxv.

relief, in the somewhat smug assurance of the contemporary press commentary: "Society Works for the Poor. It seems that the chief aim of society this winter is to do as much good as possible among the poor," by means of "charity balls, bazaars and various other affairs in the aid of the poor."[35] Lyman Abbott, the noted Brooklyn preacher, acclaimed charity for its humane qualities and particularly applauded the popular "fragment societies," which passed on discarded clothing to the poor. Henry George, on the other hand, was rather scornful of such charity as "false, futile, and poisonous when offered as a substitute for justice," and he scoffed at such proposals as would have each pupil in the public schools bring daily a cold potato and a slice of bread for the poor or provide free concerts in the churches for their entertainment.[36]

Transcending such limited and personal aspects of poor relief was the larger issue of the ultimate responsibility of government—municipal, state, and national—for unemployment and its relief by public works. Repeatedly debated in earlier depressions, the public works controversy was now raised to a new level of political agitation and demonstration. The case was reduced to its simplest terms on both sides by two men named Flower, by a surprising coincidence. In rejecting the demand for a special public works program in 1893, Governor Flower of New York regretted the prevailing unemployment but emphatically pointed out that "in this country firm lines separate our political ideas from those of European countries. . . . In America the people support the government; it is not the province of the government to support the people. . . . The security of Democratic government is its purity and simplicity. Break down those safe-guards, and you invite corruption, socialism, and anarchy." Governor Flower, moreover, objected that public works solely for the relief of the unemployed would establish "a dangerous precedent for the future, justifying paternal legislation of all kinds and encouraging prodigal extravagance."[37] Of a different mind, however, Benjamin Flower, the utopian editor of the *Arena*, protested in 1894 that many worth-while projects, such as roads and the Mississippi levees, might have saved the day, but for the fact that "gold is more precious in the eyes of our legislators than independent, self-respecting citizenship. . . . Millions for armories and the military instruction of the young, but not one cent to furnish employment to able-bodied industry in its struggle to escape the terrible alternatives of stealing or starving—such seems to be the theory of government in the United States today."[38]

Both in the East and in the West elaborate programs of public employment were offered for public attention. In Massachusetts, Edward Bellamy, author of *Looking Backward* and inspirer of the currently popular National Clubs, advocating a kind of collectivism, submitted to the Massachusetts Board on the Unemployed in 1894 a permanent and elastic plan for state workshops for the unemployed. Constituting a self-contained economic and social system with a scrip of their own, such state-supported shops would guarantee to the unemployed a decent minimum, without

[35] *Troy Northern Budget* (December 17, 1893).

[36] *North American Review*, CLVIII (February, 1894), 175 ff.; *Forum*, XVI (February, 1894), 663 ff.

[37] *Public Papers of Governor Flower, 1893*, p. 350.

[38] *Arena*, IX (May, 1894), 822.

the stigma of charity, but "nothing more."[39] From California, State Senator Dague circulated the draft of a proposed "Act To Give Employment to the Unemployed," which he complained had been pocketed by Governor Budd. Deploring the current and brutal vagrancy laws, Dague outlined a program by which the states could relieve those "who have been thrown out of employment by the modern inventions and the greed of the trust millionaires," as well as keep up wages, by providing for those now crowding the labor market. Each county would supply lodging, meals, and thirty-five cents per eight-hour day to "The Honorable Unemployed," and engage them on suitable projects. This modest beginning could, moreover, lay the "foundation for the public ownderhip of county farms, municipal waterworks, street railways, public parks, and other industries of a public nature. . . . Upon this foundation can be created, step by step . . . if desired, the larger structure of a Cooperative Commonwealth."[40]

The very nature and appeal of such schemes can best be understood, however, within the framework of alarm and interest created by the so-called "Coxey's Commonweal Army" and its march on Washington in the spring of 1894, culminating in the fiasco of the May Day demonstration on the Capitol grounds. This gathering of groups of discontented and unemployed particularly in the Far West, and their mobilization on the national capital, symbolized the eastward ebbing of the tide of western migration as well as the nation-wide impact of depression. Its impetus was suggested as arising "through some curious psychological impulse; the notion of a general crusade of squalor spread all through the country; and from every quarter of the West and the Southwest, bands of ragged, hungry, and homeless men appeared, fierce of aspect, and terrifying to the people of the hamlets and sparsely settled districts through which they passed."[41]

The progress of these so-called "industrial armies," actually rather meager in proportions and mainly inoffensive in behavior, and the antics of their leaders, "Generals" Kelly, Frye, Browne, and Coxey, were highlighted and distorted by the sensational reports in the press, and the resulting public reaction was a mixture of alarm and amusement. Censure, ridicule, and sympathy were fused into a flood of commentary and interpretation, which at once derided the ridiculous features and warned of the dangers inherent in the movement. Typical was the description of the Coxeyites by W. T. Stead, author of the depression-inspired *If Christ Came to Chicago*, as "the sandwich-men of poverty, the peripatetic advertisers of social misery. They may be the avant-couriers of revolution, maleficent or beneficent, as the case may be."[42] In the concentration upon the more colorful and personal aspects of this mass demonstration, the *Journal of the Knights of Labor* warned that its real object must not be lost from sight. This was to petition and to press upon Congress demands for the public issue of five hundred million dollars in paper money,

[39] *Report of the Massachusetts Board*, pp. 109 ff.; *Forum*, XVII (March, 1894), 81 ff.; J. Dorfman, *The Economic Mind in American Civilization* (New York: Viking Press, 1949), III, 149 ff.

[40] R. A. Dague, *An Act To Give Employment to the Unemployed* (Chicago, 1897), pp. 2 ff.; *Public Opinion*, XVII (June 14, 1894), 245; *Outlook*, XLIX (February 24, 1894), 354.

[41] H. T. Peck, *Twenty Years of the Republic* (New York: Dodd, Mead & Co., 1929), p. 373; D. L. Mc-Murry, *Coxey's Army* (Boston: Little, Brown & Co., 1929), *passim*.

[42] *Review of Reviews*, X (July, 1894), 47 ff.

to be distributed through the states and cities and to be spent for good roads: "Is there anything foolish or anarchistic or wild in the demand for good roads? . . . Coxey's demands are legitimate, practical, and, above all, American. Congress will sooner or later have to consider them."[43]

Even the conservative and hostile *Harper's Weekly*, while deriding this "sham crusade," agreed with the Coxeyites that "Up these steps [Capitol] the lobbyists of trusts and corporations have passed unchallenged on their way to committee-rooms, to which . . . the representatives of the toiling wealth-producers, have been denied." They were only following the lead of those who ride to Washington in palace cars: "the tin-plate men, and the wool men, and the iron men, and the collar and cuff men, and the cutlery men, and so on, with McKinley as grand marshal at their head, and the protection banner floating over them."[44] Addressing itself to "hard-headed practical men engaged in industrial and other economic pursuits," the *Engineering Magazine* also warned that Coxey was not merely a lunatic to be laughed at; cranks have given the country a hard time lately, but "this is a poor country for both cranks and fools. . . . What is needed just now is to publish far and wide that it is not the business of the United States to raise prices, provide work, regulate wages, or in any way to interfere in the private business or personal affairs of the people."[45]

Ironically, the last echo of the "Army of the Commonweal" came from the East, after the major demonstration had fizzled in a drizzle of rain, ending with the arrest of Jacob Coxey on the Capitol steps on a charge of trespassing. A Boston contingent of sixty men arrived in New York on May 8, under the leadership of "General" Fitzgerald and Dr. Morison L. Swift, a Boston journalist and utopian sociologist. Disclaiming any connection with Coxey, Swift released a petition to Congress, proclaiming that "the country is already a plutocracy. The wealth power must be curbed and civilized, or our days of national happiness and prosperity are numbered." A long list of demands included "farms and factories where the unemployed now and at all times may be able to employ their labor productively for the supply of their own wants; . . . steps to amend the Constitution of the United States, so that it shall affirm the right of every one to have work." There were, in addition, demands for noninterest-bearing notes, good roads, the nationalization of railroads, the telegraph, and mines, and a final one "to investigate the desirability of nationalizing the trusts."[46]

If 1894 witnessed the tragicomedy of Coxey's Army, it also experienced the more serious shock of labor and social disturbances climaxed by the Pullman strike, with its manifold economic, political, legal, and judicial complications and implications. Already in April, 1894, *Bradstreet's* expressed alarm over the "wave of industrial unrest . . . over the country"; it reported more than thirty strikes in progress, including coal miners and coke workers in Pennsylvania, iron miners in the Mesabi, brickmakers in the Hudson Valley, shoe workers in New England, silk workers, and particularly western railroad workers, whose strikes occasioned the early issue of injunctions by federal courts. Approximately 750,000

[43] *Public Opinion*, XVII (May 10, 1894), 137.

[44] *Harper's Weekly*, XXXVIII (May 12, 1894), 434.

[45] *Engineering Magazine*, VII (June, 1894), 313 ff.

[46] *Public Opinion*, XVII (May 10, 1894), 137; Dorfman, *op. cit.*, III, 222.

persons were involved in such strikes during 1894, primarily defensive in character, to check the strong current of wage-cutting.[47]

The Pullman strike proper began in characteristic fashion as a measure of desperate protest against repeated wage cuts in the Pullman car shops during 1893.[48] This local stoppage was converted into "the most gigantic strike in all history," with the threatening aspects of a rebellion in the inflamed state of press and public opinion, when the American Railway Union intervened by proclaiming a sympathetic boycott of Pullman cars on all railroad lines employing its members. Barely a year old in July, 1894, and itself a mushroom growth of depression, this early example of an industrial union embraced then a membership of some 150,000 railroad workers, under the militant leadership of Eugene V. Debs, who had rejected the "old paternal Pharisaism: 'What can we do for labor?' . . . [for] a more manly query . . . 'What can Labor do for itself?' The answer is not difficult. Labor can organize, it can unify, it can consolidate its forces. This done, it can demand and command."[49]

Whether opportunely or otherwise, there developed during July, 1894, a great trial of strength between the American Railway Union and the General Managers' Association controlling the great railroad systems radiating out of Chicago, which thus became a center of

disorder and violence, resembling and reminiscent of the railroad strikes on the eastern trunk lines in 1877. The strike took on national political significance through the dual intervention of the federal government. In the first place, the Cleveland administration, in the person of Richard Olney, the attorney-general, applied for and obtained an injunction in the Federal District Court to restrain the union and its leaders from interfering with the movement of the mails. This was accompanied by the even more militant policy of dispatching federal troops into Chicago, despite the protest of Governor Altgeld of Illinois. There ensued several days of bloody collision between the military forces and the strikers and their sympathizers. More than twenty persons were reported killed and two thousand cars destroyed, and Chicago presented the appearance of an armed camp, occupied by fourteen thousand state and federal troops.[50]

The original issues of the Pullman strike were obscured by its failure, while a bitter political and legal feud developed between the Cleveland and Altgeld factions of the Democratic party, as well as between the rival constitutional claims of federal and state authorities. As H. P. Robinson, editor of *Railroad Age*, summed it up somewhat gloomily:

It is probably safe to say that in no civilized country in this century, not actually in the throes of war or open insurrection, has society been so disorganized as it was in the United States during the first half of 1894; never was human life held so cheap; never did the constituted authorities appear so incompetent to enforce respect for the law.[51]

[47] *Bradstreet's*, XXII (April 7, 1894), 209; J. R. Commons, *History of Labor in the United States* (New York: Macmillan Co., 1921), III, 501; *Report of the Industrial Commission* (Washington, D.C.: Government Printing Office, 1901), VII, 615, 799.

[48] *Report on the Chicago Strike*, pp. 598 ff.

[49] Ray Ginger, *The Bending Cross* (New Brunswick, N.J.: Rutgers University Press, 1949), pp. 97 ff.; *Public Opinion*, XVII (July 5, 1894), 305; Almont Lindsey, *The Pullman Strike* (Chicago: University of Chicago Press, 1942), pp. 395 ff.

[50] *Bradstreet's*, XXII (July 14, 1894), 434; *Public Opinion*, XVII (July 12, 26, 1894), 330 ff., 383 ff.; Ginger, *op. cit.*, pp. 121 ff.; Grover Cleveland, *Presidential Problems* (New York: Century Co., 1904), pp. 79 ff.; S. Yellen, *American Labor Struggles* (New York: Harcourt, Brace & Co., 1936), pp. 101 ff.

[51] *Forum*, XVIII (January, 1895), 523.

More confident was the affirmation of the new role of government by the *New York Nation*, usually so critical of any effort, especially on the part of the much-derided "ethical economists," to extend the province of government. With wishful prophecy, it asserted:

The collapse of the strike is not the most important development of the week. Transcending this in significance is the demonstration that such a strike can never again be so formidable in this country. It is now universally recognized that such a strike as Debs ordered is a rebellion, and that the people of the United States will promptly suppress rebellion.

The ambitious young Republican politician, Theodore Roosevelt, characteristically thought that "it was most fortunate that the action at Washington was so quick and so emphatic," and he condemned Governor Altgeld, along with other radical governors, as "the foe of decent government, and . . . capable of doing far more damage than Tweed."[52] The idealistic *Arena*, on the other hand, pointed up the irony of the situation in which it was Cleveland, "the great historic heretic, who is to pave the way for Caesarism in the next century" and thus revive the old federalism, to the enthusiastic acclaim of the Tory and plutocratic press.[53] Aside from the established precedent of the antistrike injunction, another reported result of this disturbance was the proposed expansion of both state militias and the regular army to 50,000 or even 100,000 men, as well as the accelerated construction of municipal armories, described as "Plutocracy's Bastiles: Or Why the Republic Is Becoming an Armed Camp." The *Journal of the Knights of Labor* was, indeed, moved to reverse its previous advice to

[52] *Forum*, XVIII (February, 1895), 743; *Public Opinion*, XVII (July 26, 1894), 384.

[53] *Arena*, X (September, 1894), 530.

workers "to keep out of the militia. . . . Every workingman should join the militia, thus getting the arms and the discipline to defend the country . . . from the anarchistic railroad managers, their trust attorneys and the murderous deputies and Pinkertons whom they employ."[54] Governor Altgeld, himself the continued butt of denunciation as "essentially a European anarchist," informed the Illinois legislature in 1895 that

Russianizing a government is an expensive business and has never yet succeeded—not even in Russia. It has always resulted in choking enterprise and in the end destroying capital. Capital today does not seek investment in any country where the laborers are slaves, and where there is an ever present system of police and espionage. . . . Capital seeks those countries where liberty stimulates activity and enterprise.[55]

In the aftermath of the Pullman strike and its collapse, President Cleveland named a three-man commission, headed by Carroll D. Wright, to investigate its causes. The commission held hearings during the summer of 1894 and made mildly liberal recommendations based upon its much criticized findings that the Pullman Company was unduly harsh in its labor relations and that the General Managers' Association represented an illegal usurpation of power and was largely at fault in the ensuing railroad strike. It advised the recognition of unions and the adoption of a ban on labor contracts forbidding union membership, and it urged the enactment of some form of

[54] *Ibid.*, October, 1894, pp. 601 ff.; *Public Opinion*, XVII (July 26, 1894), 384.

[55] *Biennial Message of J. P. Altgeld* (Springfield, Ill., 1895), p. 53; H. Barnard, *Eagle Forgotten* (New York: Duell, Sloan & Pearce, 1938), pp. 295 ff.; Pingree, *op. cit.*, pp. 10 ff., reporting that some army officers met secretly and "denounced the policy of using the army to perpetuate wrongs and . . . degrade it in the eyes of the people."

compulsory negotiation and arbitration of industrial disputes. In 1895, a bill was sponsored in the House of Representatives and credited to the inspiration of Carroll D. Wright, chairman of the Chicago Strike Commission. It proposed the establishment of a five-man "United State Board of Conciliation and Arbitration" for the submission of interstate disputes and made it a misdemeanor for employees to strike or for employers to discharge workers without giving thirty days' notice while an arbitration was in progress.[56] In 1898 Congress adopted a railroad arbitration act, which Carroll Wright characterized as "practically a bill of rights for labor." Richard Olney, the central figure in the antilabor injunction controversy, was largely credited with its authorship, including a proposed clause, which permitted an appeal to a court for a Bill of Equity naming receivers for any railroad that refused to arbitrate a labor dispute. These receivers would operate the road in the public interest until proper settlement was reached.[57]

A host of other recommendations was presented for public attention both inside and outside the Chicago Strike Commission. General Miles, whose forces suppressed the strike in Chicago, advocated the restriction of immigration and the ruralization of population through soil reclamation and colonization as the best antidote against the "malarial poisons" of the Debs element.[58] A writer in the *Atlantic Monthly* pointed out the inadequacy both of force and of "govern-

ment by injunction," as well as of the puny Interstate Commerce Commission, for the regulation of the vast railroad system. He recommended a "department of transportation" to foster better services, better relations, and better results for all concerned.[59] More philosophically, Professor John Bascom, of Williams College, deduced the lesson of 1894 in warning that, while "there is a hard and unwise conservatism ready to applaud this prompt intervention of national power, yet it has in it much of the concealed virus of tyranny." Bascom concluded, moreover, that the country was in a new stage of development: "There is a fourth contention upon us . . . that springing up between classes, or . . . that between the classes and the masses."[60]

Not the least of the aftereffects of the Pullman strike of 1894 was its influence upon the intellectual and political evolution of Eugene Debs as the prototype of the national hero of labor. During his six months of rather comfortable imprisonment under the contempt conviction for violation of the injunction, Debs became an object of attention by the Socialists. These attempted to make capital out of the depression by directing organized labor into the channels of political activity and cost Samuel Gompers his only defeat for re-election as president of the American Federation of Labor in 1894. Debs resisted the socialistic pressure but joined the swing, strong particularly in the West, toward Populism and political action, advising labor to vote for an "independent people's party." With Altgeld, he participated in the Bryan campaign of 1896 but was already then toying with the utopian project of a

[56] *Public Opinion*, XVIII (January 3, 1895), 1 f., 128; *Report on the Chicago Strike*, pp. xi ff.

[57] Henry James, *Richard Olney* (Boston: Houghton Mifflin Co., 1923), pp. 65 f.; James Morgan, *The Life Work of E. A. Moseley* (New York: Macmillan Co., 1913), pp. 143 ff.

[58] *North American Review*, CLIX (August, 1894), 180 ff.; *Report on the Chicago Strike*, pp. 657 ff.

[59] *Atlantic Monthly*, LXXVI (July, 1895), 122.

[60] John Bascom, *Growth of Nationality in the United States* (New York, 1899), p. 132.

"Cooperative Commonwealth," to be established by the colonization of the unemployed in some western state. Early in 1897, following the disastrous failure of Populism, Debs announced his new conversion: "The issue is Socialism versus Capitalism. I am for Socialism because I am for humanity. . . ." A convention of the skeleton remnants of the short-lived American Railway Union resolved to convert itself into the "Social Democracy of America," through which Debs hoped to combine the dual, but divided, objectives of co-operative colonization and political action. By 1898 Debs's political evolution and emotional conversion were completed, and he had begun his new and long career as the leader of the newly formed Social Democratic party and was its first candidate for the presidency in 1900.[61]

Depression and its accompanying distress during the 1890's inspired a renewed search for causes and cures. According to the particular interests and attitudes of geographical sections and economic groups, this pursuit was directed into many specific channels, represented, among others, by the issues of money, tariff, taxation, labor, and agrarian discontent. The whole system of American government, including the Supreme Court, with its power of judicial review, was drawn into the controversy Over and beyond the rancorous clamor of political battle and election campaign, however, there were raised voices proclaiming prophetic gloom and doom or holding forth utopian promises of salvation. Motivated by a particular social outlook or perspective, they avowed concern with the more general and moral aspects of the current crisis, discovering in it the cause of decay and degradation or the hope of regeneration. Whatever their divisions and differences, both camps sincerely shared a deep-rooted American tradition and tendency to resolve the problems and issues of depression into moral terms and thus subscribed to a moralistic rather than to a Marxist interpretation of history.

Thus, for example, in 1896, *Harper's Weekly* took approving note of the great crowds attending Dwight Moody's revival meetings in New York: "Mr. Moody hopes for a revival of religion that will keep pace with the revival of business, and he is making good progress in his labors to that end." It commended Moody's message "against anarchy, against greed, against extortion and hate. He is the enemy of sectionalism and all hostility of class to class. His mission is to arouse the conscience and to awaken the spiritual side of men, to make them patient, long suffering, diligent. . . . His labors are patriotic as well as pious. Success to them!"[62] A year earlier, in a critical review of the Pullman strike and the Chicago Strike Commission, A. B. Hart, a rising young teacher of American history, had raised the rhetorical question of "Are Our Moral Standards Shifting?" and deplored the decline of "moral alertness" and the disposition to regard capital as the enemy of labor from which it needs protection. To this Henry Holt, the publisher, added such other deplorable tendencies as labor's envy of the rich and "excessive immigration from countries

[61] Ginger, *op. cit.*, pp. 162 ff., 195, 201; S. Gompers, *Seventy Years of Life and Labor* (New York: E. P. Dutton & Co., 1925), I, 355 ff.; N. Fine, *Labor and Farmer Parties in the United States* (New York: Rand School of Social Science, 1928), pp. 184 ff.

[62] *Harper's Weekly*, XL (November 28, 1896), 1163; *Bankers' Magazine* (New York), XLIX (August, 1894), 127, for a banker's injunction to place contentment above wealth, since "riches are not a guarantee of happiness."

where harder conditions than ours have given more occasion for discontent."[63]

The tide of antiforeign sentiment was swelled by the reaction against the labor disturbances of the period and was expressed most vehemently and virulently in a letter to the press by a Dr. James Weir, of Owensboro, Kentucky:

> Year after year Europe pours into the United States multitudes of degenerate human beings, who, incited by the freedom of American institutions . . . immediately give free rein to their atavistic imaginations, and . . . plunge into anarchy and lawlessness. These people are savages, and should not be treated as civilized beings. When the Indians out West go on the warpath, we know how to control them. The psychologist considers the anarchist as no better than the Indian.[64]

From Boston came almost simultaneously the announcement of a newly formed "Immigration Restriction League, non-partisan, non-sectarian, and non-political," whose object was to publicize a program for excluding "elements undesirable for citizenship or injurious to our national character." Its officers included such notable figures as former Senator Edmunds of Vermont, Henry Parkman, Col. Henry Lee, and Robert Treat Paine, of Boston, Professors N. S. Shaler and John Fiske, of Cambridge, and its secretary, Robert De Courcy Ward.[65] Scarcely more restrained or judicious was the plea of Francis A. Walker, noted economist at the Massachusetts Institute of Technology, for the "restriction of immigration" to protect "the American rate of wages, the American standard of living, and the quality of American citizenship

from degradation through the tumultuous access of vast throngs of ignorant and brutalized peasantry from the countries of eastern and southern Europe." Professor Walker pressed the argument that "in all the social and industrial disorders of this country since 1877, the foreign elements have proved themselves to be ready tools of demagogues in defying the law, in destroying property, and in working violence."[66]

In characteristic fashion, Frederick J. Turner, whose frontier theory of American development had been published as recently as 1893, also applied it in an explanation of the contemporary crisis:

> The free lands are gone, the continent is crossed, and all this push and energy is turning into the channels of agitation. . . . And now the frontier opportunities are gone. . . . Discontent is demanding an extension of governmental activity in its behalf. In these demands, it finds itself in touch with the depressed agricultural classes and the workingmen of the South and East. . . . It is a social problem on a national scale.[67]

J. Laurence Laughlin, a member of the orthodox and conservative camp in the divided world of American economics, accounted for the susceptibility of the West to the silver and other crazes as "the inevitable manifestation of an idea strongly held by undereducated men."[68]

But the veteran and expert analysts of, and moralizers about, depression continued to be, as they had been during the 1870's, E. A. Godkin, editor of the New York *Nation*, and William Graham Sumner, economist, sociologist, and ardent apostle of the natural law and its corollary, the "do-nothing" policy of laissez faire. Godkin warned:

[63] *Forum*, XVIII (January and February, 1895), 515, 665.

[64] *Century Magazine*, XLVIII (October, 1894), 953.

[65] *Century Magazine*, XLIX (February, 1895), 639.

[66] *Atlantic Monthly*, LXVII (June, 1896), 822 ff.

[67] *Atlantic Monthly*, LXXVIII (September, 1896), 296 ff.

[68] *Ibid.* (November, 1896), p. 579.

The socialist movement . . . all movements to make governments provide for the people, either by constant employment or by free silver, to make the government support the people instead of making the people support the government, are attempts to do away with the need of character, to enable the world to get on without it. They seek to make the idle and indolent as sure of the future as the industrious and energetic. I do not believe this state of things will ever come about, for it is slavery.

Godkin, moreover, carried on a long and persistent campaign against those "bellowing about trusts and monopolies," who have fomented "the craze against property that has been sweeping through the country." He was sharply critical of the new fashion of the "ethical economists" who abound in colleges, "singing 'songs of freedom' with socialists and labor agitators, and filling the bellies of the poor with the east wind," when, as a matter of fact, "never in any age of the world has there been a greater need that economists should speak with a voice of proved and provable authority." The *Nation* found occasion to rebuke President Aylesworth, of Drake University, for losing his head over the Coxey movement; and it censured William Dean Howells for his "needless provocation to anarchy," with his recently published *Altruria*, and "dream of a truer social order." Most of all, the *Nation* joined in the attack upon Richard T. Ely, the "practical ethical socialist," and questioned whether the University of Wisconsin did well to retain him as "Director of the School of Economics, Political Science, and History." It contrasted Ely with William Graham Sumner, the latter an advocate of "a tough old world," who opposed those wanting "to make the world over." Sumner himself labored at and built up his familiar thesis in essays on the "Cause and Cure of Hard Times" and "The Delusion of Debtors." In par-

ticular, he condemned the modern medicine men who "say it is the gold-bugs, Wall Street, England, who are to blame for hard times. . . . There is something to hate and denounce."[69]

In actual fact, Richard Ely successfully defended himself in this early case of academic freedom, scouting the charge that "he is generally the teacher and promulgator of socialistic and anarchistic doctrines." At most, the much maligned Ely had been an important figure in the development of Social Christianity since the depression of the 1870's, along with such ministers as R. Heber Newton, George Herron, and Washington Gladden. In 1893, Ely appealed to workers not to desert the church but to use it: "I would oppose to the war-cry of Karl Marx another, namely: 'Workingmen of all lands, find freedom in the service of Christ! Workingmen of all lands, capture the Church.' "[70]

By 1893, the Social Gospel of Christianity, as against "Churchianity," had become manifest as the unifying bond among reformers of many complexions. Richard Ely himself was president, and John R. Commons secretary, of a newly formed American Institute of Christian Sociology. A "Baltimore Union for Do-

[69] *Nation*, LVIII (May 24, 1894), 378 ff.; LIX (July 19, August 9, 1894), 59, 95; *Atlantic Monthly*, LXXVIII (December, 1896), 727; W. G. Sumner, *The Forgotten Man and Other Essays* (New Haven: Yale University Press, 1918), pp. 153 ff. For the academic freedom case of Ely at Wisconsin cf. *Public Opinion*, XVII (August 16, 1894), 462; and for that of President E. B. Andrews, of Brown University, cf. Elizabeth Donnan, "A Nineteenth-Century Academic Cause Célèbre," *Bulletin of the American Association of University Professors*, XXXVIII (autumn, 1952), 368 ff.

[70] *Outlook*, XLIX (January 13, 1894), 60; *Public Opinion*, XVII (August 16, 1894), 462; for similar manifestations in an earlier depression, see my article, "Distress, Relief, and Discontent . . . 1873–1878" *Journal of Political Economy*, LVIII (December, 1950), 511.

ing Good" was established, and a "National Union of Practical Progress," with headquarters in Boston and branches in other cities, was open to all who have "a desire for the betterment of society and the spread of moral reform." This vaguely idealistic "do-good"movement drew inspiration from both religious and secular sources; among the latter, in particular, was the influence of Henry George, Henry Demarest Lloyd, and Edward Bellamy, whose characteristically American programs attracted many types of supporters. As early as 1894, a critic of "Socialism in Its Different Forms" warned that "the Social Democrats, the Collectivists, and the Nationalists are more active in propagating their doctrines than the Socialists ever were."[71] In 1899, a Conference of Unrest, held at Buffalo and sponsored by the Rev. W. D. P. Bliss, editor of the *Encyclopedia of Social Reform* and himself the intellectual offspring of the various reform strains, brought together and attempted a merger of Georgists, Populists, Greenbackers, Nationalists, and Christian Socialists. A short-lived Social Reform Union was established, which enlisted the earnest efforts of such diverse persons as George Herron, Hazen Pingree, H. D. Lloyd, B. O. Flower, Frank Parsons, Laurence Gronlund, and W. D. Howells in a common, omnibus reform program.[72]

Politically, depression sharpened Pres-

ident Cleveland's own dilemma, which lay in his commitment to silver repeal and sound money, coupled with tariff reform. The Wilson-Gorman Tariff Act, enacted in 1894 without the presidential signature, failed to bring reform and provoked the disappointed Cleveland into an outburst against "the trusts and combinations—the communism of pelf— whose machinations have prevented us from reaching the success we deserved." The contradictions of policy were further accentuated by the fact that the same Wilson Act attempted to compensate for the anticipated loss of federal revenue, by incorporating an income tax on individuals and corporations, amounting to 2 per cent on incomes above $4,000.[73] This venture into peacetime income taxation, long a major demand of radical social and political programs, precipitated another dispute, second only to the silver agitation in violence and vituperation, as exemplified by the charges in the *Nation* that it was "concocted without notice not so much to raise money as to punish certain people for being saving and successful and for holding odious views on the currency." The income tax issue led ultimately to the Supreme Court, where Joseph Choate, as chief counsel for the defendant corporation, the Farmers' Loan and Trust Company, appealed to the court to uphold civilization regardless of "popular or Populistic wrath" and to halt "the communistic march," which might lead from an initial 2 per cent even to a 20 per cent tax on large incomes. By a 5 to 4 decision, the Supreme Court rejected the income tax

[71] *American Journal of Politics*, IV (April, 1894), 438; *Public Opinion*, XVII (May 24, 1894), 164; A. I. Abell, *Urban Impact on American Protestantism* (Cambridge, Mass.: Harvard University Press, 1943), pp. 61 ff., 88 ff.; James Dombrowski, *The Early Days of Christian Socialism in America* (New York: Columbia University Press, 1936), pp. 50 ff.

[72] R. B. Nye, *Midwestern Progressive Politics* (East Lansing: Michigan State University Press, 1951), pp. 169 ff.; T. H. Greer, *American Social Reform Movements* (New York: Prentice-Hall Book Co., Inc., 1949), pp. 3, 38.

[73] *Public Opinion*, XVII (September 6, 1894), 23, 539; S. Ratner, *American Taxation* (New York: W. W. Norton & Co., 1942), pp. 172 ff.; Allan Nevins (ed.), *Letters of Grover Cleveland* (Boston: Houghton Mifflin Co., 1933), pp. 3, 65; Allan Nevins, *Grover Cleveland* (New York: Dodd, Mead & Co., 1933), p. 666.

as unconstitutional in 1895, and its opinion added fuel to the fires of controversy in a year of depression. While the *Nation* acclaimed the court's rebuke to Justice Harlan's minority exposition of the "Marxist Gospel," the *Salt Lake Tribune* compared the decision with the Dred Scott Case, and a Georgia newspaper, the *Augusta Chronicle*, would "not accept it as a final disposition of the question involved."[74] Governor Pennoyer of Oregon made a rather frenetic proposal in 1895 to check

the judicial oligarchy. The time has now come when the Government should be restored to its constitutional basis. . . . If Congress at its next session would impeach the nullifying judges for the usurpation of legislative power, remove them from office, and instruct the President to enforce the collection of the income tax, the Supreme Court would never hereafter presume to trench upon the exclusive powers of Congress.[75]

No such drastic treatment was, of course, considered seriously; instead, the income tax was eventually legalized by the Sixteenth Amendment to the Constitution, ratified in 1913.

The highly controversial role of the Supreme Court and of the courts generally was expanded in proportion as there were increasing pressures for labor and social legislation, paralleled by resort to judicial intercession for the resolution of industrial conflicts. None put it more succinctly than F. J. Stimson, an early commentator on these trends and compiler of a *Handbook to the Labor Law of the United States*, first published in 1896: "If 'hard cases make bad law,'

hard times make radical legislation." In part, he blamed the political opportunism of state legislatures for adopting such laws and thereby shifting responsibility to the courts; and he cited the extreme case of Kansas, with its Anti-Blacklist and Anti-Contempt legislation, aimed at the nullification of labor injunctions. In a paper on "Democracy and the Laboring Man," presented to the Social Science Association in 1897, Stimson summarized and classified some 1,550 labor acts as passed in the states during the preceding decade. He applauded the civic courage of the courts for having disallowed about 60 per cent of them, and he complained that "the unexpected weakness of democratic government, as shown in the crisis through which we are now passing, is its belief in the efficacy of law-making. It seems possessed with the idea that statutes can amend both nature and human nature."[76] The attitude of labor in supporting legislative supremacy was understandable, as was exemplified by an attempt in 1896 to commit the convention of the American Federation of Labor to a resolution calling for the abolition of judicial review by constitutional amendment. The liberal *Outlook* thought this extreme, but suggested an alternative possibility of submitting to a popular vote laws vetoed by judicial opinion.[77]

In the traditional manner reminiscent of previous periods of depression, creditor-debtor relations, especially those affecting farmers and small business, also became a source of discontent, politi-

[74] *Public Opinion*, XVIII (May 30, 1895), 594; *Nation*, LX (May 23, 30, 1895), 394, 417; *American Journal of Politics*, IV (May, 1894), 496; *Forum*, XIX (March, July, 1895), 48, 513 ff.

[75] *American Law Review*, XXIX (July–August, 1895), 558.

[76] *Journal of Social Science*, No. 35 (1897), p. 167; *Yale Review*, V (November, 1896), 251; VI (August, 1897), 184 ff.

[77] *Public Opinion*, XXI (December 31, 1896), 856.

cal pressure, and controversy. Western states adopted stay laws to allow varying degrees and rights of exemption, delay, and redemption in cases of foreclosure, and these became subject to judicial tests and nullification as impairments of contract. More particularly, there was renewed agitation in Congress to enact a federal bankruptcy law, which entailed a prolonged debate and a conflict of debtor-creditor interests that was finally resolved in the bankruptcy legislation of 1898. The principal issue was as between the original Torrey bill for involuntary bankruptcy favoring creditors, and a substitute measure providing for voluntary insolvency in the interest of debtors. In the background of prolific business failures induced by depression during 1893, the Torrey bill was rejected in Congress with the argument: "Such a bill should never be enacted when a business depression exists." The opposition to the proposed substitute bill favoring debtors, however, argued that

there is no fixed class of debtors and creditors. The largest body of creditors are the working-men, with savings in the banks. . . . Let us have done with this class talk about the money power and the poor man. Whatever weakens credit increases costs and raises rates of interest. The one thing that the South needs today is the confidence of men who have capital—the very men whom some of you stigmatize as the "money power," "gold bugs," etc.

The compromise measure finally enacted in 1898 ushered in a period of continuous federal bankruptcy legislation and represented the increasing recognition of the national idea that it is in the common public interest not merely to collect and distribute assets but also to preserve them and to keep business going.[78]

The major outlet for economic and regional discontent during the 1890's

was to be found, however, in protest politics and in the struggle for power, which helped to determine the alignment of major and minor parties, the shaping of platforms, and the outcome of elections. Experience in this period validated the political truism that "No party in power has ever won an election occurring amid bad times." Despite the auspicious inauguration of President Cleveland in 1893, the new administration quickly ran into the storm of financial panic and the emergency repeal of the Sherman Silver Purchase Act. This, together with the persistent and costly policy of supporting the gold standard and replenishing the gold reserve funds of the Treasury by private loans, tended to elevate silver into the central issue, widening rifts and divisions in both major parties and providing a common rallying cry and binding cement for the fusion of parties of protest. Just before the mid-term congressional elections of 1894, F. L. Stetson, the president's law partner, warned Cleveland: "We are on the eve of a very dark night unless a return of commercial prosperity relieves popular discontent." The inevitable "avalanche of 1894" returned a Republican Congress, while Populist congressional candidates polled nearly one and a half million votes, exceeding the million votes cast for the presidential candidate, General Weaver, in 1892. President Cleveland resigned himself to the trend, while stubbornly committed to the policy responsible for it: "In our hand to hand conflicts our triumphs are many, but I am afraid, as we triumph, our party loses and the

[78] *Bradstreet's*, XXI (August 19, 1893), ·530; *Public Opinion*, XVI (November 2, 1893), 117; *Harper's Weekly*, XLI (December 25, 1897), 1278; Charles Warren, *Bankruptcy in United States History* (Cambridge, Mass.: Harvard University Press, 1935), pp. 134 ff.

country does not gain as it should; and yet what would the condition be without us?"[79]

In the years between elections, continued depression, despite a brief and deceptive revival in 1895, and the crucial issues of money, tariff, and taxation fed the flame of controversy and intensified political conflict. The gathering forces of opposition pointed toward the great showdown in the election campaign of 1896. In the meantime, a tremendous outpouring of written and oral diatribe, in Congress, the press, the pulpit, and all other available media, revealed the ubiquitous articulateness of American political opinion; and it culminated in the unprecedented volume of violent propaganda which characterized the campaign of 1896. "Gold-bugs" and "Silver lunatics," Wall Street and Populists, supplied both sides with visual symbols for vituperation and caricature. The Populists, in particular, became "a subject for psychological research and wonderment, baffling and discomforting to mental classification and analysis." It was agreed that "at present, 'hard times' and business depression are their main support"; but there was the warning that "the socialists, the communists, and anarchists have already chosen that party for a home to harbor. . . . With present tendencies . . . it is very doubtful if one can be a full member of that party and a good citizen at the same time."[80]

Such an identification of Populism and silver with communism proved con-

venient and popular during the campaign of 1896, and the very fusion of the protest parties in the candidacy of William Jennings Bryan enabled *Harper's Weekly* to hail it as "The Triumph of Sectionalism and Communism" and to depict in a full front-page cartoon the face and figure of Governor Altgeld, bearing a blazing torch labeled "Anarchy," and lurking behind the bland mask of Bryan and "Free Silver." It bore the injunction: "Leave Altgeld and His Mask."[81] In his celebrated editorial on "What Is the Matter with Kansas," William Allen White summarized the essence of the campaign: "The American idea is today in balance. The Republicans are upholding, the Populists and their allies are denouncing it. The election will sustain Americanism or it will plant Socialism." In the tremendous pressures of the campaign, McKinley was pictured as "the Advance Agent of Prosperity," and *Bradstreet's* threatened rather than merely warned that "in the event of failure next November to stem the threatening tide of repudiation and national dishonor, the reverses and depression of 1893–94 are likely to be only foretastes of what will follow." It quoted the *Philadelphia Press* on "What Bryan's Panic Would Be," and concluded: "The world has never seen such a panic. We trust it never may. . . . No one, not even Mr. W. J. Bryan, has ventured to deny that panic would follow the first adoption of the Chicago plan. He says it is worth a panic. Do you?"[82] Republican victory, however, nullified this threat; it

---

[79] M. Josephson, *The Politicos* (New York: Harcourt, Brace & Co., 1938), pp. 591, 602, 618; B. F. Andrews, *The United States in Our Own Time* (New York, 1912), p. 773; M. S. and S. W. Stedman, *Discontent at the Polls* (New York: Columbia University Press, 1950), pp. 6 ff.; J. D. Hicks, *The Populist Revolt* (Minneapolis: Minnesota University Press, 1931), pp. 337 ff.

[80] *American Journal of Politics*, V (December, 1894), 653; *Harper's Weekly*, XL (July 18, 25, September 12, 1896), 698, 722, 889; W. H. Harvey, *Coin's Financial School* (Chicago, 1894), pp. 3 ff.

[81] *Harper's Weekly*, XL (July 18, 1896), 698.

[82] *Bradstreet's*, XXIV (July 11, August 29, 1896), 433, 558; Josephson, *op. cit.*, pp. 662 ff.; Nye, *op. cit.*, pp. 118 ff.

was hailed as the "crushing defeat of free coinage and lawlessness" and, somewhat ironically, as "the President's Triumph" and the vindication of Grover Cleveland, the deposed and defeated leader of the Democratic party. The country was congratulated on its escape from Altgeldism and socialism, with the renewed caution that "the people should be made to understand that Mr. Bryan and his party are not loyal citizens of the republic."[83]

In his disillusionment with the Democratic debacle of 1896, Brooks Adams, bimetallist and author of the depression-inspired *Law of Civilization and Decay* in 1895, became convinced that Darwin's law of selection favored the "gold-bugs" and Republicanism. He concluded prophetically that a new struggle for world power was beginning.[84] In actual fact, an awakening expansionism offered the prospect of world trade and territorial acquisition; and America's destiny was expressed by Albert Beveridge in April, 1897:

American factories are making more than the American people can use; American soil is producing more than they can consume. Fate has written her policy for us; the trade of the world shall be ours. . . . And American law, American order, American civilization and the American flag will plant themselves on shores bloody and benighted.[85]

A prolonged debate over imperialism had begun, and there were repeated warnings against the "jingo" spirit and its illusory promise of relief for depression. The St. Louis *Age of Steel*, indeed, cautioned that expanded foreign trade might encourage "territorial greed, as in the case of older nations, the price of which in armaments and militarism offsets the gains made by the spindle and the forge."[86] The *Iron Age*, in a year-end review of moderate recovery for 1897, somewhat wishfully looked ahead to the "Future of Business" and the start of a new era:

The most abiding effect of the panic of 1893 was the sudden and complete severance with our commercial past . . . the happy-go-lucky methods of buying and selling, the unquestioned belief in regularly recurring cycles of boom and speculation, the lack of economy in production and the extravagance in distribution . . . and the blind confidence that the future was an inexhaustible fund, against which we could always draw in the way of constant multiplication of machinery and of factories.[87]

[83] *Harper's Weekly*, XL (November 14, 1896), 1114; Nevins, *Cleveland*, pp. 712 ff.; Nye, *op. cit.*, p. 89.

[84] Thornton Anderson, *Brooks Adams* (Ithaca, N.Y.: Cornell University Press, 1951), pp. 58 ff., 76; Brooks Adams, *America's Economic Supremacy* (New York, 1900), *passim; The Law of Civilization and Decay* (New York: Alfred Knopf, 1943), pp. 4 ff.

[85] Pratt, *op. cit.*, p. 227; A. K. Weinberg, *Manifest Destiny* (Baltimore: Johns Hopkins Press, 1935), p. 395.

[86] Pratt, *op. cit.*, p. 256; *Nation*, LVIII (April 12, 1894), 267; LX (March 28, 1895), 1; LXI (December 26, 1895), 458; LXII (January 9, 1896), 22, citing a letter in the *Portland Oregonian* that "business is at a standstill and will remain so until something happens"; cf. Richard Hofstadter, "Manifest Destiny and the Philippines," in Daniel Aaron (ed.), *America in Crisis* (New York: A. A. Knopf, Inc., 1952), pp. 173 ff.

[87] *Iron Age*, LX (December 23, 1897), 19.

EPILOGUE AND
BIBLIOGRAPHICAL NOTE

To present at this point a complete bibliography covering the full century of American experience with depression would be neither practicable nor particularly profitable. It would largely reproduce and duplicate the references contained in the footnotes accompanying each essay in the volume. These are as full and as comprehensive as was possible at the time and considering the circumstances under which they were respectively prepared.

A bibliographical note such as this may, however, consider the special problems peculiar to a volume of this character. The principal problem is the great volume and diversity of bibliography involved in these studies, both in a chronological and a topical sense. Since each essay deals with a specific period of time, related to the rest only in their common character of depression, it is evident that the primary sources will be basically different in each case. Only the general and secondary references might be similar or even the same for more than one depression. Even these are, however, of a progressive and cumulative character, reflecting in each case the views and speculations of a particular time or situation. This is well illustrated in the notes accompanying the introductory essay on the sociology of American depressions. Here is recorded a significant sample of theoretical as well as occasional literature concerned with the nature and consequences of depression.

For the rest, the bibliographical problem has been one of sampling and selection out of a great volume and variety of available materials, and it is hoped that this has been adequately achieved in and for each essay. By way of clarification and simplification, these references arrange themselves on several planes or levels as to their value or relevance to the specific depression in question. In the first place, there is the first or fundamental level of materials supplying the manifold data illustrating the state and reality of depression. These must

199

come from many kinds of sources, and must obviously represent as random a sampling as possible of single, scattered items comprising a cumulative pattern of depression. Such references would include primarily newspapers, published both in large and small cities, and as far as possible, from different sections of the country. But they would also embrace the recollections and records of many men of affairs, ranging from politics to business and even literature. There are many such sources, in the form of diaries or other accounts.

On a second level are the journals of interpretation and opinion. These, too, vary from period to period and differ in orientation and purpose, from those directly concerned with business, industry, and banking, such as *The American Museum, Niles' Register, Hunt's Merchants' Magazine, De Bow's Commercial Review,* and *Bankers' Magazine,* to the more general journals of opinion, such as the *Atlantic Monthly. Democratic Review,* and, particularly for the post-civil war generation, the *Nation,* under its vigorous and voluble editor, E. A. Godkin.

There is virtually no limit to these and other resources available for the nineteenth century, and any presentation must be selective but, hopefully, also significant and relevant to each period of depression. Added to the private and personal materials, there is also the public sector, consisting of public documents and publications, both legislative and executive, on the state and federal levels. Beyond these bibliographical components of almost infinite dimension and proportion, lies still another, containing contemporary analyses and interpretations, whether by professional economists or by other commentators, both ministerial and lay. These are either apologetic or critical, but scarcely neutral. Here is a vast and growing literature, which again can only be sampled and used illustratively, both in text and bibliography. In it is reflected the current state of mind and opinion, in individual and distinctive form, but all ultimately comprising the total and representative pattern of the whole community.

This mass of contemporary writings expands and shades off into the broader, if more secondary excursions into theoretical expositions of depression as a stage of the business cycle. This has become an important and growing part of the systematic literature of economics, which engaged the thought of the most noted economists during the nineteenth century, from Sismondi to Marx, from Henry George to

Thorstein Veblen. It extends into the present century and gains in theoretical breadth and statistical precision of exposition and interpretation, although it may lose in ultimate relevance to the actual reality of depression. In this connection, the research activities and published output of the National Bureau of Economic Research, under the direction of Wesley C. Mitchell, in the generation following 1920, are particularly significant.

It is noteworthy, and illustrative of the historically close relation between economic facts and economic theory, that, since World War II, the efforts of economists, including those of the National Bureau, have shifted from the study of the business cycle, including depressions, to the analysis of the secular forces of economic growth, with or without fluctuations. This may be related to the apparent decline of the business cycle and the stabilization of economic activity in this postwar period of growth and affluence. It may be that the changing character of economic thought and analysis in the present period represents the close of an age of sharp, recurring economic and social fluctuations extending back into the nineteenth century. In this heyday of the business cycle, the phenomenon of depression in its many manifestations played a significant and growing role. In some degree, the essays contained in this volume have been intended to delineate and illuminate the pervasive influence of depression, especially during the nineteenth century, its period of germination and evolution. The long depression following 1929, omitted but not ignored in this volume, was perhaps its most complex and troublesome example. Possibly it was the last great experience of mankind in this painful accompaniment of modern industrialization. It is to be hoped that it was also the best teacher, whose lesson was one of prevention and avoidance of the extreme swings of the business cycle by the application of a new social and political philosophy of constant vigilance and concerted effort toward a more equal and equitable system of production and distribution.